MUSLIM INSTITUTIONS

MUSLIM INSTITUTIONS

MAURICE
GAUDEFROY-DEMOMBYNES

TRANSLATED FROM THE FRENCH
BY JOHN P. MACGREGOR

NEW YORK

BARNES & NOBLE, INC.

Publishers • Booksellers • Since 1873

FIRST PUBLISHED IN 1950
SECOND IMPRESSION 1954
THIRD IMPRESSION 1961

Translated from the original French
Les Institutions Musulmanes

Printed in Great Britain
by Bradford and Dickens
London, W.C.1

PREFACE

The Muslim world is today made up of a number of communities. each striving to raise itself to the dignity of statehood, but seeking, at the same time, to preserve a measure of spiritual unity. This unity was, for centuries, confused with the idea of political unity, the caliph combining in his person temporal power and spiritual authority. During that period there existed a single Muslim community, the institutions of which were permeated with the spirit of religion. It is those institutions that we have endeavoured to describe, without omitting to point out that they have evolved, and that, at the period of their apparently most perfect unity, they were subject to the modifying influence of changing human moods and varying traditions.

The bibliography printed in the earlier editions has been omitted. The reader is referred to the work of Jean Sauvaget: *Introduction à l'histoire de l'Orient Musulman: Essai de Bibliographie* (1943), references to which in the footnotes are preceded by the letter S, with the recommendation that he should read and ponder the first fifty-six pages. It has been here thought sufficient to refer, at the foot of each chapter, to a few easily accessible works and to certain articles in *L'Encyclopédie de l'Islam*—indicated by the letters E.I.

TRANSLATOR'S NOTE

This English edition has been read and approved by the author. A few errors which had been overlooked in the French edition have been corrected, and a number of passages introduced covering developments in the Muslim world since 1945.

CONTENTS

PREFACE *Page* 5

I. The Muslim Dominion 9

II. The Muslim Community 13

III. The Movement of Ideas 29

IV. The Islamic Dogma 47

V. The Sources of Muslim Law 61

VI. The Cult 70

VII. The Caliphate 108

VIII. The Family 127

IX. Property 139

X. Justice 148

XI. Social Life 159

XII. Economic Life 177

XIII. Intellectual Life 192

XIV. Modern Islam 208

CHAPTER ONE

THE MUSLIM DOMINION

Its extent—Its language and institutions.

THE institutions of the Muslim world are those that are common to the peoples who have accepted the religion of the Qur'ān, either as a result of conquest or as a fruit of the peaceful propaganda of its missionaries and brotherhoods. Islam has still a considerable place in the religious life of humanity: it comprises two hundred and fifty millions of the faithful, scattered over a very wide area, from China to Morocco.

The first Arab conquerors of the 7th century carried it to Syria, Egypt and Iraq, to peoples who were by no means strangers to them, and whose religious differences offered no obstacle to the formation of a quickly converted, Arabic speaking community. From Egypt Islam spread to the Berber world which, however, it won with difficulty. The orthodox creed finally vanquished the dissident sects, and the language of the Qur'ān, Arabic, became the ruling idiom. In spite of this, Berber Africa retained its individual characteristics and was destined to pursue its own evolution under the intellectual guidance of France. For seven centuries, from 711 to 1492, Muslims exercised a decisive influence on the destiny of Spain; they left the imprint of their artistry on her cities, her language retains traces of an Arabic vocabulary, her social life still preserves something of the manners of the Orient, but, on the other hand, the history of the reconquest of Spain and that of the rule of her Catholic kings still lingers with tenacious rancour in the memory of the native population of North Africa. Filtering into Africa along the channels of trade, and spread by the teaching of Muslim brotherhoods, Islam penetrated into the land of the negro as far as the regions of the equator. But here there is more of surface than of depth.

In Asia the conquest of Persia followed immediately on the first successes of the Companions of the Prophet, and the 'Abbāsid caliphate owes to the Persians its most enduring glory. But Persia, by adopting Shī'ism, emphasised her originality and, by retaining her Indo-European language and trend of thought, preserved her personality and her right to a destiny of her own. She is threatened by powerful neighbours, and by the rivalries of nations anxious to secure for themselves her reserves of oil. The seventy millions of Indian Muslims continued to occupy an isolated position within the immense Indian Empire; their reaction to the freedom that Great Britain has granted to them has been to separate themselves from the other peoples, and to form an independent State consisting of two fragments and called Pakistan. The Malay group is important by its mass (fifty millions) and by its commercial activity. Its ethnical origins, its geographical situation, and the Dutch protectorate, gave to it a lasting individuality; the breach with the Netherlands, however, makes its future uncertain. However important they may be (eight millions), the Muslim colonies of China are lost in the giant Chinese nation: Arabic is for them a church language known only to educated Muslims.

From Persia Islam advanced northwards, across the Oxus and beyond, to the Tatar peoples that still retain the faith. By the agency of the Ottoman Turks it conquered Asia Minor and Asiatic Turkey, and advanced towards the Danube and the Adriatic. In the North the Tatars carried it to Russia, where it is still a living force. They are, for the most part, grouped into Soviet republics the state of whose culture is unknown. We may here neglect the small Muslim groups, of various origins, which exist here and there throughout the world.

None of the important groups that we have mentioned has lost, by conversion to the Muslim faith, the original characteristics that derive from its geographical situation, from its past, or from the qualities peculiar to the individuals of which it is composed. Those characteristics manifest themselves clearly through the language of each, and it is only a slight exaggeration of a just observation to say that the institutions of a Muḥammadan people are the more strictly Muslim according as the language spoken by them approaches more closely to that of the Qur'ān. Adopting this principle, we can place in the foremost ranks of Islam those peoples who speak Arabic, even if they have done so only since their conquest, as in the case of the inhabitants of Syria, Mesopotamia, Egypt and the Maghrib. Yet it must not be thought that those people speak identical tongues, nor that their customs are similar: the language and customs of a Syrian Bedouin differ markedly from those of an inhabitant of Marrakesh. But the resemblance between them is much closer than that between Arabic speaking peoples and those races which, by the preservation of their ancient tongues, demonstrate the persistence of their national individuality. The borrowings of the latter from the language of the Qur'ān have an artificial character: they consist of religious expressions, expressions used in administration, and abstract words; in other terms they include only those expressions which a people receives from a civilisation that dominates and governs it. Beyond that, Arabic has forced its written characters on Persian, Turkish, Malay, etc., completely displacing the ancient alphabets. An exception is the case of Hindustani (Urdu), a mixed tongue, formed in the 12th century, in which the Sanskrit alphabet has maintained itself alongside certain Arabic characters. But each language has kept its own nature, derived, not only from the words themselves, but from the manner of using grammatical inflections and of building up sentences, that is to say, from its morphology and its syntax. Persian has added approximately one third of Arabic words to its Indo-European vocabulary, but has kept its peculiar conjugation of the verb and its own way of constructing a sentence. The Osmanli Turkish language, that of books and official documents, has gone very far in its borrowing: it has naturalised Arabic and Persian words, retaining only about a third of the words of popular speech. But it has forced the newcomers to adopt the verbal laws of Turkish, which are far removed from those of the Semitic and Indo-European languages. Analogous statements can be made in the case of Hindustani, Malay, Berber, Somali, etc. In the linguistic domain, as elsewhere, Muslim influence has impressed itself on the intellectual life of the peoples who have been more or less touched by it. In theory every Muslim ought to read the Qur'ān in the Arabic text; Arabic is the religious language of Muslims, their fraternal idiom, as was Latin to the Catholic church of the Middle Ages; it has given to the tongues of its domain a religious and abstract vocabulary, which has in no way disturbed the natural development of each of them. In Chapter XIII we shall deal with the defects of the Arabic alphabet.

Thus the institutions of the peoples who have been converted to Islam keep their originality, and a description of them would be a history of a section of the human race. We are not bold enough to undertake that task here. We shall seek merely to make clear the principal features of the institutions that those peoples owe to Islam, which are common to them all, not because they derive from the universal laws of human thought, but because they are a product of Muslim doctrine. No doubt there will be confusion at times, in the case of facts which are not directly religious, of Muslim and Arab customs: the distinction will be too subtle to be drawn in a cursory study such as this.

As it seems impossible to understand the Islamic doctrine without a knowledge of the broad lines of its history, we shall begin by recalling the essential points around which Muslim thought grew in the Middle Ages, and the various directions in which it developed. We shall then describe the essential dogmas of Islam, and pass on from there to the religious duties of the Muslim, his 'cult'. Finally we shall endeavour to make clear those facts of his social, economic and political life which seem to be characteristic of Muslim society. Some of those institutions, that of marriage for example, follow customs and rites which, although adopted by the Muslim world, are none the less a product of ideas of magic that, in spite of local variations, are common to the human race.

SOURCES

1 L. Massignon: *Monde Musulman*, 3rd Edition. Paris, 1929.

CHAPTER TWO

THE MUSLIM COMMUNITY

Ancient Arabia—Muhammad—The Umayyad Caliphate—The 'Abbasid Caliphate—The Sunnite Renaissance—The Turks.

ISLAM is a syncretism which has manifested itself through a known medium, through a book, the Qur'ān, which has been preserved in a form of which there is no need to dispute the authenticity. The teachings of the holy book have been supplemented by a Tradition, the Sunna, the Ḥadīth, which has been carefully collected by the learned men of Islam. To it have been added historical and literary documents, with the object, it would seem, of ensuring a perfect knowledge of the origins and early years of Islam, a period of which, however, our knowledge is still very incomplete.

With rare and meagre exceptions there exist today none of those documents and epigraphic texts which are the solid foundations of history to tell us of the far away days of Northern and Central Arabia. Those of Southern Arabia (Yaman, Ḥaḍramaut) are few in number and ineffective to conjure up a life that is past. And yet they supply evidence of a settled existence and a religious and social development that was more active than that of the remainder of the peninsula.

So it is that we must turn to an ancient poetry and to an historic literature that were not collected until the 9th century if we would trace some of the features of the religious life of Arabia before the Qur'ān. In this "period of ignorance" (*Jāhilīya*) gods, of imprecise nature, ruled feebly, each over a clan of greater or less importance. The worship that was accorded to them was hardly distinguishable from that given to the sacred stones, to water springs and trees. Everywhere were to be found rites of circumambulation, of stationary attitudes, of rapid processionary movements, of illumination, all of which seem to have belonged to the cult of the sun.

But other heavenly bodies were honoured, and there lingered at Mecca a rite of salutation to the first crescent of the moon which is evidently pre-Islamic. Each year, at the period, varying from region to region, when the rains bring forth the tender grass, a new-born lamb was chosen from the flock for sacrifice in a ceremony (*mausim*) of marking the newly weaned young. Man felt himself to be surrounded by a rude and capricious nature and carried forward by a destiny of which he ceased to try to discover the ultimate end. His gods granted him only occasional oracles, and the world was peopled by invisible jinns whose caprices and spites are still feared in this 20th century, and whose favour one seeks to win by presents and acts of homage. They haunted especially the holy places and the bottoms of valleys, the passage through which called therefore for haste. There was a vague feeling that, after death, one left behind a *doppelgänger* who continued to lead a pale and wretched existence. This double, in the form of a funeral bird, hovered most frequently about the tomb of him whose passing had been violent, uttering loud lamentations, until such time as his death was avenged.

The oracles of the gods were spoken by the mouth of a soothsayer (*kāhin*) who interpreted them. There were men gifted with peculiar vision, who explained hidden things and foretold the future. Those mysteries were embodied in a rhythmical and rhyming prose, the *saj'*. The poet, the *shā'ir* "he who knows", employed, even before the 7th century, a rich variety of rhythms, and played the part of the inspired defender of the honour (*'irḍ*) of the tribe by chanting its glory and hurling invectives against its enemies.

In Arabia, Nature lends itself to a settled life only in a few regions of the south and north-east. Elsewhere, except in a few oases, the Bedouin are in constant movement, not only following the regular and peaceful movements of the flocks, but subject also to sudden displacements, during which battles re-shape some social groups and destroy others. Between the settled communities and the Bedouin proper, the inhabitants of Mecca formed a mixed group of town dwellers, occupied in trade, and travelling in caravans. It would seem that the connections they had formed with Syria and the Yaman, and along the roads leading thither, had enabled them to add greatly to the fame of their little shrine, the Ka'ba, which profited further from the vicinity of the holy places of the religions of the Bedouin. The city of Mecca had thus become the centre of religious life in Central Arabia and in the Ḥijāz, into which there gradually entered ideas taken from other cults. Christianity had long since spread among the tribes, either propagated by Abyssinians, or through Persian influence in the form of the Jacobite doctrine, that of the Syrian Monophysites. There were groups of Jews or of Judaised Arabs who, although their religious culture was rather meagre, were greatly attached to their laws and their own form of worship.

In the beginning of the 7th century various currents of foreign ideas penetrated into the Ḥijāz, and certain souls were sufficiently influenced by them to seek to raise themselves to a religious plane higher than that on which rested the animism of the Bedouin. In the peaceful trading assemblies of the tribes, held at various points in the Ḥijāz during the holy months of inter-tribal truce, Christian voices had been raised, it would seem, to utter the threat of the Last Judgment, announcing, at the same time, the joys of Paradise and the pangs of Hell. The Jews of Yathrib were awaiting a prophet, and many men, anxious as to their own fate, longed to find a guide. Manichaeism had spread throughout all the East the conception of the struggle between good and evil, of which traces may possibly be found in the ideas of Muḥammad.

It may be that we shall never have a knowledge of the life of the Prophet sufficiently accurate for us to understand how, after a life spent in the ordinary activities of a Qurayshite merchant, he was able, when about forty years old, to convince himself that he was the man predestined to bring to the Arabs the words of Allāh, the supreme deity whose name was beginning to be spoken.

It can be imagined that he had been impressed by the Judeo-Christian doctrines which were no doubt professed in Mecca by some, and which inclined the minds of others towards monotheism. Feeling himself freed by his marriage from the material cares of life, he seems to have given himself up wholly to meditation. The Tradition shows him wandering on the hill of Ab ū Qubays which dominates Mecca; he has visions which end by taking the concrete and visible form of Gabriel (*Jibrā'īl*), the angel of the Christian Annunciation, who became in Islam the Angel of the Revelation.

He received from the angel Gabriel, towards the year 610, the revelation which he communicated to his wife, Khadīja, then to a few believers. This revelation took the shape of the brief but urgent warnings which form the shortest sūras of the Qur'ān, the last according to the order that was later adopted by the editors of the holy book. Muḥammad's prophesy was received by the mass of the Qurayshites, first with indifference, then with irritation when they understood that it was not satisfied with the addition of a new deity to those that had up to then assured the safety and the wealth of Mecca, but that it sought to replace them by an unknown god. Although such important people as, for example, Abū Bakr, 'Uthmān, and 'Umar were converted, the Muslim community was only a small group made up of members of the Hāshimite family and of persons belonging to the humblest circles of the city. Muḥammad thought that he would be better understood by Christian Abyssinia, in which country several of his adherents made a prolonged stay. He himself went to Al-Tā'if, two days journey south-east of Mecca, where he tried in vain to convert to his faith an active group of settled farmers and gardeners.

On the other hand, an inquiry into the opinions of the inhabitants of Yathrib-Medina convinced him that they were ready to welcome an invitation from outside, which would put an end to the intestinel quarrels on which they were wasting their energies. They were an unstable mixture of two Arab and three Jewish tribes who contested the leadership of a settled community well protected from the Bedouin, occupying land sufficiently watered to permit of continuous cultivation. Just then victory had lain with the Arab tribes, Aus and Khazraj; but the constant rivalry between the two threatened to transfer authority to the Jewish tribes. Muḥammad interviewed members of the Arab tribes who had come to take part in the religious celebrations that were held annually in Mecca and the vicinity. They undertook to adopt his faith and to share his lot. In 622 the Moslems left Mecca (the Hegira) in small groups, and were followed in the end by Muḥammad and Abū Bakr, later by 'Alī.

During the difficult years that the Prophet had spent in

Mecca, the Revelation had continued to proclaim, in words of fire and splendour, the coming of the hour of the Resurrection and of the Judgment which should reward the good by giving them eternal life in the gardens of Paradise, and punish the evil by burning them for ever in the fires of Hell. It insisted on the oneness of God which had been denied by the Qurayshites. It prescribed, although still without defining its form and frequency, the duty of ritual prayer. Gradually the divine word lost its fire as it proceeded to enunciate rules for living and, more especially, to tell stories of the prophets of old whose successor Muḥammad was, and whose example demonstrated the unity of the truth faith, broken only through the wickedness of the Jews and the Christians. Muḥammad did not claim, in fact, to reveal a new religion: he was only one who uttered warnings against error, the last prophet after Jesus (*'Isā*), and sought to confirm and restore the ancient religion of Abraham. His doctrine was open to the adhesion of the Jews of Medina.

In the course of the negotiations that he had undertaken during those past years, and in the difficult task of guiding the little flock of the faithful, Muḥammad had assumed the role of a judge, a lawgiver, and a chief, functions for which it would appear that he had become fit, suddenly and miraculously, as soon as he had planted his foot in Qubā', at the gates of Medina. His revelation had possessed him so thoroughly that, henceforth, his own thoughts seemed to him to be the thoughts of God. Without effort and with complete sincerity, he solved by the divine word, not only all the problems raised in the process of organising the Muslim community, but even the difficulties arising in his own life, and that in ways contrary to reason. It is probable that, when the Qur'ān, in the earliest sūras, threatened the Qurayshites with imminent punishment, Muḥammad believed in an early end of the world, and we are struck by the resemblance to the prophesies of Jesus. But, at Medina, the Qur'ān abandoned its apocalyptic tone and turned to the lawgiving that organises what is real and lasting.

Thus it is that, in their matter as in their form, the Medina sūras of the Qur'ān have appeared to Muslim, and later to European, exegetists, to stand out from among the Mecca passages, in spite of the extreme chronological disorder of the final text of the Qur'ān.

On arriving in Medina, Muḥammad concluded with the local Arab tribes a pact which, without providing absolutely for their conversion to Islam, bound them to recognise his personal authority, which his position as the Prophet gradually transformed, in the eyes of the faithful, into that of God. As for the Jews, Muḥammad, supported by a revelation favourable to his designs, strove to bring them to himself, but in vain. However poor the dogmatic culture of the Jews of Medina may have been, it was well enough grounded to keep them from accepting, in the person of Muḥammad, a prophet of the law or a Messiah. Muḥammad's resulting disappointment soon turned to hatred; favourable circumstances allowed him, encouraged by his revelation, to destroy or to expel the Jews.

The agreement, implying moral and material brotherhood which the Qurayshite "emigrants", i.e. the *Muhājirūn* had made with certain Medinites, the "assistants", i.e. the *Anṣār*, had still not incorporated the newcomers in the economic life of Medina, Their existence was dependent on a hospitality which might well become a burden to the inhabitants. They therefore took up the habitual trade of the Bedouin, which consisted in stealing the goods of their neighbours and pillaging the flocks of those who were not of the faith. An expedition directed against a Mecca caravan, bringing from the north a rich consignment of merchandise, and defended by a guard of Qurayshites, led to the skirmish of Badr, which tradition has turned into the defeat of polytheism, achieved by the Muslims with the assistance of the angels. Two campaigns undertaken by the citizens of Mecca against Medina did not prevent Muḥammad from enriching his followers with the spoils of the Jews, nor from consolidating his authority in Medina, and extending it to the Bedouin tribes. At the same time the Qur'ān declared the Abrahamic and sacred character of the holy places of Mecca; it was towards the Ka'ba that the Muslims turned for their ritual prayer. The Qurayshites felt the necessity and the advantage of an agreement which was negotiated by prudent men, Al'Abbās, the uncle of Muḥammad and Abū Sufyān, the father of his wife, Ḥafṣa. In 630 Muḥammad entered Mecca in triumph and destroyed the idols of the Ka'ba, which became the empty house of an ever-present God.

On his death in 632, as if he had really thought that the

world would end before him, he left his Muslims leaderless. The Muslim community was a haphazard group that he had brought together by the unity of the faith, by his reputation as a prophet, and by his personal ascendancy. He had been a tribal Shaykh, a supreme judge, inspired by God doubtless, but without the authority that dynastic tradition and political custom can confer on a king. His revelation had not declared the power that should succeed him and which should ensure the continuity of the Muslim community. It seemed about to dissolve in apostasy and revolt. The hereditary idea, foreign to the political habits of the Arab, was, moreover, excluded by the fact that Muḥammad left no male child; it was only at a later period that the idea was revived. Instinctively, recourse was had to the palavers that accompanied the election of a Shaykh by the tribes. An attempt was made to reconcile individual ambition, tribal vanity, and ordinary instincts, and it was wonderfully fortunate for the future of Islam that Abū Bakr, companion of his beginnings and father of 'Ā'isha, the Prophet's favourite wife, was chosen to be the lieutenant of the Envoy of God (*khalīf atu rasūli llāh*). Just as he had left his succession unprovided for, Muḥammad had not thought of collecting the passages that the revelation had scattered abroad during twenty years, and which the practice of the cult had repeated and mingled in men's minds. The text of the Qur'ān was first definitely fixed under 'Uthmān.

Meanwhile, the Muslim community was in possession of the elements of a new social and family organisation and, when the text of the Qur'an had been fixed, they had a legal code which, at times, condescended to the most minute detail, although it laid down no general rule or constitutive principle. Muḥammad had been nothing more than a supreme arbitrator between social groups, which had preserved their customs, in so far as they were not contrary to the divine law. The Qur'ān found itself supplemented, moreover, by a new way of life in which the religious ideal (*dīn*) of Islam was substituted for the manly virtues (*muruwwa*) of Old Arabia. This was the way of life of the Companions of the Prophet, born of his example and of the anxiety of the Companions to copy him. It was the straight way in which walked the four caliphs (*rāshidūn*), Abū Bakr, 'Umar, 'Uthman, 'Alī. But the smashing victories of the caliphate of 'Umar transformed, in a few years, the intellectual and material life of the Muslim community. There arose a great Muslim state. Dwelling, up to then, on the fringe of oriental civilisation, Arabia had suddenly hurled her tribes, newly initiated into a new religion, into the middle of an unknown world. In that world old beliefs and fine cultures had either mixed or fused, and Hellenism had stamped on them imprints that were by no means superficial. Manichaeism had left some marks on them. The glory of Alexandria had only just been dimmed; Antioch had still its schools; Gundēshāpūr was a great Monophysite centre. On this terrain, so rich in memories, and still so full of energetic life, Persia had faced, first Rome, and then Byzantium; and the Qur'ān speaks of their alternating successes of which the last, that of Heraclius, had fired the imagination of the people of Mecca. According to the legend, Muḥammad had called upon the emperors of Byzantium and the Sāsānid king to embrace Islam. Their struggle for supremacy manifested itself in the hostility of the minor rulers of the two Arab marches in the Syrian desert, the Lakhmids of Ḥīra who, on the lower Euphrates, reigned under the protection of Persia, and the Ghassānids of Baṣra, who held for Byzantium the south of Syro-Palestine. In a few years the Arab flood menaced all, both Persians and Byzantines, and the Arabs ruled over populations that had long been accustomed to changing masters: Islam looked to them like one more Christian heresy.

The conquerors who, for the most part, were neither saints nor proselytisers, were eager to enjoy their conquests in peace, and, after the loot of the battlefield, to gather the fruits of the soil without the necessity of cultivating it. The Bedouin were accustomed to hold to ransom the settled inhabitants of the oases. The protectorat for gain was a formula of tolerance and collaboration that the Qur'ān had invented for the benefit of the "People of the Book" (Jews and Christians), and which was applied to all the peoples who accepted a régime of submission and tribute, in exchange for the safety of their persons and their goods, for respect of their customs and beliefs, and for the maintenance in office of their magistrates. The conquered possessed, moreover, a culture superior to that of their conquerors; but the latter rose quickly to a realisation of the need for order in the government of men and the enjoyment of things, perceiving that this must take place on a higher plane than that reached in the development of religious thought. At the same time they acquired a feeling for art which nothing hitherto had awakened in them. The Qur'ān was no longer a sufficient guide for Muslims brought into touch with new needs which the rigidity of the text did not permit them to satisfy. A new law was required, in harmony, no doubt, with the essential principles of the original code, but more supple, and capable of modification and retraction. They found it in the prophetic Tradition that, under the first four caliphs, had been looked upon as the straight road, the road on which the Prophet had, by his example, set the feet of his community.

This Tradition, like the Qur'ān, had been passed from mouth to mouth, gathering up incompatible memories and apocryphal and tendentious matter, destined to provide arguments for the disputes that grew ever more animated in the new society that was being built. When the traditionalist scholars of the 8th and 9th centuries collected and codified them, they had to separate the tares from the good grain. In the following chapter the reader will learn how they understood their task. This Tradition, incorporated into the Doctrine, is the *sunna*, expounded in an immense collection of short narratives (*ḥadīth*).

The authority attributed to the *sunna* appears to be only a confirmation of that of the Qur'ān. But the transmission and even the putting into words of the *ḥadīth* implied an element of personal judgment and of choice. There was here a turning aside from the sole word of God, revealed to Muḥammad and transmitted by him, in order to follow the word of Muḥammad by his Companions or by the generation that came after them. It was, when one considers the exclusive reverence that had been paid to the Qur'ān since the assassination of Caliph 'Uthman (656), *the* great breach in the Moslem community. 'Alī, husband of Fāṭima, daughter of the Prophet, and the father of his two grandchildren, Ḥasan and Ḥusayn, became caliph, and, after having been forced to fight some of the Companions of Muḥammad with whom his scheming widow, 'Ā'isha, had associated herself, found himself, in 661, confronting Mu'āwiya's Syrians. The latter forced him to consent to an arbitration which went against him, and which was indignantly rejected by the Khārijites, resolved to hold to the judgment of God's book. They deserted the camp of 'Alī who was assassinated soon after, the caliphate passing to the Umayyads (661–750).

The Umayyad century is undoubtedly the most interesting, as it is the least known of all Muslim history. It was the time during which the foundations of Muslim institutions were laid, when men's thoughts began to reach outwards, a time of soul searchings amidst the splendours of an opulent material existence, an epoch in which 'Abbāsid society (after 750) became a brilliant centre of intellectual life. The princes of the Umayyad dynasty whom the 'Abbāsid historians have belittled were, for the most part, skilful and resolute rulers, who prepared the way for the absorption into the Muslim community of those who had hitherto merely paid tribute to it.

The Muslim Empire which, in a few decades, had expanded from Khurāsān and Sind to Morocco and Frankish Gaul, had neither a constitution nor an organised administration. The Caliph, representative of the Prophet and of the Law, delegated his limitless powers to his agents, to the provincial governors and army chiefs, to his tax gatherers and qāḍīs, whose respective duties were to ensure the defence of his borders, to maintain civil peace, and to see to the regular collection of dues and tribute. It was a régime that had neither traditions nor principles, in which the energy and judgment of the chiefs took the place of formal regulations. The great territorial divisions were those that Nature delimited. Arabia, "Cradle of Islam", was now on the outer fringe of the Empire, and the efforts that Ibn al-Zubayr made to play the caliph at Mecca were fruitless (692). The House of Allāh continued to be the religious centre of the world, and the tomb of the Prophet at Medina soon became the object of as great a veneration. In the 8th century the city of Medina was still a centre of juridical studies, of which Mālik Ibn Anas is the most illustrious figure, and contained, in addition, a famous school in which female slaves were trained as musicians and singers.

But the centre of the Empire was Damascus, and the Arab bands of the subdivisions of Syria (*jund*), whose war services had been rewarded with grants of land, the so-called "Syrians", constituted an army that was long faithful to the Umayyad caliphs whose peace was disturbed by the Arabs of the North (*Qays*) and those of the South (*Kalb*). Mu'āwiya had maintained in his capital the Byzantine administration, the personnel of which his successors strove to win for Islam, without however damaging its mechanism.

'Irāq, disturbed by the opposition of Khārijite and Shī'ite bands, was meanwhile developing its material resources under the direction of a succession of distinguished governors, such as Ziyād ibn Abīhi and Al-Hajjāj, who, at the same time administered through a lieutenant the vast spaces of Iran and Khurāsān.

Egypt furnished plentiful supplies by which the caliph profited after he had satisfied the appetites of a numerous colony of Southern Arabs who had settled in that country, under governors of whom 'Abd al-Malik's brother, 'Abd al-'Azīz, was one.

The Muslim West was still in the first stage of its organisation.

The Umayyad court still had two aspects, the one of civilised refinement, the other purely Bedouin. The caliphs loved the Damascus *ghūta*, the well-watered plain which, a few miles to the east, is lost in the desert. Those people from Mecca, although doubtless accustomed to a settled life, had been men of the caravans, who had crossed the desert too often not to have kept in their blood the taste for the wide open spaces. Moreover, their mothers were often of Bedouin stock. Several of them built, on sites that had been cleverly irrigated, their farm-houses and hunting lodges, palaces, the recent discovery and examination of which enable us to reconstitute today the history of Umayyad art and civilisation.

Mu'āwiya, after having based his right to the caliphate on an arbitration which, accepted at Siffīn by the unhappy 'Alī, took the place of an appointment by general consent, introduced into the method of handing on the caliphate the idea of heredity, a conception that was foreign to Arab tradition. In the course of a meeting of tribal chiefs and of the principal personalities of the Empire, he secured the acknowledgment of his son Yazīd as heir apparent. The new doctrine was maintained by the 'Abbāsids, but it was frequently tempered by assassination.

The 'Abbāsids came to power after a struggle of complicated origin, which, however, brought about a complete change in the caliphate. The Umayyads had adhered to the Qurayshite traditions; in spite of their intelligent adaptation to a novel situation, they had remained essentially Arab. They had known the art of using the tributary Christians of Syria and Egypt who had been later converted in large numbers to Islam, but the new Muslims of the eastern provinces of the Empire had, for the most part, attached themselves to the party of the 'Alids, who maintained their identity, although decimated by war and without chiefs worthy of the name. They were attracted thereto by the doctrine of the legitimate caliphate upheld in the family of the Prophet, a doctrine that conformed to their former conception of a royal line inheriting a divine emanation. An uncle of the Prophet, 'Abbās, had moved very skilfully among both Muslims and Qurayshites, and had helped to secure the surrender of Mecca in 630. His descendants, who had inherited his talent for intrigue, had, during the 8th century, created a centre of agitation in 'Irāq, by means of which they seemed to seek to further the return of the 'Alids, while yet working entirely in their own interests. They were able to rally to their cause the party of the Mu'tazilites who had come to have considerable influence in intellectual circles, as we shall see in the following chapter, an influence which was sharply anti-Umayyad, although it rejected the teachings of the Shī'ite extremists who professed to have, through the line of 'Alī, inherited the divine light. In 750 Abū Al-'Abbās al-Saffāḥ proclaimed himself the legitimate lieutenant of the Prophet, and received, at Kūfa, the oath of fidelity of an important gathering of tribal chiefs.

With the 'Abbāsids, the new converts, and principally the Iranians, attained power, and introduced into the community tastes and tendencies that affected every sphere of action. Damascus was abandoned in favour of Bagdad. That, too, was a sign. The Caliph was turning his back on the Mediterranean and breaking with the West, which now, from Egypt to the Pyrenees, became independent and paid the caliphate only an occasional and formal homage—a mere courteous gesture.

The Caliph turned his eyes to the East, to his Iranian provinces, which were destined to break away from him, and from which were to come his masters, and towards the Persian Gulf and the waters of the Indies from which his merchants were to bring to him the riches of the further Orient.

The 'Abbāsid Caliph's first effort was to bring the Muslim community back into the straight path from which, under the impious Umayyads, it had strayed; for his principal claim is piety and respect for tradition. Like the Prophet, he is the inspired interpreter of the holy book, either by himself or through the theologians and jurists who enjoy his confidence. Historians draw a contrast between his piety and holiness and the irreligion and vices of the Umayyad caliphs—a tendency to polemics by which we must not allow ourselves to be deceived. But he is also a sovereign in the Persian style, an ostentatious and resplendent king, around whom there grows up the luxury familiar to the peoples of Iraq and Persia, who have never forgotten the artistic past of their race. The court of the Caliph gathers to itself a strange concourse of pious doctors, singers, qāḍīs, poets, pedants and conjurors. The exquisite nights of Bagdad are the hour of royal assemblies. After the pious observance of evening prayer, songs are sung and, between the songs, the wine cups are emptied. The air, already perfumed by the sweet vapours that rise from the incense bowls, and trembling to the murmur of tinkling fountains, vibrates to the sweetly powerful voices of the singers and to the tones of the lute. Sometimes an unexpected incident gives variety to the daily feast, the questioning of a prisoner of quick retort and lively speech, the visit of a proud and churlish beggar monk, maybe a head lopped off the while the cups go round. The night draws to an end, drunken hearts grow sad, tears fall, someone laments in verse the brevity of life. At last the dawn dimly lights the scene, and those of the guests who can still remain erect piously perform the morning prayer. It is a life full of sensations, both violent and tender, of coarseness and refinement, the like of which is to be found, but with greater vigour and more splendour, in our own Renaissance, and which is excellently depicted in The Thousand and One Nights, the Book of Songs, the Golden Meads, in the descriptions of historians, and in the words of poets.

But, behind this romantic façade, there lives a people, among whom are some who think; and it will be their thoughts and struggles that will be the subject of our next chapter. The 9th century sees the culmination of the Muslim effort to understand God, man, and life, and to reconcile faith and reason. It is, too, the flowering time of Arab literature while it sees the beginning of a second, momentary, resurgence of Islamic art. In it all the possibilities of intellectual brilliance and material splendour are realised. In its last years the hour strikes that marks its decline and the decay of all this glory.

The Muslim Empire broke asunder under the weight of geographical and historical necessity. In the 10th century its western borders, facing the Byzantine Empire, were still intact, except for the occasional consequences of momentary incidents, but all the Iranian provinces had finally broken away, and it was Iranian amīrs who came to Bagdad and took control of an impotent caliph (946). Shī'ites themselves, they helped to propagate a moderate Shī'ism, while the Qarmaṭs spread disorder and ruin from Mecca to Bagdad, and the Ismā'īlians founded in Ifrīqiya (Tunisia) the Fāṭimid dynasty which, for two centuries, ruled over Egypt and Syria. Spain remained independent and hostile under a dynasty of Umayyad caliphs, but followed, none the less, all the phases of eastern thought.

In the 11th century the Caliph had a change of masters. The Turks who, since the end of the 9th century, had got to know the way to Bagdad, seized it in 1056 and governed, without intermediary, 'Irāq, Mesopotamia, and a part of Syria, where the Saljūq amīrs had divided up the country into small rival principalities. The dispersion of the Muslim forces, the wretched state of the 'Abbāsid caliphate, and the decadence of the Fāṭimid caliphate made possible the extraordinary adventure of the Frankish crusade of 1097. But the very presence of the crusaders, who likewise owed their failure to disorder and personal rivalries, contributed, by a sort of reaction, to the re-grouping of Islam under the Zangid and Ayyūbid amīrs, first Nūr al-Dīn, and then Ṣalāḥ al-Dīn (Saladin) who, in 1187, recaptured Jerusalem. The new masters of the Orient restored Sunnite orthodoxy and, since this time, save only in Persia, Shīʿism has been the faith of none but a schismatic minority. Through the expansion of the *madrasa* they formed a numerous class of *fuqahā'*, trained in the good doctrine.

The Sunnite revival accentuated the narrow character of Muslim orthodoxy. In a society where reactions are quick, opposing tendencies could not fail to be aroused. These showed themselves in the rapid advance of Ṣūfism which, in the 12th century, covered the Orient with monasteries and centres of mystical preaching. Looked upon with suspicion, or condemned outright by orthodox Muslims, whose ritualism was incapable of adaptation to its redoubtable individualism, Ṣūfism united itself with Sunnism, thanks to the teaching of Ghazālī, who died in 1111. Ṣūfism infused into Islam certain possibilities of tenderness, an appeal to the heart, calculated to seduce lofty spirits, and established its influence over the masses by extending the worship of the saints, both of the dead and of the living, by urging an increased reverence towards the shaykhs, by all that Maghrib calls the Marabouts and Zāwiyas. Ṣūfism was, for several centuries, the most living form of Islam. In the West, in Morocco of the 11th and 12th centuries, the Almoravids and the Almohads had set in motion a religious reformation which gave some living religious force to the struggle against the Spanish *reconquista*.

In the 13th century, the 'Abbāsid caliphate was, in 1258, overthrown by the Mongols and, in the tremendous confusion of their invasions, the intellectual life of the Muslim stagnated until as late as the 19th century. Yet, during no moment of this period of slumbering, has Islam lacked men who cared for spiritual values. In the 14th century the ardent attempts of Ibn Taymīya to bring Sunnism back to the pure Ḥanbalite doctrine of the 9th century, and even the extent to which his efforts were resisted, gave proof of the vitality of religious thought.

The Ottoman conquest brought to the East order and unity; the sultans treated dissident thinkers with a kind of indifferent tolerance, alternating with the scaffold and the galleys. This treatment destroyed nothing vital or stimulating to the new moral life. Meanwhile, Islam, lulled by the monotonous rhythm of prayers that had long since become mechanical, and for long careless of every effort towards religious revival, has suddenly awakened to a realisation of its material weakness and intellectual poverty. That it has thus reacted is a remarkable event, and no less remarkable is the fact that it must be given its place among the moral values of tomorrow, a fact with which we shall deal more thoroughly in chapters XIII and XIV.

SOURCES

Halphen: *Les Barbares* (S.98); Diehl & G. Marçais: *Le Monde Oriental* (S.99)—Gaudefroy-Demombynes: *Le Monde Musulman jusqu'ax Croisades* (id.);—H. Massé: *L'Islam* (S.86); Tor Andrae: *Muḥammad* (French translation by Jean Demombynes (1945);—Bühl: *Muḥammad*;—Muir: *Moḥammed*.

CHAPTER THREE

THE MOVEMENT OF IDEAS

RELIGIOUS events are, perhaps more in Islam than elsewhere, intimately related to the political. The rapid historical summary that we have just completed reveals the constant confusion of the temporal with the spiritual. This is an essential characteristic of Muslim institutions. Muslims, whose daily life was steeped in the essence of religion, never ceased to discuss the gravest questions within the purview of human knowledge, an aspect of their history which those few pages must strive to recall.

Muḥammad was a prophet, not a theologian, a fact so evident that one is loath to state it. The men who surrounded him and constituted the influential élite of the primitive Muslim community, contented themselves with obeying the law that he had proclaimed in the name of Allāh and with following his teaching and example. They had a simple, robust faith that was satisfied with a small number of formulae and a few rites.

A few decades of life in contact with peoples who were given to constant religious disputes sufficed, however, to cause the sons of those same men to take a passionate interest in the essential questions that are raised by the mystery of human fate and are involved in the need for understanding the world. They brought to the inquiry such an extreme variety of contrivance and such a plentiful wealth of ingenuity, that one hesitates, after sketching the outlines of the great movements of Muslim thought, to assign to any one thinker a definite place in a dogmatic category.

It would seem that the polemics that so greatly agitated the Christian church found a place in Muslim thought, even before the tributary Christians became, by conversion, a part of the Muslim community. It was not only in the mind of

Muḥammad that the Qur'ān is a turning back and a restoration of the Pentateuch and the Gospel; it is so in actual truth. And the same thing can be said of a tradition that is steeped in Judeo-Christianity. The vigour of the controversies that revolve around it are evidence of the vitality of the religious and political thought that it aroused, just as the flabbiness of modern speculation is a clear sign of indifference and mechanical piety.

Muslim thought occupied itself with the loftiest questions of human destiny, questions which, for the most part, had been merely hinted at in the Qur'ān which, it must not be forgotten, is a revelation and not a manual of theology. The problem of predestination and free will, enunciated so early as in the Umayyad period, was, however, frequently touched on in the Qur'ān and all its aspects stated. Historians have insisted on the formlessness of this Qur'ānic thought, and on contradictions which could not fail to provide arguments for all parties. We think, on the other hand, that one should admire the richness of Muḥammad's mind that enabled him to gather from without, or to draw from his own mental stock, the essential points of the problem, and to put forward a number of solutions. Although we hesitate to risk a comparison that could be justified only as a result of a lengthy exposition, it may be said that all the elements of the successive theses of St. Augustine are to be found in rudimentary form in the Qur'ān, and that all that is lacking is the constructive reasoning of the theologian.

The whole judgment of Muḥammad seems to have been dominated by the almighty nature of the one God who is all powerful, in the past, the present and the future, or even, to express more clearly Muḥammad's imprecise conception by the use of an idea evolved since his day, in the absolute that is outside the idea of time. It is outside time that God determines, or has determined the destiny of man. One might say that language itself conduces to this imprecision, language that gives to the verb an aspect of completed or uncompleted action, independent of the idea of time. God orders the destiny of man by showing him the good way (*hudā*). Some follow it, profiting by the grace that God has granted to them. God has stopped up the eyes and ears of others so that they understand not; and in this way are drawn up the formulae which predicate an unmodified predestination, against which all man's efforts are vain.

But the Qur'ān proclaims also the justice of God; and it was the application of this justice, that is, the reward to be bestowed on the day of the Last Judgment, that formed one of the principal themes of earliest and most enthusiastic preachings. God cannot do man a wrong; He will reward him according to his deserts. There appears to be here a violent contradiction with the earlier notion of a prearranged destiny, and an attempt is made to discover how and why some men were pre-destined to good, and others to evil, and why they can be punished for the one or rewarded for the other, seeing that they had no responsibility for what they did. Christian doctrine takes refuge in the ignorance of man and the divine mystery; one cannot see why similar reasoning should not be valid for Islam.

Another mystery is encountered when the attempt is made to explain the origin of good and evil. The Qur'ān has contributed nothing definite on this subject. It is not known whether God created, or endured, or was ignorant of evil, nor whether man is sullied by it from his birth, or whether life brings it to him. Islam, moreover, equates good and evil to obedience to God and rebellion against His commands.

Indeed, in order to appreciate the solutions given by the Qur'ān, we must remember that, in dealing with high questions of human fate and in explaining the world, as also in considering the commonest events of human life, the Revelation followed the circumstances of the life of the Muslim community, solving difficulties as they arose and in so far as they were a hindrance to Muḥammad's work. The predestination that prevents the Qurayshites from giving ear to his preaching consoles the Prophet for his failure with them; it allows him unregretfully to abandon the wicked to their fate, and to make the hesitant tremble at the thought of their eternal damnation. If they have the will, their actions will prove that they are not predestined to evil. Passages telling of the infinite goodness of a merciful God and of the rewards for good deeds promised by Him are a corrective to threatenings and an encouragement to follow the Prophet's instructions. We do not believe in a sudden massive development of Muḥammad's mind, although excellent modern historians have thought to detect it, even if that was how the teaching of St. Augustine took shape. But we are of opinion that Muḥammad became aware of the various aspects of the problem through the influence of circumstances which we may at times vaguely perceive.

It would seem that, under Judeo-Christian influence, Muḥammad formed a conception of the origin of man which we can state as follows: Adam, God's ultimate creation, received from Him the light (*nūr*) at the same moment in which he was given life. He knew the names of things and was given power over them. He was accepted by the angels who, on the command of God, prostrated themselves before him. Nothing remained, therefore, for him to do but to enjoy, in paradise and with Eve as a companion, all created things. But a rebel angel, Iblīs, who had, through pride, refused to bow down before Adam and whom God had driven out, revenged himself by giving Adam knowledge, that is, evil. Although God forgave Adam, he sent him out into the world while continuing to grant him the grace of his light and the hope of a return to paradise. On the other hand, he gave to Satan the power of deceiving men until the day of the Last Judgment. The race of men, which then multiplies and covers the earth, has in it a spark of the light of God, but is in constant danger of losing it by following the suggestions of Satan. God comes to its aid by sending His prophets, who bring to it His revelation, which is the full light, and by pointing out the good way. Since God does not send His prophets to all men, it would appear that He has a chosen people, which is always that of every prophet, from Noah until Jesus. The rest of humanity is abandoned and lost, through a divine abstention which is pre-destined. As to the time when this predestined fate was determined by God, tradition put into the mouth of Muḥammad divergent views; one *ḥadīth* put this moment fifty thousand years before the creation of the world; another, of popular inspiration, showed God watching over the development of the embryo, gradually giving it its form, and finally deciding its fate. Yet the conception of man's course that we have just described does not brand him definitely with evil from his beginning; it permits of the belief that man is weak, but that, aided by the divine mercy, he may succeed in resisting the power of Satan: all men have the possibility of salvation. But the Qur'ān says that God did not wish to save all men, and that He "swore against Himself" that he would fill Gehenna; God has His elect and those whom He has rejected; and, in the end, we always come face to face with a mystery.

The divergencies of the *ḥadīths*, confirming the contradictions of the Qur'ānic text, serve as a basis for the discord that rules men's minds from the beginning of the 8th century under the Umayyads. The majority favoured the idea of predestination, and it was this idea that prevailed in the orthodox doctrine. In the beginning its partisans were called Jabarites (*'jabarūt*, "the compelling power of God"). But a considerable minority professed the liberty of human action. By a verbal derivation which is still imperfectly explained, these were called Qadarites (*qadar*, predestination), their opinion acquired a body of doctrine with the Mu'tazilites, of whom we shall speak in the next chapter; we shall also add a word about the Murji'ites who left God's decision in suspense until the day of the Last Judgment. The belief in predestination, fatalism, is consequently, in the general opinion of Europeans, the essential characteristic of the Muslim. We shall not here attempt to determine to what extent the idea overcame, among Muslims, the life instinct and brought about a slowing down of their activity.

In the controversy that arose concerning predestination the Umayyad caliphs favoured the doctrine that denies the freedom of men's actions. Their authority grew out of the secession from the Muslim community of the *fitna*, which, at the same time, brought about the formation of the three great heterodox doctrines of Islam: Khārijism, Shī'ism and Mu'tazilism. The adherents of the first movement left (*Kharajū*) the camp, renounced obedience to the 'Alids, and gave themselves an *imām*, guardian of the pure doctrine; the second was the 'Alid party (*shī'a*) properly so-called; finally the leading Companions of the Prophet kept themselves apart (*i'tazalū*), a fact which seems, together with the other facts, to have given the name Mu'tazilism to their position outside the other two parties.

They were definitely anti-Umayyad, since they acknowledged the right of 'Alī to succeed Muḥammad; but they recognised the legitimacy of the first three caliphs, rewarding the part they played with a respect which was imitated by certain moderate Shī'ites and also by some of the Khārijites. This middle, but anti-Umayyad, attitude it was that, according to Nyberg, brought together the numerous party of reflective spirits who worked, during the first half of the 8th century, for the overthrow of the Umayyads and their replacement, not by the descendants of 'Alī who were guided by the extreme partisans of the transmission of the divine light within the family of the Prophet, but by the 'Abbāsids, to whose political skill was added the true wisdom of sound judgment. However that may be, the Mu'tazilite doctrine was maintained by the 'Abbāsid caliphate from the origin until the coming to power of Mutawakkil (847). It was thus a state doctrine, as far as this idea can be understood in Islam. Mu'tazilism was an authoritarian doctrine, active, dominating, not the rational liberalism the earlier European historian saw in it. It defended energetically the foundations of the faith, the Qur'ān, and the Tradition, but it repudiated the vulgarly traditional belief of the *ahl-al-ḥadīth,* and used reason as an aid to faith. Borrowing the reasoning processes of Greek philosophy, the Mu'tazilites created Moslem scholasticism; they are the first logicians of Islam, the *ahl al-kalām* or *mutakallimīn.*

Mu'tazilism believes in the absolute oneness of God, opposes all dualism, Manichaean or otherwise, rejects anthropomorphism and denies in God any attribute apart from His essence (dhāt). All its moral teaching is dominated by the idea of the justice of God, who did not create evil but permitted it in the workings of His creation. Welldoing consists in obedience to the commands of the Qur'ān; the acts of man are free and he receives the reward earned by them. His graver sins are contraventions of the prohibitions of God, and the man who is guilty of them (*fāsiq*) is considered to be placed in a situation intermediary (*al manzila bayn manzilatayn*) between the infidel (*kāfir*) and the true believer (*mu'min*). Contrary to what we have stated above, the name given to the doctrine has been thought to be derived from this position "apart" from the world. The Mu'tazilites found themselves opposed to Shī'ism, especially so to the fanatics of that party who had gone so far as to assign a sort of divinity to the 'Alid *imām,* as well as to the often rude traditionalism of the doctors in canon law, who were at that time the organisers of the practices of the religious life of Islam. They had also put up a show of opposition to the Umayyads who professed the Jabarite conception of absolute predestination.

In adopting a definite position regarding the question of the divine attributes, the Mu'tazilites had decided against their eternal duration, and particularly against that of the word of God. This doctrine, which constituted only a secondary element of the controversies in which the Mu'tazilites took part, had a concrete and tangible side that so captured the attention of the masses as to become the slogan of Mu'tazilism. The doctrine generally accepted until then had held that the Qur'ān, the Word that had come forth from the glory of God, could not be other than eternal as He was, and that it had had no place in the act of creation; various solutions had been put forward which should distinguish between the Qur'ān itself, the divine Word, and its material embodiments such as copies and the recitation of extracts from it. The Mu'tazilites, on the other hand, maintained that the Qur'ān had been created at the same time as other earthly things. This was the official doctrine that Caliph al-Ma'mūn (813–833) tried to impose by force.

Al-Mansūr (754–775) had set up an inquisitorial organisation which pursued heterodox tendencies manifested chiefly among groups of new converts of Iranian origin. It had imprisoned, executed, but more often murdered, all those who were suspected of being *zindīg*, a Persian word which had been earlier applied to the Manichaeans. The lasting influence of Manichaeism on Muslim thought is a fact the importance of which has yet to be determined. The caliph had, therefore, submitted to a test (*miḥna*) the opinions of all those who, by their occupations or by their intellectual activity, occupied positions of influence. Under Al-Ma'mūn the *miḥna* was directed against the opponents of Mu'tazilism, and all important persons, the *qāḍīs* for example, had to affirm their immutable faith in a created Qur'ān. Imām Ibn Ḥanbal was pursued by the mob and imprisoned for having refused to make this declaration. Later, Caliph Mutawakkil inaugurated an era of pure traditionalism and of persecution of all heretics, schismatics and unbelievers; the same *qāḍīs* or their successors had to declare their indefectible belief in a

Qur'ān that was *not* created—one of those reversals of opinion such as are often seen in communities where passions are strong and reasoning weak. The fall of Mu'tazilism was, however, so complete and so sudden that we must conclude that the attempt to make reason accord with faith had interested only a very restricted circle, and that it had actually not greatly affected them. One eminent Mu'tazilite, Ibn al-Rāwandī, passed over, without transition, to extreme Shī'ism. Mu'tazilite thought was, however, not dead, and, although the systematic destruction of the works of the sect leaves us with an imperfect knowledge of its outward form, it had expressed itself forcibly enough to have a continuing action on certain minds that the dominant traditionalism could not wholly satisfy. It had a powerful influence on Al Ash'arī, the author of the compromise that was henceforth to control the official theology of Islam. Mu'tazilite schools were active in the time of the Būyids, in the 10th century, in 'Irāq, Persia and Khurāsān, and the doctrine had a beneficial effect on moderate Shī'ism.

The other two large religious parties of Islam, the Khārijites and the Shī'ites, were constituted, as we have seen, after the "rupture" of the battle of Ṣiffīn, and for a political reason; the first were believers who left (*Kharajū*) the army of 'Alī and separated from him when he had accepted the arbitration which had taken from God the decision of the struggle, in order to put it into the hands of two arbiters. Under an elected chief, who kept only the title of Imām of the community, they gathered in the region of Baṣra, and formed later offshoots in Arabia. Opposed to the authority of Mu'āwiya, as well as to that of 'Alī, they contributed, by means of the disorders and campaigns for which they were responsible, first to the success of the Umayyads over the 'Alids, then to that of the 'Abbāsids over the Umayyads. By the end of the 8th century they had disappeared from the main stream of history, but islets of Ibāḍites and Nakkârites, still full of life, were still to be found in 'Umān, at Zanzibar, and in the Maghrib (Mẓab and Jabal Nafūsa). Their teaching on the subject of the government of the Muslim community continues to be the principal cause of their isolation. The entry of numerous converts into the first groups of Khārijites strengthened among them the opinion that the *imām* is not necessarily a Qurayshite, nor even an

Arab, but that he can have been a "black slave". They venerate Abū Bakr and 'Umar, and repudiate 'Uthman and 'Alī.

Some historians have called the Khārijites the "Puritans of Islam"; they have among them, indeed, a party who strictly observe the Qur'ānic law, who claim to preserve in the Muslim community its ancient concern for social unity and brotherliness. It is by their interpretation of certain moral facts that they depart from orthodoxy. The man who commits a mortal sin (*kabīra*) is treated by them as an apostate (*murtadd*), and consequently as an unbeliever (*kāfir*); his person and goods are no longer protected, and he is excluded from the community. Ibāḍite society is governed, according to a severe moral code, by a body of *fuqahā'*. The Algerian Mzabites join to great skill and tenacity in affairs a remarkable honesty. They are disdainfully dubbed "men of the fifth rite", which is an involuntary way of acknowledging that they are not far removed from Sunnite orthodoxy.

Shī'ism has a quite other political and religious import and it plays a considerable part in history. It is the party of those who, after Ṣiffīn and arbitration, remained true to 'Alī when the Ḥijāz abandoned him under pressure from such Companions of the Prophet as Al-Zuhayr and his son, and when Syria and Egypt adhered firmly to Mu'awiya. Widely distributed throughout Iraq and the Iranian provinces, the Shī'ites proclaimed the legitimacy of the caliphate within the family of 'Alī, even in favour of descendants by a wife other than Fāṭima. Checkmated by the Umayyads, deceived by the 'Abbāsids, Shī'ism was originally, and continued to be, a party of the discontented. The first 'Alids gathered together in Iraq the new converts, the *mawālī*, whom the "Syrian" caliphate placed in a secondary social rank, and who maintained in activity fermentations of "Nabataean" and Persian particularism. In the 9th century it was with an 'Alid label that the slave revolt of the Zanj broke out. The Qarmaṭs, like the Ismā'īlians, were Shī'ites, as were some small sects of obscure origin such as the Nuṣayrīs. 'Alism and Shī'ism are therefore expressions which, behind a more or less sincere adhesion to the *imāma* of the descendants of the Prophet, include very diverse religious and social tendencies.

The position of being an opposition party was, however,

suddenly changed in the 10th century for that of a party supporting the caliphate. The caliphate was, in fact, dominated, from 946 to 1055 by the Būyid amīrs, Shī'ite princes, who stopped short of the revolution that was implicit in their doctrine, and which would have involved the substitution for the 'Abbāsid Caliph of a representative of the hidden Shī'ite imām. After the disappearance of the Qarmaṭs, it was a moderate Shī'ism that spread widely, in a quasi-official form, throughout all the cities of the Near East, not without continually causing disorders. Meanwhile the Shī'ite extremists, the Ismā'īlians, had founded, in Ifrīqiyạ (Tunisia), in 910, a Mahdist caliphate which transferred itself to Egypt in 969, then conquered Syria, and which claimed to control the whole body of the Shī'ites, while appearing as opponents of the Sunnite caliphs of Bagdad. But, in 1055, they fell under the dominion of Saljūqian amīrs who proclaimed themselves zealous defenders of Sunnism. The Crusaders were involved in the last Ismā'īlian manifestations without profiting by them, as they might have hoped to do, and, in 1169, Saladin put an end to the Fāṭimid caliphate of Cairo. Shī'ite communities have, however, continued to exist almost everywhere in the East; in Persia Shī'ism has assumed the form of a state doctrine since the date of the coming to power of the Ṣafavid dynasty (1502).

Its essential dogma is political; the first three caliphs were illegitimate; the fourth, 'Alī, ought to have assumed the caliphate immediately on the death of Muḥammad, and all the Umayyad and 'Abbāsid caliphs were usurpers. The rights of 'Alī and his descendants had been determined by Qur'ānic texts which orthodoxy falsified, or of which it gave a false interpretation. It is within the scope of those corrections that there exists a Shī'ite Qur'ān, a variant of the orthodox Qur'ān. According to Shī'ite opinion the Divine Light (*nūr*) which, since Adam, has been transmitted from prophet to prophet, illuminated at the same time the fathers of Muḥammad and of 'Alī, then fell on them and their descendants and consequently on the children that 'Alī had by a wife other than Fāṭima; they are the people of the house (*ahl al-Bayt*), a vague expression which has permitted of the formation of several groups having each a different imām. But, they having died without posterity, the doctrine was adopted of the return of the imām (*raj'a*), which has no doubt its origin in Judeo-Christian beliefs. After the end of the little absence (*ghayba*) in 939, during which the hidden imām had been replaced by four locum tenentes (*wakīe*), the great *ghayba* began, during which the Friday prayers cannot be said since the imām is absent; he will appear only when the time is opportune. While awaiting his coming, a Shī'ite body, finding itself lost in a Sunnite environment, submits to the rule of an illegitimate sovereign, and hides (*katmān*) its real beliefs behind the outward observances of those around them. Shī'ism has thus acquired the aspect of a secret society that has been developed by the extreme sects. There one finds again the Qarmaṭs and the Ismā'īlians.

We have once again put the terms "Shī'ite" and "Sunnite" in opposition; but this must not be taken to imply that the Shī'ites have no *sunna*, or prophetic tradition; they have their own collections of *ḥadīths*, composed during the 10th century, at a time when the Būyid amīrs were masters of Bagdad. The Ṣafavid princes set up a shaykh al-islam, guardian of the tradition.

The Shī'ite imām, when he truly has the qualities laid down by the doctrine, is infallible (*ma'ṣūm*); the sects give different forms to the supernatural power which they acknowledge to be his. The Zaydites, who are the most moderate of the Shī'ites, and who admit, in a roundabout way, the legitimacy of Abū Bakr and 'Umar, think that their imām is directly guided by God; the extremists (*ghulāt*) believe that there is hypostasis (*ḥulūl*) and that the human element in the imām is reabsorbed by his divine nature; for the Imāmites the imām remains a man, but a partial *ḥulūl* causes a portion of the divine to enter into him.

The Imāmites, who are the principal sect, admit twelve imāms, the line ending with Muḥammad b. al-Ḥasan; they are called the "Twelve" (*Ithnā 'asharīya*). The Zaydites or Imāmites substitute for the fifth of those imāms Zayd, son of 'Alī Zayn al-'ābidīn, who became the hidden imām: it is to this branch that the Idrīsid dynasty of Fez (791–926) and the imāms of the Yaman belong; there are still Zaydites in Southern Arabia.

The Ismā'īlians, who take their name from the seventh imām, Ismā'īl b. Ja'far al-Sādiq, who is the last in the list of legitimate sovereigns, have not only played a considerable role in the history of North Africa with Mahdī 'Ubayd Allāh and the Fāṭimid dynasty which the illogicality of fate caused to rule in Tunisia and subsequently in Egypt, but the history of the East and of the Crusades is full of their exploits and their wondrous works. It was in this form that Shī'ism most fully developed its role as a secret society, characterised by absolute obedience to its head, and by a religious initiation which, carrying to the extreme limit the allegorical interpretation of the Qur'ān, brought those who fully accepted it to a state of complete religious and moral independence.

The Shī'ite doctrine is distinguishable from Sunnism only in questions of detail the answers to which vary according to the sect. So far as human liberty is concerned, the Shī'ites, in general, came near to Mu'tazilism, and declared their belief in a created Qur'ān. Groups, such as the Ikhwān al-Ṣafā' and the Qarmaṭs, leaned towards a gnostic philosophy. Shī'ism held aloof from Ṣūfism, although it resembles it in certain external aspects and by the variety of its trends; the duty of following the imām, inspired by God, and His representative on earth, is completely incompatible with the conception of individual striving to find God. At times the Shī'ites were in violent opposition to the Ṣūfis, to Al-Ḥallāj for example. The practice of Shī'ism has certain peculiarities, in the call to prayer, in the *tarāwīḥ* of Ramaḍān, etc. Shī'ite law has its own peculiar solutions, some of which will be indicated in their proper context.

Qarmaṭism is linked with Shī'ism by certain external similarities. It is essentially a gathering together of social and philosophical trends originating in Lower Mesopotamia in the 9th century; in its philosophical opinions it is linked with the Ikhwān al-Ṣafā'; in its social aspect it recalls the communism of the slave war of the Zanj and, as happened in that case, it gave as a recommendation the name of an 'Alid imām. But the Qarmaṭs refused to accept the conception of the inheritance of the Divine Light within the family of 'Alī, an idea which they replaced by that of the guidance of the Muslim community by any initiate whatever who might be individually favoured by the divine inspiration. The Qarmaṭs were directed by visible chiefs who declared themselves to be the agents of a hidden master, and in this, as in the case of their initiation ceremony, they borrowed from Shī'ism. The Qarmaṭ doctrine of inspiration, which derives from Hellenism and Manichaeism, determined the constitution of the sect, which consists of superimposed categories of beliefs and practices, from those of the simplest of Muslims to the intuitive perception of a divine monism which rejects the very idea of religious observances. In its diversity, Qarmaṭism combines, at its summit, philosophy, at the base, the crudest features of extreme Shī'ism. Moreover, it was never capable of anything but destruction. We have only to recall Abū Ṭāhir's expedition which, in 930, carried off from Mecca the black stone which was not returned until 951, and then only, it would seem, thanks to the intervention of the Fāṭimid caliph. In Khurāsān the Qarmaṭs built the fortress of Alamūt which became the strong place of the Ismā'īlians and was destroyed only in 1258 by the Mongols of Hūlāgū, and, in Syria, built Salamīya, which passed likewise into the hands of the Ismā'īlian Hashshāshīn (Assassins). To resume, Qarmaṭism interests the historian of Muslim institutions only by the way in which it contributed, concurrently with Shī'ism, to the development of associations of craftsmen and groups of initiates. The latter were of various tendencies: the *futuwwa* of the 13th century are Anti-Ismā'īlians.

The Neo-Ismā'īlians of India, who derive from a son of the Fāṭimid caliph Musta'min (d. 1094), form a compact community under their Āghā Khān. Lastly, there is to be found in Persia a group of Shī'ite extremists (*ghulāt*), the 'Alī-Ilāhī who, by their complex beliefs and observances, are in downright opposition to Muslim law.

The Druses are a still living branch of extreme Shī'ism; they owe their doctrine to an individual who, in Cairo, taught the divine nature of the Fāṭimid caliph Al-Ḥākim (d. 1120). It is still the fundamental doctrine of the sect whose higher degrees of initiation appear to admit neo-platonic elements, such as the active mind (*'aql fa''āl*) and the universal soul (*nafs kullī*). This violent body of a hundred and fifty thousand souls, which is still in isolation within Islam, made a stir in the East in the 19th century. Their minds are completely devoid of originality.

The Nuṣayrīs constitute, in Northern Syria, in Jabal

Anṣārīya, an important schismatic group whom Arab writers class with the Ismā'īlians and who do, indeed, profess some of the latter's doctrines. Their origin is, however, unknown. An inquiry on the spot, when that should prove possible, will doubtless confirm the existence of the pagan substratum pointed out by Dussaud. They profess the theory of the divine emanation transmitted to hierarchical groups of men with 'Alī at the top. There is initiation in three degrees and observances peculiar to themselves.

The three great sects of Islam and the bodies allied to them have all a political character, and it is the question of the imāma that has divided them. For the Khārijites, the office belongs to the believer whom the community thinks most worthy; for the Shī'ites, it is an inheritance within the family of 'Alī, enjoying a special divine favour; for the Sunnites, it is a position of power which God has bestowed on the Qurayshite tribe and which cannot be held outside it.

The Ṣūfī movement is outside all politics. It arose in Islam as a result of the spontaneous evolution of certain Qur'ānic trends, a development that was favoured by the atmosphere of 8th century society. On the subject of the rule that should be followed in practical life, whether of indulgence or asceticism, the Qur'ān appears to have recommended men to adopt a middle course, an equilibrium, which later teaching sought to make one of the outstanding qualities of the Prophet. The Muslims of the conquest naturally obeyed those precepts which allowed them to enjoy, without qualms of conscience, the immense wealth that an unexpected good fortune had placed in their hands; some ḥadīths depicted a Muhammad appreciative of perfumes, of fine raiment, of magnificent weapons, of horses and good cheer. That is only one side of the diptych; the other panel exalts the poverty of the Prophet, who suffers hunger, is always frugal even to extreme, careless of all enjoyment other than that of women. Those reactionary hadīths satisfy, doubtless, a taste for antithesis; they are in harmony, too, with a new sentiment that causes religious minds to rebel against the scandalous fortunes of certain of the Companions and their successors, against their greed and appetite for pleasure: that was not what God had commanded. Further, Syria and Egypt still contained solitary Christians, models of asceticism, and when, under the 'Abbāsids, Buddhist thought was introduced to the Muslim world, it contributed to the extension of asceticism and mysticism. As early as the 8th century Ṣūfī communities were formed at Kūfa and at Baṣra, coupled with the name of Ḥasan of Baṣra (d. 720). Muḥāsibī (d. 837) was, in Bagdad, a master of Ṣūfism whose teachings are known to us. It is no longer a question only of asceticism as an end in itself, but rather as a means of stripping the soul of all that ties it to the world, and of thus facilitating its journey towards God.

As a symbol of simplicity and purity the ascetics adopted the costume of white woollen cloth (*ṣūf*) to which they owe their name.

Ṣūfism was not accepted without resistance on the part of the politico-religious parties that succeeded each other in the governance of the Muslim community. In order to achieve their desire for inward purification, and to realise their aspiration towards the divine love, the Ṣūfīs turned aside from the customary ritualistic practices set up by the Qur'ān and the Sunna, in order to have recourse to personal methods of achieving asceticism and ecstasy; this individualism could not fail to offend the Shī'ites in particular, seeing that they think that the intervention of their imām is necessary to the believer, before he can attempt to draw near to God. The Khārijites considered it to be contrary to the conscientious observance of the cult, and, therefore, to be incompatible with the qualities that make a true believer. The Sunnite doctors were less sharply hostile but were reticent; the Mu'tazilites quoted logical reasons to explain their position. The position of the Ṣūfīs in the Muslim community was therefore exposed to many hazards according to the attention that each individual drew to himself, and depending on the temperament and interest of the masters of the hour. It was Ghazālī that brought about a reconciliation between Ṣūfism and orthodoxy, by including it in the framework of the current beliefs, and by enforcing the observance of ritual practices; he shed on the rigidity of the rites, which could hardly be said to be spiritualised by the purpose (*nīya*) for which they were imposed, the rays of the divine love, and gave a new life to compulsory observances which tended to become mechanical. It was not for nothing that this "revivification of knowledge and religion" was expressed in writing and with infinite poesy in a form that has scarcely its equal in Arab prose.

In the East as in the West the Ṣūfī communities have their monasteries and their meeting places in which they perform spiritual exercises, from pious exhortations, recitations of the Qur'ān, litanies with music and singing (*samā'*), to vertiginous dancing and savage macerations. In the 13th century the Orient possessed numerous *ribāṭ*, *khānaqāh*, *zāwiya*, where instruction was given and disciples trained.

No simple formula would suffice to give an understanding of the past and present of Ṣūfism. The political intrigues of certain brotherhoods and the jugglings of others bring hasty judgments which satisfy the limited thinking powers of the mob; to it pictures of dancing Dervishes and 'Īsawīya are acceptable as being a complete and final representation of Ṣūfism. Other minds fear the adverse effect on the stability of the human reason of ecstasy-producing exercises that lead to a close communion with God, conceived, doubtless, with deep humility, but, even then, in a spirit of boundless egotism; and they think that an ego which absorbs the ultimate all is very near to losing itself in a hypertrophy which is a root cause of the most commonplace dementia. But to picture Ṣūfism in this manner would be to indicate only its outward manifestations; it would be to forget that, in lifting the soul up to a knowledge of God, in compelling it to purify itself before attempting to unite with perfection, Ṣūfism achieves a deliverance from the mechanical religious observances which satisfy neither the senses nor the reason, and that it drives the inward life to new efforts and moral regeneration. It may be said that Ṣūfism, in its day, revived the life of the spirit in Muslims who saw that the forms of religion had become the whole of faith, and had put conscience to sleep, and who were grieved by the paganism of the spreading cult of the saints. Yet, by a curious irony, it is in connection with this very cult that we shall, later on, come back to Ṣūfism.

It seems to be reasonable to connect, to some extent, with mysticism attempts at syncretism which arose in Islam at a late period, and which are valueless unless we consider them to be a sincere effort to unite all men of good will in a common movement of the heart towards God. No doubt the fruitless attempt made in the 17th century by that ruler of originality, Akbar, has left no living memory in India, and it is not to him that we must attribute the present tendencies of the Islam of Hindustan; although it is probable that all his efforts were not lost, and that other religious reformers have profited by his example.

Persian Shī'ism, stagnating, like the orthodox creed, in rigid formulae, and bound within the narrow and mechanical intellectual life of a clerical clique, the Mullās, suffered, in the 19th century, a very violent assault which left it for a long time much weakened. An individual who was both learned and inspired, Mīrzā Muḥammad 'Alī, claimed to perceive within himself both a manifestation of the hidden imām and of the divine spirit: he declared himself to be the gate (*Bāb*) that opened on a perfect humanity. Having turned away from the traditional outlook, he sought, not to bring Islam back to the old principles, but to give it new ones. Steeped, on the other hand, in the ideas of the Ismā'ilians, who cared little for the rites, and leaned, now towards rationalism, now towards mysticism, he showed Islam a future of continuing divine manifestations, each one of which, according to him, would bring fresh knowledge of the Beyond. To a somewhat vague theology the Bāb added a practical system of ethics which, more precise than that of Islam, claimed to develop in a special way the stability and moral strength of the family by securing the freedom of women. He even ventured to enter the political field in definite opposition to the ruling classes of Persia. The Mullās had him thrown into prison, then tortured (1850), a course which merely emphasised the greatness of his personality, and seemed at first likely to ensure the success of his teaching. But, after his death, his supporters fell apart, the group that gathered about Ṣubḥ-i-Azal keeping inviolate the ideas of the master. It would seem to be difficult to estimate the present-day influence on the religious evolution of Persia of that branch of Bābism. The other Bābists have accepted the direction of Bahā' Allāh, who has assumed the role of reformer and prophet, and whose teaching is expounded in works that have been translated into several European languages: they take the place, either of the Qur'ān or of the traditional teaching of the Prophet and his Companions. In this last form, Bahāism, which appears to have had but moderate success in the East, but which has been carried as far as America, has assumed the shape of a composite doctrine to which each of the great human religions brings its contribution, and which strives to "discourage" neither scientific rationalism nor the mystical tendencies of certain contemporary bodies.

It is needful to avoid exaggerating the impression of spiritual torpor which, until the 19th century, the Muslim world seemed to convey; the study of the law and theology has been constantly cultivated by bodies of conscientious men, among whom are to be found some lofty minds. Ibn Taymīya, who died in 1328, clung tenaciously to a Ḥanbalite doctrine of integral respect for the Qur'ān and the Sunna, in which he thought to have found the direct and intuitive solution of all the questions which the logical reasoning of dialectics, of *kalām*, found it so hard to answer. He further rounded off his point of view by a remarkable care for the interests of the Muslim community (*maṣlaḥa*), seeing them as maintained by a sort of practical providence. He took up a position sharply adverse to the worship of the saints. Those points of view were copied, at the end of the 18th century, by an Arab Shaykh of the Najd, Muḥammad Ibn al-Wahhāb, who preached the return to Islam of the first caliphs and the suppression of all the innovations that time had brought, as well as of the ancient pagan practices that time had not removed; he was especially emphatic in his opposition to the worship of the saints, and when, having passed beyond the borders of the Najd and the region of the Persian Gulf, Wahhābism descended like a storm on Mecca and Medina, it destroyed the monuments of the worship given to the Prophet and his family. Only the intervention of Egyptian troops could drive from the Ḥijāz reformers whom we shall find as the masters of Arabia in the 20th century.

SOURCES

Goldziher: *Dogme et Loi de l'Islam,* translated Arin (S.86); E.I.: Nyberg: *Mo'tazila,* 3.840; Wensinck: *Murdjiya,* 3.784; Massignon: *Carmats,* 2.813; *Moçairis,* 3.103; *Tasawioref,* 4.715; *Terriqa,* 4.700; Strohmann: *Shia,* 4.368.

CHAPTER FOUR

THE ISLAMIC DOGMA

Islam and kufr—The Divine Oneness—Angels, Demons and Jinns—Prophets Resurrection—Last Judgment—Paradise—Hell—The Worship of the Saints—The Brotherhoods.

THE Islamic dogma, the principles of which are to be found in the Qur'ān, was formulated at various periods by Muslim doctors, in documents after the manner of catechisms, professions of faith which claim to be in strict conformity with the Qur'ān and the Sunna. They are none the less the result of a choice which could not have been made without some personal effort (*ra'y*) of interpretation and judgment. It is therefore not strange that those catechisms (*'aqīda*) differ singularly one from the other, according to their dates and the personal inclinations of their authors. The first tentative efforts at compiling them are found in the *ḥadīth*, later in the *fiqh* attributed to Abū Ḥanīfa, and lastly, in the *'aqīda* of Al-Nasafī (d. 1142); the one that Ghazālī inserted in his *Iḥyā' 'ulūm al-dīn* is an imitation of this last.

The believer is called, in the Qur'an, either *Mu'min* or *Muslim*, without anything to indicate a distinction between the two expressions. The Qur'ān goes on to add to *īmān* and *islām* the word *birr*, "the good", piety (2.172): "Piety does not consist in turning your faces to the East or to the West; but piety consists in believing (*āmana*) in God, the Last Day. the angels, the Book, the Prophets, in giving your possessions, while loving him (can also be construed as: for the love of God) to your neighbour, to the orphans, the unfortunate, to travellers, beggars and (for their ransom) to captives; in performing the duty of Prayer, in delivering up the legal alms, in carrying out your undertakings, in remaining patient in adversity, suffering and danger." Taken up again by a *ḥadīth*, this passage brings together in a single formula the prescribed beliefs and actions.

Another *ḥadīth*, which seems to set up a distinction between *īmān* and *islām*, says that *īmān* consists in believing in God, in His angels, His book, in the reunion with Him, in those He has sent, and in the resurrection, a rather confused list; and that *islām* consists in serving God without associating any person with Him, in performing the duty of prayer, in paying the legal alms, and in fasting during the month of *ramaḍān*. We might conclude from this that *mu'min* is he who has faith in the dogmas, and the *muslim* he who performs the acts that confirm the faith. But there is really nothing of importance in this apparent distinction that need be remembered; it was merely of use to Ghazālī in attributing to the *muslim* the upsurging of the heart through which he thought to give new life to Muslim observances. No account will be taken of it in the explanations that follow.

In an early form the doctrine based the faith on the combination of three elements: an inward conviction of profound knowledge (*ma'rifa*), acquired by prophetic revelation or by the use of reason (*'aql*); a profession of faith (*shahāda bi-al-lisān*); the carrying out of the fundamental duties of the believer (*'amal bi-al-arkān*). It is those three essential elements that the orthodox doctrine has formulated thus: conviction (*taṣdīq*), confession (*iqrār*), and works.

The question of acts, of works in the faith is, in Islam, as in Christianity, of capital importance. We have earlier pointed out that Muslims have discussed the position of the believer without works, who is the damned (*fāsiq*) of the Mu'tazilites and the Ash'arites, for whom the Murji'ites "suspend" the divine decision until the Day of Judgment, whom the Khārijites declare to be an unbeliever (*kāfir*). According to the Murji'ites evil actions cannot make a *mu'min* become *kāfir*, since good actions succeed only in making of a *kāfir* a hypocrite, a *munāfiq*. The practical key to the common teaching is the idea that he who performs the Prayer (*ṣalāt*) while turning towards the *qibla* is accepted as a believer (*mu'min*), just as he who omits the Prayer (*tārik al-ṣalāt*) is declared to be *kāfir*. It is this last expression that is applied to unbelievers in general (plur. *Kuffār*) and which is understood to be comprised in the term *mushrikīn*, "associators", applied to those who associate another god with Allāh.

The essential dogma is that of the oneness of God; He was neither born nor had any son, says the Qur'ān. This is generally believed to be the meaning that the doctrine gives to the word *tawḥīd*. But when it came to deal with the attributes of God, that is, with the significance that should be given to His faculties of knowing, of doing, of hearing, of seeing, etc., and when the question was raised of the relationship of His attributes to the essence of God (*dhāt*), the doctors understood that, by assigning a separate value to the attributes of God, they limited to some degree the conception of His oneness. They therefore taught that the attributes of God are only emanations of His essence; it is in this sense, for example, that we must understand the *tawḥīd* of the doctrine of the Almohads (*al-Muwaḥḥidīn*).

Allāh is the creator of the universe; He made it in six days, and did *not* rest on the seventh (Q. 40.37). Out of a vapour that filled all space Allāh created the waters, the earth, the mountains, then living creatures, and, finally, on the Friday, Adam. There are seven heavens and seven earths, as there are seven regions in Paradise and seven divisions of Hell. The Tradition is sparing of details concerning the creation; among the numerous legends which claim to explain the world the following is current: Allāh created an angel who carries the earth on his mighty shoulders; his feet rest on a ruby borne on the horns of a bull, that stands erect upon the fish Bahamūt, which swims in the waters that cover the unknowable. The angels (*malak*, plur. *malā'ika*) are creatures of Allāh, are without sex, and made of light (*nūr*); they are generally ranked below the prophets, since the latter acquire special merit as a result of the fight they have to sustain against human nature. At the head of the angelic band there are four archangels (*Karūbīyīn*), Gabriel (Jibrīl), the messenger of Allāh, whom the Qur'ān seems to call the "breath of holiness", (*rūh al-quds*); Michael (Mīkā'īl), who watches over the order and the life of Nature; Isrāfīl, who will sound the trumpet on the day of the Last Judgment, and 'Azrā'īl, the angel of death, who comes and draws away the final breath from the lips of the dying.

Angels watch over man: the two "guardians" (*ḥāfiẓayn*) and the two writers (*kātibayn*) who take note of good and evil actions: there is doubt as to whether those angels are different persons, or the same persons with different functions. The two guardians of the night give place, at sunrise, to other two, and again at sunset: there are here two moments of danger for the faithful, in which they must fear the assaults of Satan (*al-Shayṭān, Iblīs*) and his acolytes. The *Kātibayn* are also confused with the angels of the tomb, *Nakīr* and *Munkar*. Paradise is guarded by the angel *Riḍwān*, Hell by the angel *Mālik*.

Demons prowl about the earth and in the lower heavens and seek to surprise, on the borders of the seventh heaven, the secrets of the angels, who continually beat them off by hurling against them the stones that are the shooting stars; they stone them as the pilgrim stones the *jamarāt* of Minā, in imitation of Abraham who, according to tradition, chased Satan into it by hurling stones at him—hence Satan's surname of "He who is Stoned" (*al-rajīm*). The meaning of those various beliefs is still uncertain.

The demons of Iblīs's army bear a number of names: *jinn*; *shayṭān*, plur. *shayāṭīn*; *'ifrīt*, plur. *'afārīt*; *mārid* or rebel. They were created before man, and are made of fire (*nār*): they are male or female, and they are able to unite with human beings. Some are Muslims; but the greater number are enemies of humanity and of Islam. The popular belief which, as we shall show later, has brought about an extensive development of the cult of the saints, has peopled the earth too with jinns, grouped in seven armies, of which each has its leader, its own duties, its own territory; man has to fear from each its own individual form of attack, and against each he possesses individual means of defence.

The head demon, Iblīs (*diabolos*), was a favourite angel of God, who had sent him to fight on earth against jinns who were in rebellion there. When God had created Adam, he tested the fidelity of the angels by commanding them to prostrate themselves before his last creation. All obeyed save only Iblīs, whose pride asserted the superiority of his own nature. Driven from Paradise, Iblīs avenged himself by beguiling Eve and causing the exile of the first human pair. He has continued, in the life of this world, to be the tempter of man; after the Qur'ān, Muslim beliefs, influenced by Manichaean memories, added further to the importance of Satan-Iblīs.

The believer must believe in the envoys of God and in the

scriptures which it is their mission to reveal. After the fall of Adam God pardoned him and placed within him the divine light, which then passed from prophet to prophet until Muḥammad, and which, according to the Shī'ite doctrine, was even transmitted after him from imām to imām in the family of 'Alī. Adam is the first of the prophets (*nabī*, plur. *anbiyā*; *rasūl*, plur. *rusul*), who form an uninterrupted chain. The prophets are even marked by certain essential virtues: truthfulness, intelligence, etc. They have protection from grave wrongdoings (*kabā'ir*) and they usually have the power of working miracles. Theologians are not agreed as to the number of prophets; it is generally allowed that one hundred and thirteen of them contributed books which are nearly all lost. The six principal prophets are Adam, Noah (*Nūḥ*), Abraham (*Ibrāhīm*), Moses (*Mūsā*), who contributed the *Taurāt* (the Pentateuch), Jesus (*'Isā*), who handed down the Gospel (*Injīl*); finally, Muḥammad, who is the last and the greatest of the prophets. Although one tradition that appears to be authentic makes Muḥammad say that he did not receive the gift of miracles and that he performed one only, the greatest of all time it is true, the revelation of the Qur'ān, popular belief attributes to him a few minor miracles, especially that of splitting the moon in two.

The books given to men by the prophets of old did not differ from the Qur'ān. They laid down the laws which the servants of God had to obey (*'abd*, plur. *'ibād*); but the Jews and Christians, for whom the books were intended, falsified them. The Qur'ān restored the true text of the revelation for the last time before the end of time itself. Muḥammad is the seal of the prophets.

Finally, the Muslim faith consists in believing in the Resurrection and the Last Judgment. The successive opinions which, in Judaism, have encouraged a belief in an earthly punishment of the wicked, or in a punishment that would follow immediately on death, or in a general bringing to account at the end of time, have brought the popular belief of Islam to accept the idea of a chastisement of the tomb. The Qur'ān had recalled the cataclysms that destroyed the peoples of 'Ād and Thamūd; the *ḥadīth* treated at length the drama of the tomb. The sound of the steps of those who have shut him in the grave has scarcely died away when he who has died is visited by two awful angels, Nakīr and Munkar, who question him: "Who is thy Lord?" If he answers by reciting the Moslem confession of faith, the *shahāda*, which was repeated around him before he died, and must have been the subject of his last words, the angels softly leave him, and open for him a door through which he can see his seat in Paradise. If he fails to answer, or answers wrongly, the angels beat him with iron clubs and, in his tomb, a door opens which shows him his place in Hell.

This belief has given rise, in Egypt for example, to a custom which is justified by the ḥadīths in which Muḥammad speaks to the dead. A man, known for his piety approaches the still open tomb and instructs the dead man in the answer he will have to give to the two angels.

The dead remain in their graves until the day of judgment, except for the prophets, who, immediately after death, have access, either to Paradise itself, or to some intermediate place (*'araf*).

The day of the Last Judgment will be heralded by awful events. First, all things in human society will be thrown into confusion. The faith will perish. Wickedness, violence, war, will ravage the earth. Government will be put into the hands of the least worthy, etc. Meanwhile there will appear, in order to restore order and peace, the Mahdī, the "Well Directed" of Allāh, the inheritor of all the messianic teachings of the East. Already he has appeared several times in Muslim lands, and has vanished, for it was not He whom Islam Awaits.

But the false Messiah (*al-masīḥ al-dajjāl*), the "Anti-Christ", will rise up between 'Irāq and Syria, one-eyed, terrible, bearing on his brow the letters signifying "unbelief" (*k f r*), mounted on an ass, and followed by seventy thousand Jews from Iṣfahān. There will also descend from Central Asia the fierce peoples of Gog and Magog, who, after having drunk up the Lake of Gennesareth, will march on Jerusalem.

Jesus (*'Isā*), descended from heaven, will appear in the mosque at Damascus, at the hour of the midday Prayer, in the angle nearest to the eastern minaret; the imām will give up his place to him and he will lead the Prayer. Then he will slay Dajjāl at the gates of Lydda, and he will obtain from God the destruction of Gog and Magog. He will marry, have children, and will reign on the earth for forty years, where he will cause peace to prevail among men and beasts.

We are apt to feel somewhat lost among those events, the announcement of which comes from different sources, and of which the chronology is uncertain; we do not know where to place the arrival of the Beast, the dense smoke which will cover the earth for forty days, the destruction of the Ka'ba, the rising of the sun in the West. Moreover, they represent the putting together of old traditions which have not all been accepted by the Doctrine. Ghazālī ignored them while he allowed his pen to be hurried on by the spirit of the poetry with which he filled his descriptions of the following scenes.

At last the Angel of the Judgment, Isrāfīl, will blow the first blast on the fateful trumpet (*nafkh al-faz'*); all beings will perish and will remain in an intermediate state (*al-barzakh*) for forty years. But a fruitful rain will prepare, in the soil, the return of life, until the second blast of the trumpet (*nafkh al-ba'th*) restores all beings to life. This is the solemn reunion (*nashr, yaum al-qiyāma*). Reunited on an immense plain that Allāh has prepared to this end, perhaps at Jerusalem, men (and doubtless also the beasts) will await the hour of judgment, naked all, burned by the sun, covered by a sweat that will drip down from their bodies, forming vast pools, standing erect in the fearful expectation of the divine decision. Then, at last, the angels will give to each the book in which are written his good and evil actions; the faithful will hold it in the right hand, the unfaithful in the left. Then man will appear before Allāh who will cause his acts to be weighed in the balance (*mizân*; Q. 21.48, which gives *mawāzīn* in the plural) after the final account has been established (*hisāb*). The faces of the faithful will be white; those who have denied the faith will have black faces (Q. 3.102). It is at this moment that the Prophet will intervene, whose intercession in favour of the Muslim community will be accepted by Allāh. Judgment having been pronounced, all men will pass over the bridge (*ṣirāṭ*) that is finer than a hair and sharper than a sword. The good will cross it with the speed of lightning; the damned will fall into Hell.

The blessed, after having slaked their thirst in the pool of the Prophet (*ḥauḍ*), are admitted into Paradise (*janna*) which, too, tradition has divided into several parts, if we interpret literally the different expressions used in the Qur'ān: one of these is *firdaus* (*paradisos*). The Qur'ān, added to by tradition, has described in detail Paradise and the existence that the blessed will there enjoy. From the very beginning of the Prophet's preaching, it appears as the place dreamed of by men who have led, in a parched land, the rough and primitive life of the nomad; gardens, says the Qur'ān again and again (76.12; 18.30; 10.9; 4.60; 2.268, etc.) in which there gush forth and flow on all sides brooks, brooks of delicious water, streams of milk, rivers of wine (Q. 47.16), streams of honey (Q. 47.17), gliding in the deep shadows of great trees (Q. 4.60); the Holy Book names three of those water brooks, the *kauthar* and the two springs that have their source beneath the throne of Allāh, Zanjabīl and Salsabīl (Q. 76.17). Tradition has popularised the splendour of the tree (*ṭūbā*) which spreads afar its immense shade: an outside legend that has adapted itself, by a play of words, to Q. 13.28. In magnificent tents those Muslims will find sumptuous couches where they will long recline, leaning on their elbows (Q. 76.13; 18.30, etc.). Clothed in precious stuffs, adorned with rare jewels, they will eat exquisite foods and delicious fruits (Q. 52.22), held out for them to pluck on the branches of palms and vines (Q. 76.14). "Eat and drink at your ease, as a reward for your deeds on earth." (Q. 52.19). They will drink of wine that is not hurtful (Q. 76.21), that handsome slaves, eternally young, will pour out for them (Q. 76.19; 52.24). As for their fair companions, the Tradition has, with much satisfaction, expanded the brief hints of the Qur'ān; these are spouses purified, that is, freed from all the defects of the human body; then come the *ḥūr al-'ayn*, the houris, women whose eyes sparkle with a dazzling brilliance of white and black (Q. 52.20), and who will remain modestly within the tents. Those of the faithful who would wish to have children will have this joy too, a touching indication of the love the Arabs have for the little ones, and also of their pride in fatherhood: their education will be as easy and as rapid as their birth.

The ideal dwelling place of the Bedouin, greedy for shade and fresh running waters, for brilliant clothing, sparkling gems, perfumes and women, has haunted the imagination of Islam for twelve centuries; we have not here, and we should not fail to note the fact, the weapons which, in other Walhallas, the warriors clash against the flagstones of their halls. It is not seemly that we should smile at the naïveté of this picture, for it seems to be built up in reality from Christian teachings that caught the imagination of Muḥammad. It has never satisfied those lofty spirits who, in Islam, have not been wholly captivated by the monotonous material realities that strict orthodoxy promises; they hope that blessedness will, for them, consist in contemplation of the face of Allāh.

Hell, to which the Qur'ān most frequently gives the name of *al-nār*, the fire, is composed, according to the exegetists, of seven zones which respectively take their names from certain imprecise words in the Qur'ān. The highest zone, *Jahannam*, Gehenna, is that in which Muslims who have sinned will suffer a punishment of restricted duration; the other zones are reserved for Jews, Christians, Sabaeans, Zoroastrians, idolators, and, lastly, the hypocrites and false prophets with whom the Prophet had to contend at Medina. The traditions have not worked out, in any considerable degree, what the Qur'ān tells concerning the tortures to be endured by the inhabitants of Hell: they will be consumed by a thirst that they will seek to assuage by imbibing stinking liquids, by drinking at the infernal wells of tar (*qatrān*) and of molten pitch (Q. 47.17 and 14.51), their skin will dry up, their entrails will be roasted, etc. The Muslim legends dealing with Hell lack originality, and are derived, like the Christian legends, from the Jewish Haggada. We have pointed out that guilty Muslims will not remain eternally in Gehenna, which, consequently, will one day cease to exist; some theologians believe that this is true also of the whole of Hell.

The believer awaits, doubtless, with confidence or resignation, the reward that will be his at the hands of his just Master; he does not know whether the worth of his actions will modify the fate that predestination has fixed for him. God is so high, so remote, so impersonal, that the believer is never certain that the invocation he has addressed to Him in his ritual Prayer has reached Him. The gods of old were weak, but they were near, and one could be sure of being heard, if not pardoned. Muslims, like Christians, have been happy in the feeling that their familiar deities had been able to resist the Qur'ān itself, and that, behind a disguise, they were ready to listen to their desires. The place of the ancient gods has been taken by the saints (*walī*, plur. *auliyā'*).

The worship of the saints occupies a considerable place in Muslim life. It is the survival of the practices by which man, filled at the same time with the consciousness of his physical weakness, and with that of his intellectual power, seeks to bring into harmony the dominant forces of Nature; popular belief keeps them definitely within the organised religions which have created a symbol of those forces in the shape of a single entity whose metaphysical greatness puts him very far away and very high above his worshipper. Buddhism and Christianity, although they have brought man nearer to a sheltering divinity, made familiar and concrete in pictures and images, have not escaped, any more than iconoclastic Islam, from the worship of saints and relics. The sanctuaries of the Islamic saints occupy the sites of ancient holy places: water springs, trees, stones, hill tops, which had already been chosen for their dwelling places by the ancient gods and the saints of Jews and Christians.

The growth of the worship of the saints has been subject, logically, to geographic and economic influences: the custodian of a sanctuary, if it had contributed to the prosperity of the city in which it was erected, benefited as a result of its importance to the life of the nation. Political events, in their turn, were not without importance. Morocco furnished an example of this when, after the fall of Granada (1492), catholic Spain, invaded once, became, by a sort of recoil, a conqueror in Africa. There then rose up, in all parts of Morocco, men who declared themselves able, by a gift of supernatural power, to expel the infidel invader; they derived this power, either from their kinship with the Prophet (*Sharīf*, plur. *Shurafā*), or from their mystic relations with a famous saint. We shall return later to those "marabouts".

Whatever his origin, the saint has, for an essential attribute, the *baraka*, the sacred emanation. Through it he brings to those who worship him, prosperity, happiness, all the good things of this world; he can bestow his gifts, passing beyond the individual, upon a whole district, and even beyond the confines of this world, through his powers of intercession with Allāh. It is not even necessary that the will of the saint should be exercised for the *baraka* to be effective; his presence and his touch are enough; so the beneficent emanation flows out and is even helped on its way by the instrumentality of the servants of the saint. It flows out from the body of the saint during his life; it remains after his death; for his dead body miraculously pours it out into the tomb that encloses it, and imbues with it, not only the grave clothes that cover it, but the very soil that surrounds it. The protecting influence of a saint has, moreover, a varying field in which it operates; it is usually regional, and extends to a group of tribes or to a limited geographical territory. When the saint, like 'Abd al-Qādir al-Jīlānī (*al-Jīlānī* = of Gīlān), dominates with his countless qobbas a part of the Muslim world, his cult assumes a general character, but it seems to be clear that each qobba is an independent oratory and constitutes a local sanctuary.

The saint is thus a familiar deity; his feast is celebrated on dates fixed from time immemorial and determined by natural causes (seedtime, harvest, drought, etc.), the origins of which are often forgotten today. The most splendid rejoicings are reserved for a date which is looked upon as being the anniversary of the birth of the saint, his *maulid* (in the Maghrib *maulūd*). It is also named *musem* (*mausim*), an interesting expression, for it is the one formerly used to designate the pilgrimage to Mecca, in commemoration, doubtless, of the propitiatory sacrifice of a new-born of the flock and of the ritual marking (*wasm*) of the young beasts; in a very different sense it brings us to the French "mousson", the Monsoon. Those pilgrimages gather together around the sanctuary, the tents of the faithful, the horsemen's mounts, the thronging pedestrians. Sacrifices are offered up; special prayers are recited; a whole cult is celebrated with its age-old rites.

By a slow extension of his personality, Muḥammad won the first place in the cohort of the saints. The Tradition depicts the veneration of the Companions for the Prophet as near to worship, and attributes to him a special emanation, a *baraka*. This idea took on in course of time a wide extension: Muḥammad was, in the beginning, the perfect man, fit to serve all Muslims as a model; then he became their protector in this life, in which he appears to them in dreams to lead them by his advice, as in the next life, when he will intercede for them with God. It is no exaggeration to say that Muḥammad, in popular belief and worship, has almost attained the importance which Christianity, for much sounder reasons, attributes to Jesus. The visit to his tomb at Medina has become a rite that is almost as compulsory as the pilgrimage to Mecca The tombs of the Companions of the Prophet, of the first two caliphs, Abū Bakr and 'Umar, who lie at his feet in the mosque of Medina, and of certain other personages eminent in Islam, are visited for the purpose of receiving the *baraka*, although they are not saints properly speaking.

The cult of the saints came into contact with Ṣūfism. From the 10th century onwards, the Ṣūfīs have their meeting places where they hold seances (*samā'*), and which eventually become monasteries (*ribāṭ, zāwiya, Khānaqāh*). The name *ribāṭ* was given to the monastery stronghold from which the volunteers of the faith conducted the holy war on the borders of the territories of Islam, and the word was transferred to the houses from which the Sūfīs likewise conducted their struggle for the faith; *zāwiya* designated literally the "corners" in the mosques where gathered the disciples of a master or the adherents of a doctrine. Those monasteries which served as rest houses for travelling monks were classed under orders, each inspired by an illustrious shaykh. At this point in its evolution Ṣūfism came to resemble the monastic congregations of the West. Each Ṣūfī community had its "way" (*ṭarīqa*), that is, both a moral and religious aim and a practical discipline, consisting in recitations from the Qur'ān (*dhikr*) or litanies, and in the repeated utterance (*wird*) of formulae such as *yā laṭīf*, "Oh Benevolent One!", in hundred thousandfold repetition. The novices (*murīd, gandûz*) became adepts (*faqīr*, plur. *fuqarā'*; *darwīsh*) after an initiation (*bay'a, talqīn*): the adepts are also called "brothers" (*ikhwān*, vulg. *khwān*).

Each of the Muslim brotherhoods has its own method of initiation, its formulae for prayers, its mother house and its secondary houses which are centres of religious exercises and of teaching. But in this particular domain, as in all others, Islam made no distinction between the clerk and the layman: in the same way as an imām may be, at the same time, a dealer in Arab cloaks, the shaykh of a congregation of Ṣūfīs may be a maker of sandals. The Muslim brotherhood has thus developed very widely the organisation of the Third Order that Catholicism attached to its congregations. It has become a real secret society of the faithful left in the world, and able to respond to any religious or political watchword. It is well known that, in Africa particularly, the religious fraternities, the gatherings of brothers (*khwān*), have been studied and watched, and that contrary opinions of their importance and activities have been maintained with equal administrative authority. According to some, all Muslim policy consists either in a struggle against the brotherhoods or in an agreement with them; and, contrariwise, their adversaries would not require much inducement to make them declare that the brotherhoods are of no importance at all. Others, again, have seen in the brotherhood a living organism, so much living that it was born, grew, divided and died before their eyes, an organism well adapted to the mind of the Berbers and nurtured, doubtless, by the reaction to foreign domination; they have observed, moreover, that Muslims did not hesitate to join a European brotherhood, that of freemasonry. The Muslim brotherhoods have been viewed by them as interesting manifestations of a public opinion that it was possible to guide, and that there was no good reason to oppose. No doubt political circumstances may add to the importance of the part they play; from the conquests of Rabah to the 1914 war, the Sanūsī occupied an important place in the affairs of the Sahara and their chiefs have succeeded in creating an embryo State, but they are little noticed today. Their very achievement made them vulnerable.

The mystics, sincere illuminees or humbugs, are not all affiliated to the Muslims brotherhoods; the divine breath manifests itself where it pleases, and is to be observed in the most diverse individuals, in the inspired who devotes himself exclusively to the practices of the ascetic, but also in the degenerate, half mad, half pretender, who, by conjuring tricks, exploits the public credulity, and likewise in the madman and imbecile, whose stammerings a clever producer knows how to turn into divine oracles. It is the living form of the cult of the Saints. To all those various beings custom has given a name which fits many of them but poorly, that of marabout (*murābiṭ*, vulg. *mrābeṭ*): its exact meaning is the faithful of the *ribāṭ*, the monastery fortress of the Muslim borders, who can be compared to the soldier monks, the Templars for example, of Christianity. It is in this sense that the term has been properly applied to the Almoravids of Morocco (*al Murābiṭīn*). The marabouts play an important part in Muslim social life: they spread around them a magical moral influence which they owe either to their personal worth, or to the authority of their ancestors, or maybe to the physiological defects that led them to illuminism. The marabout may be a solitary who leaves nothing after him, but he may also attach himself to a brotherhood; he may be the originator of a new cult, which a *moqaddam* will maintain about his tomb, and which will perhaps serve as the rallying place of a new confraternity.

SOURCES

Wensinck: *Muslim Creed* (S.86); E.I.: Macdonald: *Imām*, 2.504; Carra de Vaux: *'Aqīda*, 1.239.

CHAPTER FIVE

THE SOURCES OF MUSLIM LAW

The Qur'ān—Commentaries on the Qur'ān—The Sunna—The *ijmā'*—The *qiyās*—The *fiqh*—The Orthodox Rites.

THE principal outlines of the Islamic dogma were traced in the Qur'ān, in sūras revealed at Mecca. It was the Medina passages that fixed the rules governing worship, family and communal relations. Those rules, which are the foundations of Muslim law, did not, in spite of their occasional minute detail, suffice to provide the Companions of the Prophet with the means of deciding all the problems which fell to be solved by the leaders of the Muslim community. They fell back, therefore, on their own recollections, on the prophetic tradition, on the *Sunna*, which last was an aid all the more precious because it lent itself, better even than the Qur'ān, to a certain variety of interpretation, and because it could even be created out of nothing. The doctors of the law later added two other sources of the code: the consensus of opinion in the Muslim community (*ijmā'*), and analogical reasoning (*qiyās*). Those are the four sources of the canon law (*uṣūl al-fiqh*).

Since the disappearance of Mu'tazilism Islamic doctrine agrees that the Qur'ān is uncreated. It was written outside of time, together with the whole life of the world, on the well-guarded table (*al-lawḥ al-maḥfūẓ*): the revelation of it came down into the lower heaven, from whence it was conveyed, in the course of events, to Muḥammad in fragments of varying lengths, and at a rate that was similarly varied; during the Mecca period long silences had filled the Prophet's soul with despair. The Revelation usually came to him through the agency of the angel Gabriel; but sometimes the Prophet heard only an impersonal voice, or else he received the divine word by means of a kind of inward perception, which appears to have made him believe that it came directly from God. Each coming of the revelation was accompanied by an interval of ecstasy, during which, following an ancient custom, observed by diviners, transmitters of oracles, he wrapped himself in his cloak. Afterwards he proclaimed the word of God.

During the first years the divine word took the form of an urgent call to believe in the essential truths, the divine oneness, the Resurrection and the Retribution, and of an announcement of the approach of the awful Day of Punishment. Those early sūras are, as it were, blown on the winds of a great tempest which breaks in thunderous threats and curses, interspersed with promises and grandiose images, in rhythmical rhyming language which recalls that used in the oracles of the soothsayers of Old Arabia. This splendour fades away as the Mecca revelation continues, and the resulting variations in tone help modern criticism to complete the classification of the passages into successive periods, which had been begun by the learned men of Islam. It had completely died out, but for an occasional burst of colour, during the Medina period when the verses turn to a definition of the rules of practical life and to repetitions of the essential precepts of the Mecca revelation. The main lines of the chronology of the Qur'ānic verses, which does not in the least correspond to the place they occupy in the universally adopted text, were determined by Muslim erudition. European criticism has accepted them. Indeed, the history of Muḥammad and of the early days of Islam rests on one single trustworthy document, the Qur'ān.

Muslim savants have given much attention to defining the circumstances which gave birth to, and which explain, the various parts of the revelation. Each verse, so to speak, was given its more or less exact place in the history of the primitive Muslim community; commentators have a prejudice which leads them to try to explain everything by an event in the Prophet's life; it is only by minds that function in another atmosphere than theirs that divine intervention in all cases, even the most trifling, can be regarded as an indifferent conception of the nature of God. This rather paltry interpretation of the Revelation is at least valuable for the historian, who can find in it, in its proper place and correctly dated, the explanation of a political decision or of the formulation of a rule. Of course we must not accept all such references in a wholly uncritical spirit.

From the first days of the Muslim community, the Prophet gathered his disciples together for the purpose of informing them of the revelation, and of performing certain pious exercises of whose nature the Tradition gives us no definite indication. It is at least probable that they were, in fact, gatherings for the purpose of worship, at which the Qur'ān was recited, perhaps commented on, and so impressed on the tenacious memories of the faithful. It was, indeed, those reliable memories that were the first vehicle and the chief treasure house of the Revelation. Memory still remains the most honourable channel for the transmission of the Qur'ān; it is an excellent thing to be a *ḥāfiẓ*, that is, one who keeps the whole Qur'ān in his mind. Yet, in the days of Muḥammad, the art of writing was more widely practised in Mecca than modern criticism was long inclined to admit, and written fragments of the Qur'ān were preserved among the very unequal material that was at the disposal of 7th century Arabia; on parchment, on pottery in the Assyrio-Babylonian style, on the shoulder blades of camels—the papyrus of Egypt seems to have been unknown in contemporary Arabia.

It does not appear that, during the lifetime of the Prophet, any attempt was made to do more than gather together a part of the Revelation; there was no complete collection of the verses of the Holy Book, nor was there any continuous effort to make a rational classification of them. The material difficulties of the task caused, doubtless, an unwillingness to undertake it. But, during the caliphate of Abū Bakr, the need was felt of possessing an authentic and more reliable text than that which was entrusted to the memory of men, and more complete than the fragments that had already been given a permanent written form. The favourite secretary of the Prophet, Zayd b. Thābit, was instructed to prepare a text which, however, Abū Bakr does not appear to have made generally accessible. The various groups of the warriors of Islam, in Syria, Egypt, Iraq and Iran, soon found themselves in possession of written versions which differed rather seriously one from the other. Circumstances threatened to accentuate those differences; discussion began of certain awkward verses, or it was proposed to insert in the sacred text traditions that were thought to be particularly inspired, the *ḥadīth qudsī*. Moved by piety, as well as by the spirit of conciliation, Caliph 'Uthmān decided on the appointment of a commission which, co-operating with Zayd b. Thābit, put together a definite Qur'ān, drawn up in four copies, one each for Medina, Damascus, Basra and Kufa, and from which were copied, without variation, the copies that were circulated throughout the whole Empire, and which served as models for the oldest existing manuscripts dating from the 10th century. According to the legend, Caliph 'Uthman had written the copies with his own hand or, at least, one of them, which he was reading when he was murdered. The libraries of mosques and those of the dwellings of princes long preserved blood-stained pages of it. In 1184 Ibn Jubayr saw, in Mecca, a Qur'an that had belonged to 'Uthman, and which was exhibited at the gate of the Ka'ba during prayers for rain.

The Qur'ān is divided into one hundred and fourteen chapters, or sūras, each of which bears a name referring to some part of its contents, and contains a varying number of verses (*āyāt*, miraculous signs). The ceremonial practice of reciting the Qur'ān in equal sections which is employed in Muslim ritual, was therefore not able to adhere to the division into sūras which are of unequal lengths, and it has adopted a division into thirty *juz'*, sixty *ḥizb*, and one hundred and twenty *rub'*. The first sūra, the *fātiḥa*, "that which opens" the book, and the last two, the hundred and thirteenth and the hundred and fourteenth (*al-mu'awwidatāni*, "the two through which one seeks refuge from Satan"), are very short and are not really a part of the Revelation; the *fātiḥa* is a prayer, the *mu'awwidatāni* are ancient formulae of exorcism; they enclose the book within a protective fence. The other hundred and eleven have been arranged in descending order, from the longest, which is the second, to the shortest. In a general way those which are the last in the book contain the earliest revelations. The first in date appears to be the ninety-sixth; the long sūras at the beginning are from the Medina period. Criticism has further brought to light in the sūras of the Medina period early verses which, no doubt forgotten under their proper date, but repeated later—it is not clear in what circumstances—have been incorporated in other and later verses.

The text of the Qur'ān, although officially established, still gave cause for hesitancy in the reading of it and in its interpretation. The variants in reading, after having been the subject of numerous controversies, have been accepted in part as valid for the Doctrine. They arise not only out of differences in the pronunciation of the readers, or out of variations in dialect, but also from varying readings of the written texts. It is right to recall that it was only in the time of Al-Ḥajjāj, under the caliphate of 'Abd al-Malik b. Marwān, in the last years of the 7th century, that the diacritical points were invented which, for example, alone permit of a distinction between *b*, *t*, *th*, *n* and *y*, and that the three signs denoting the short vowels were introduced even later: those improvements in the Arabic script are contemporary with the Massoretic reform of Hebrew script. The variants in reading (*qira'āt*) accepted by the Doctrine are, moreover, of little importance to Qur'ānic exegesis.

The relative divergences in the interpretation of the Qur'ān have been studied in the commentaries (*tafsīr*),) which sought to fix the sense of the words and to explain the meaning of the verses by having recourse, for the language, to ancient Arabic poetry and, for the ideas, to the Tradition (*ḥadīth*) and to reasoning. The commentaries have thus developed special branches of learning: the science of the rare terms (*gharīb*) used in the Qur'ān, that of the lapsing and the lapsed (*al-nāsikh wa al-mansūkh*) which decides, as between two contradictory verses, which is the one that remains valid, etc.

The second source of Muslim law, the Tradition, the *sunna*, the *ḥadīth*, appears to provide, even today, inexhaustible documentary material for the study of the institutions. Little familiar narratives, to which the use of the direct style gives a peculiar reality, initiate the reader into all the details of Muhammad's life, and admit him into an intimacy with the social life of the Arabs of the 7th century. No doubt many of them are apocryphal and were invented in the 8th century in order to justify innovations and tendencies which were very foreign to the intentions of the Prophet. Such as they are, and observing a little critical care in their use, they are documents of surpassing interest. Each of them is connected with the

Prophet or one of his Companions by a narrative chain: A reported, according to B, who had it from C, that the Prophet. . . . It is what is called the "chain of supporting points of the Tradition" (*silsilat al-asānīd*, sing., *isnād*). Muḥammad's acts and abstentions, his words and his silences, are given in this way the force of rules.

The learned men of Islam made, in the 9th century, compilations which are the basis of all traditionalist studies. Some were made by arranging the ḥadīths according to the chronological order of their successive authors (*isnād*). The most famous arranged the traditions in the order of their subject matter. The "*jāmi' al-ṣaḥīḥ* of al-Bukhārī (d. 870) has been often published in the East and has had added to it numerous commentaries, of which the best known are the '*Umdat al-qāri'* of Al-'Aynī (d. 1451) and the *irshād al-sārī* of Al-Qasṭallānī (d. 1517). A second compilation is the *ṣaḥīḥ* of Muslim (d. 875). Four others were essential: Ibn Māja (d. 886), Abū Dā'ūd (d. 888), Tirmidhī (d. 892) and Al-Nasā'ī (d. 915). Some more recent works are popular: the *maṣābīḥ al-sunna* of Al-Baghawī (d. 1122) and his revision, *mishkāt al-maṣābīḥ* of Al-Ṭabrīzī, the *kitāb al-arba'īn* of Al-Nawawī (d. 1278), and the *jāmi' al-ṣaghīr* of Al-Suyūṭī (d. 1505). For criticism of the ḥadīth the *taqrīb* of *Al-Nawawī* is important.

Although the authors of the collections of ḥadīth tried to bring them into some kind of order and partially succeeded, the Qur'ān and commentaries, the Sunna and commentaries, constituted a mass of material to make capital out of, rather than an epitome of principles and rules of conduct. Discussion was endless, and a time came when it was scarcely possible to secure the acceptance of new facts by the help of manufactured ḥadīths, particularly so since a watchful, if superficial, criticism had begun to hunt down the apocryphal ḥadīths. The value of personal opinion (*ra'y*) had always been acknowledged; through the influence of the *mutakallimīn*, and of the more active among them, the Mu'tazilites, force of law was allowed to the effort of personal interpretation (*ijtihād*), but the practice of it was confined, with the title of *mujtahid*, to a small number of elder scholars of Islam. It is still hard to know to what extent the *ijtihād* was possible after them.

But, if an isolated opinion did not suffice to create a doctrine, it became authoritative once it had gained the adhesion of the Muslim community; for, according to a ḥadīth of the Prophet, the community could not possibly give its general assent (*ijmā'*) to a mistaken theory. But we must not take the word *ijmā'* to mean the harmonious opinion of the masses, but only that of the theologians and jurists of any one time; an attempt has even been made to confine its application to the scholars of Medina in a given period.

Individual judgment is accepted only to a limited extent, being given an analogical application, *al-qiyās*. This source of the law, still drawn upon today, allows a jurist to apply to a novel case a ruling made to fit analogous cases. The right of so deciding is to be found chiefly used in legal and theological consultations (*fatwā*, plur. *fatāwā*) recorded by persons whose learning is generally recognised, but who do not necessarily occupy an official position (*muftī*). The collections of *fatwā*, which are very numerous in manuscript form, and of which the publication has begun, will be an important source in compiling a history of the institutions.

The variety of the doctrines that sprang from those various sources, amidst fierce legal and theological quarrellings, prevented them from achieving, even within the bounds of orthodoxy, a perfect unity. The schools of law, founded in the 9th century on an orthodox basis, have maintained their differences until this day; they share among themselves the government of the orthodox Muslim world. Their differences, manifested in their mental attitudes, have a real practical importance; but those *madhāhib* (sing. *madhhab*) are orthodox rites, not dissenting sects; a Muslim may pass from one of the four *madhāhib* to another without committing a sin. It is even possible, in certain cases, to follow the rules of a rite to which one does not belong: a Mālikite, for example, may, on contracting a marriage, declare that he will conform to the rules of Ḥanafite law in so far as they affect the legal consequences of that marriage, but on the condition that he accepts all its decisions whether they be favourable to him or no.

The Ḥanafite rite, founded by the imām Abū Ḥanīfa (d. 767), is the least rigid of Islamic rites. It was adopted by the Turks, and has continued to prevail in Central Asia and India. Traces of it are to be found in the countries that have been under Turkish rule, in Tunisia and Algeria for example. Shāfi'ism, the school of Muḥammad b. Idrīs al-shāfi'ī, born in Bagdad, died in 820, was the official rite of the 'Abbāsid caliphate and, through merchants and sailors of the Persian Gulf, spread to the coastal regions of the Indian Ocean. It still prevails on the coasts of the Persian Gulf, of Southern Arabia and India, and among the important Muslim communities of the Sunda Isles. The same commercial influences carried it to East Africa. It has been specially studied by Arab scholars in Holland, late mistress of the East Indies. Traces of its authority are to be found in Lower Egypt. Mālikism, originated by the Medina imām, Mālik b. Anas (d. 795), is dominant in the Maghrib (Tunisia, Algeria, Morocco) and in Central Africa. It has been the subject of important studies by the French school. The Ḥanbalite rite, founded by Aḥmad b. Ḥanbal (d. 855), has only a small number of adepts in Central Arabia and on the shores of the Persian Gulf; it is the strictest of the orthodox rites. In modern Arabia it seems to have fused with Wahhābism.

The combined total of the rules that are the result of this great effort of traditionalism and of reasoning makes up the Muslim law (*fiqh*), and the jurists (*fuqahā'*, sing. *faqīh*) constituted, in the Muslim State, a considerable body of men, a corporation in which the principal public officials enlisted, and which, in certain troublous times, knew how to stir up the mob. The *fiqh* is, in effect, the methodical knowledge of the law (*sharī'a*) contained in the Qur'ān and the Sunna, co-ordinated and explained by reasoned opinion. It can, following the temperament of the doctors, lean towards personal interpretation or hold to the Tradition. The oldest legal treatise known today is the Muwaṭṭa' of Mālik b. Anas. In Syria, Al-Auzā'ī (d. 774) founded a school of *fiqh*, of which no written works have survived, but the authority of which, all-powerful at the time, was well established in Umayyad Spain. After Abū Ḥanīfa came the qāḍī of Hārūn al-Rashīd, Abū Yūsuf, author of a "Book of Land Taxation" of which the matter goes far beyond the limits of the title.

But legal practice which, as we shall emphasise again, had to submit to the demands of local customs, encouraged specialisation in studies which strayed ever farther from the sources, to lose itself in the "branches" (*furū'*). There was a tendency, therefore, to reduce the older, lengthy treatises to short manuals which provided the magistrates with a code, the phraseology of which was copied in their judgments. Mālikism has the *Mukhtaṣar* of "Sīdī" Khalīl (d. 1365) with numerous commentaries (Kharashī, Dasūqī, etc.). The manual of Shāfi'ism is the Minhāj al-Ṭālibīn of al-Nawawī (d. 1278) with its commentaries, the Tuḥfa of Ibn Ḥajar and the Nihāya of al-Ramlī. Among current works in Ḥanafism we may mention the Jāmi' al-Rumūz of Al-Khurāsânī, and the Kanz al-daqā'iq of al-Nasafī.

Those practical manuals, none the less, take no account of local custom (*'āda*, *'urf*, *'amal*), which has yet thrust its way, not only into the ordinary judicial life that leaves no written record, but even into many of the regular acts and judgments of the qāḍīs; their collection and publication has been begun.

The divine law (*Sharī'a*) thus finds itself contained in a mass of books and documents, a knowledge of which constitutes the *fiqh*. This includes rules of worship (*'ibādāt*) and measures of family and social law (*mu'āmalāt*) and of penal law ('Uqūbāt). Those regulations are not all of equal value, and are divided into five legal categories (*'aḥkām*): what is compulsory (*farḍ*, *wājib*) and earns a reward or a punishment; a distinction is drawn between individual duty (*farḍ 'ayn*), for example that of prayer, and a collective duty (*farḍ kifāya*), with which one can dispense if it is sufficiently performed by others, for example the jihād; and secondly, what is recommended (*mandūb*, *mustaḥabb*), the performance of which is rewarded, but the omission unpunished; thirdly, what is permitted or immaterial (*mubāḥ*), and is neither rewarded nor punished; and lastly, what is forbidden (*ḥarām*) and which is punishable.

SOURCES

Juynboll: "*Handbuch des Islamischen Gesetzes*" (S.88); Goldziher: "*Loi et Dogme*" (S.86); "*Muhammedanische Studien II. Hadith*" (S.29): Buhl: "*Koran*", E.I., 2.1184; Schacht: "Sharia", E.I., 4.331; An Nawawi; "*taqrib*", translated by W. Marçais (S.).

CHAPTER SIX

THE CULT

The Profession of Faith—Prayer: mosques, special prayers—Pilgrimage: 'Umra and Hajj; the Ka'ba and the Circumambulations, the Sa'y, 'Arafa and Minā; Medina and the Tomb of the Prophet—Fasting—Legal Alms.

MUSLIM law lays on the faithful a small number of ritual duties which constitute "the angles or pillars of the faith" (*arkān al-dīn*). These include the recitation of the confession of the Muslim faith (*shahāda*), the ritual Prayer (*ṣalāt*), the fast (*ṣaum*), the pilgrimage (*ḥajj*), and the legal alms (*zakāt*). Some authors put in place of the *shahāda* either the purification (*ṭahāra*), or the holy war (*jihād*).

The *shahāda* is, in fact, a normal manifestation of Islam rather than a religious duty; it is as much a part of the faith itself (*īmān*) as of the works that are its outward sign (*'amal*). It is a witness to the faith expressed in the two statements: "I give witness that there is no god but Allāh, and that Muḥammad is the envoy of Allāh" (*ashhadu anna lā ilāha illa llahu wa anna muḥammadan rasūlu llāh*). To utter this phrase is to profess Islam, and the Doctrine declares that the title of Muslim must be recognised as due to whoever does so. The dying are made to say it, and the fighter in the holy war is supposed to have had it on his dying lips and is therefore called *Shahīd*. It is an essential element of the Prayer (*tashahhud*).

The ritual Prayer (*ṣalāt*, plur. *ṣalawāt*) is *the* essential element of Muslim worship. It is an assemblage of rites, gestures and words, laid down by the law. One ought, therefore, to keep, in speaking of it, to the Arabic word *ṣalāt*, reserving the term "prayer" for the translation of the Arabic *du'ā*, which is applied to the personal and variable appeal that is addressed to God. Here we shall use Prayer.

The execution of the duty of Prayer does not necessitate the presence of the worshipper in the mosque, except on

Fridays at midday; such presence is recommended only because it reduces the chances of its being performed in a manner contrary to the law, and therefore invalid.

The Prayer is the principal duty of the Muslim and, when it is desired to express the fact that a man is not a Muslim or has ceased to be one, it is said that he is a "neglector of the ritual Prayer" (*tārik al-ṣalāt*).

The Prayer was observed, at the beginning of the teaching, only at the rising and setting of the sun; the Tradition insists that it should be neither at the actual rising or setting of the orb; it seeks thus to destroy the memory of an ancient solar cult. But the number of the daily Prayers has been finally fixed at five: they occur at hours of the day (*waqt*, plur. *auqāt*) comprised between two instants that are determined by astronomic facts. The *ṣubḥ* takes place in the morning, between the moment when the sky is finally filled with light—the true dawn—and sunrise: it is of no value if said after the moment of sunrise. The "time" of the *ẓuhr* falls validly between the moment when the minimum shadow of a man standing begins to grow—immediately after midday—and that when the shadow cast by a man is equal to the stature of that man, added to his minimum shadow: in reality, it takes place immediately after midday. The *'aṣr* is said between that moment and that in which the sun sets; in practice, between three and five o'clock in the afternoon, varying with the season and local custom. The *maghrib* is placed between sunset and the disappearance of the yellow light that illumines the horizon. Neither of those last two Prayers must overlap the instant of sunset. The "time" of the *'ishā* extends from the end of the *maghrib* to the beginning of the time of the *ṣubḥ*, which means that it may take place at any hour of the night: in practice, in the evening, in the first moments of nocturnal darkness.

Through the observance of the Prayer the worshipper draws near to Allāh, and that fact gives to his person a momentarily sacred character. He must prepare for this act by submitting to special conditions of personal and external purity. We shall later give some details as to the place in which the Prayer may be validly observed. In his person the worshipper must be in a state of legal purity (*ṭahāra*): he must be free of every defilement (*ḥadath*), great or small. Sexual intercourse, which is the great defilement (*janāba*), can be compensated for by general ablution (*ghusl*); the small defilement, which arises from the satisfaction of the calls of nature, from sleep, from simple contact with a person of the other sex, etc., is removed by ablution following a definite ritual (*wuḍū*) which is that which Muslims commonly perform before they pray, either in the dependencies or in the court itself of the mosque. With water that is legally pure the worshipper washes his face, then his hands and forearms to the elbow. He then passes the wet right hand over his head; then he washes his feet; all in that order. Besides this, the worshipper must not approach Allāh wearing a garment that is stained with blood, with excrement, etc., and any defilement, spittle, bleeding of the nose, etc., incurred during the Prayer, destroys its efficacy.

In a state of legal purity the believer may answer the call (*adhān*) of the muezzin (*mu'adhdhin*) who, in the towns, calls out from the top of the minaret the formula that invites to prayer, and announces that the time for it has come: "Allāh is great (four times); I bear witness that there is no other God but Allāh (twice); I bear witness that Muḥammad is the messenger of Allāh (twice); come to the *ṣalāt* (twice); there is no other God but Allah." Outside the towns the believer must be his own *mu'adhdhin*.

If the worshipper cannot go to the mosque where he would only have to conform to the arrangement of the building and the postures of the *imām*, he must first make for himself a sanctuary, a *templum*. He takes up his position, standing, his face turned towards Mecca, where the Ka'ba is the centre of attraction, the *qibla* of the Muslim world. At the beginning of his stay in Medina, the Prophet, by an instinctive or, it may be, politic, imitation of the Jews, had recommended that one should pray with the face turned towards Jerusalem. Having changed his policy, he adopted as *qibla* the House of Allāh which occupies the centre of the mosque of the Holy City. A little mosque at Medina preserves the memory of this reversal and is called the mosque of the two *qibla* (*jāmi' al-qiblatayn*). The direction in which the *qibla* lies, which, in towns, is determined by the orientation of the mosques, is everywhere else fixed by the observations and the opinions of the "scholars".

When he has decided the direction in which he must face,

the worshipper makes certain that the ground around him is not defiled and that he may validly perform there the ritual of the Prayer. He marks the limit of his holy ground by plunging his lance into the ground in front of him, according to the older texts, or by the mere laying down of some clearly visible object. It is within the point thus marked that he will touch his forehead to the ground in the act of prostration. If, during the Prayer, a human being or an animal should traverse the sacred enclosure, the rite would be null and void.

Standing, turned towards Mecca, the worshipper repeats the call to prayer (*iqāma*) and puts into words, either silently or in a low voice, his intention (*nīya*) to repeat, for example, the Prayer of the *ṣubḥ* or the *ẓuhr*. This intention is essential to the validity of the Prayer, and it is well to insist on the importance of this element of conscious will in each of the rites of Islam.

Then, raising his open hands to the level of the shoulder, the worshipper utters the *takbīr*, the formula *Allāhu akbar*, "Allāh is great", more exactly, "Allāh is greater" (than all others). This formula, which is used in many circumstances, assumes here a special importance, for it marks the beginning of the period during which the worshipper devotes himself completely to the observation of the Prayer, and enters into communion with the Deity. From that instant he breaks off all connection with earthly affairs; a word or a gesture foreign to the ritual cancels the Prayer, for they interrupt the union of the worshipper with Allāh. Muslim jurists have accurately defined the importance of this formula, and have called it *takbīr al-iḥrām*, that is to say, "recitation of the *takbīr* of sanctification".

Still standing, the left hand placed in the right, the worshipper recites the first chapter of the Qur'ān, the *Fātiḥa*. He then inclines the upper part of the body, repeating another *takbīr*, and places the palms of his hands on his knees in an obeisance called *rukū'*, he then resumes the erect position (*i'tidāl*). He then assumes the posture of greatest surrender to Allāh, the "prostration" (*sujūd*), which is, so to speak, the culminating point of the Prayer, and appears to correspond to the Christian attitude during the elevation of the Host. The worshipper then kneels on the ground, then stretches out his hands and, between them, touches the ground with his brow, at the root of the nose. He then raises his body, but remains in a kneeling position, his hands stretched along his thighs, in a "sitting" (*julūs* or *qu'ūd*) position. Then he prostrates himself a second time, this being, as the first time, preceded and followed by a *takbīr*.

Those successive postures, from the recitation of the *fātiḥa* to the end of the second prostration, constitute a whole, called *rak'a* (plur. *raka'āt*), and each of the daily Prayers contains a ritual number of *raka'āt*. The Prayers of the *ẓuhr*, the *'aṣr*, and the *'ishā*, of which the "moments" are prolonged, have four *raka'āt*, those of the *ṣubḥ* and the *maghrib*, the period of which is shortened by the necessity of avoiding any coincidence with sunrise or sunset, have two and three *raka'āt* respectively. Each group of two *raka'āt* concludes, in obedience to the Sunna, with the recitation (*tashahhud*) of the Muslim confession of faith (*shahāda*).

When the last *rak'a* is ended, the worshipper, after the second prostration, resumes the *julūs* position; he then repeats an obligatory *shahāda*, then the formula of the intercession for the Prophet (*ṣalla llāhu 'alā sayyidinā Muḥammadin wa sallam*). Then, turning the head over the right shoulder, then over the left shoulder, the worshipper pronounces the formula of the salutation, the *taslīm*: "May the salutation rest upon you, and the mercy of Allāh" (*al-salāmu 'alaykum wa raḥmatu llāh*). This formula ends the sacred period (*iḥrām al-ṣalāt*) that the *takbīr al-iḥrām* had opened, and, for this reason, it has been given the name of "the salutation of the de-sanctification" (*taslīm al-taḥlīl*). If the worshipper remains in the mosque in order to perform the supplementary devotions, he may break off occasionally to converse with neighbours, give orders, etc.: he is desanctified.

The rites just described are completed, in the case of pious persons, by the recitation of invocations and verses of the Qur'ān, the number and variety of which depend on the religious culture of the worshippers and the rite (*madhhab*) to which they belong. Muḥammad recommended, in addition, the voluntary performance of supererogatory Prayers (*nāfila*, plur. *nawāfil*).

The Prayer is therefore an individual religious act which the believer must perform alone and wherever he may be. But, preferably, it should be performed in company (*jamâ'atan*), that is, under the direction of a pious Muslim, learned in the ritual, behind whom the worshippers take position in parallel lines, and whose gestures they copy. This prayer leader, the *imām*, has, it should be noted, no religious character; he has undergone no initiation; he is not a clerk. The imām is a man who, in private life, practises any profession whatever, it may be a very humble one, but who is put over his co-religionaries only because of his reputation for knowledge and piety. It is also recommended that the faithful should so gather together in a mosque where the material installation of the edifice is so arranged as to remove the most serious risks of invalidation of the Prayer. It is a collective duty of Muslims to ensure, by the presence of a certain number of them, the celebration in the mosque of the daily prayers.

Once a week, on Friday, at the hour of the *ẓuhr*, the faithful must take part in a special ceremony, the "Friday Prayer' (*ṣalāt al-jum'a*), during which the shops in the sūqs are closed and economic life is suspended. A general purification (*ghusl*) is recommended in preparation for it and the donning of newly washed garments: this is a rule observed by Muslims who have "good manners" and who, in the towns, throng to the ḥammāms on Friday morning.

The essential element of this ceremony is a sermon (*khuṭba*) preached by a special imām called *imām khaṭīb*. This *khuṭba* is in reality made up of two parts (*khuṭbat al-na't*, and *khuṭbat al- wa'ẓ*), which include: the first, a general eulogy, the formula for which is almost uniform, and the second, pious exhortations in which the *khaṭīb* can display his eloquence, unless he prefers to repeat one of the model addresses of which special collections have been made. The Prayer of the *ẓuhr* with four *raka'āt* is not held on that day; or at least it is made up of only two obligatory *raka'āt* which come immediately after the *khuṭba*; but the traditional usage is that two more *raka'āt* should precede the *khuṭba*.

In the first *khuṭba* the worshippers pray that the blessing of Allāh may be on the reigning sovereign: this old custom was an important practical act, for it was the public manifestation by means of which the people not only publicly recognised an individual to be their immediate ruler, but also acknowledged, together with him, the sovereignty of a higher chief, a caliph. When, in 1183, the Spanish traveller, Ibn Jubayr, is present at Friday Prayer in the mosque at Mecca, the *khaṭīb* calls down the blessing of Allāh on the amīr of Mecca, then on his mighty sovereign lord, Sulṭān Saladin, and lastly on the ʿAbbāsid Caliph to whom the latter has promised his homage and his aid. In the Muslim world the name of the Turkish caliph dominated the *khuṭba,* save in those countries of which the ruler, like the Moroccan Sharīf, lays claim to the title of *amīr al-muʾminīn,* "Prince of all Believers". Since the fall of the caliphate the ritual varies. Algeria and Tunisia have a common form of praying for, and calling for blessings on, the Muslim community and its masters. The Wahhābites pray for the "King-Amīr". In Egypt there is also a common formula which follows the name of the Egyptian King. In the Sudan prayers are still said for the four orthodox caliphs.

The ceremony of the "Friday Prayer" must be performed in the presence of at least forty worshippers; it is permissible only in cities of some size, where the community is large enough to ensure that it will be celebrated with due solemnity. Large cities only are allowed several mosques authorised for the *khuṭba,* provided the number of the faithful is too great to permit of their gathering together in any one of them. The mosques in which Friday prayers are said are called *jāmiʿ*, plur. *jawāmiʿ*).

The origins of the mosque are complex. They are not imitations of the temple at Mecca which consists essentially of the Kaʿba with Zamzam, which the caliphs later caused to be surrounded by a large courtyard, enclosed within encircling galleries. The mosque, according to the Muslim tradition which we must partly accept, has grown out of the court in which, before the house of the Prophet in Medina, the faithful gathered for the Prayer, to listen to the Revelation and to receive the exhortations, a part of which was soon roofed in by an awning so as to protect the worshippers from the sun's heat or foul weather. To some extent also, the mosque was modelled on the Christian churches which were greatly admired by the first conquerors, who adapted a number of them to suit Muslim usage.

The mosque is a rectangular construction comprising a court (*ṣaḥn*) and a covered hall which, in the older buildings, has a flat roof resting directly on columns or pillars, placed on the abaci of the capitals of the columns. Finally, the vaulted cupola made its appearance in several parts of the mosque. The orientation of the building is determined by the direction in which Mecca lies; the Ka'ba is the *qibla* of the Muslim world. An apsidiole, a curved recess, is sunk in the middle of the rear wall of the mosque, at the far end of the hall of prayer, marking the direction of the *qibla*, so that the worshippers may assume the correct position for the Prayer. This apsidiole, which is more or less richly ornamented with marbles, mosaics, stucco carvings, or tiles, is the *miḥrāb*. It was an offence to the eyes of the pure worshippers of the Umayyad period, as being an innovation borrowed from the Christians, recalling the recesses for the reception of the images of saints, or a bishop's stall.

The pillars or columns form, at the same time, aisles that extend from the court to the wall of the *qibla*, and galleries at right angles to them, in which the worshippers form long lines parallel to this wall. The hall of prayer, in the majority of mosques, is wide open to the court from which it receives the light and air that has direct entrance only through narrow *claustra* piercing the three walls. Through these pass concentrated rays of light which play over the decorations of the pillars and on the carpets that cover the floor. In the more handsome buildings the walls, bare on the outside, are covered, within the hall of prayer, with plaques of marble, with mosaics, porcelain tiles and stucco carvings. The roofs are flat and lead covered, or domed, or composed of arches covered with lead or green tiles. The court is surrounded by galleries of little depth, on which the worshippers like to sit. It is into the court that the main gate usually opens, under the minaret or beside it; direct entrance from outside into the hall of prayer is provided by two doors facing each other.

The central aisle that runs from the court to the *miḥrāb* is, generally, wider than the secondary aisles and of the same width as the gallery which forms, along the wall of the *qibla*, the far end of the hall of prayer and which is a transept. The intersection of those two galleries is, therefore, a square, or at least a rectangle, which, frequently domed, is specially decorated. It is there that the floor is covered with the best mats or the newest carpets. The light cluster, which depends from the vault, is sometimes still a beautiful example of the work of the old coppersmiths. It is there that the imām (*antistes*) "places himself at the head" of the worshippers to conduct the Prayer, surrounded by the most important personages of the neighbourhood or of the city.

The caliph who, in person or through his representative, presides over the solemn Friday Prayer, abandoned, in the early days of Islam, the custom of taking his place amidst the faithful; to the protection provided by his guard he added that of an enclosure of wood, a *maqṣūra*, on the construction of which the cabinet makers of Islam expended every resource of their art. Women were admitted to the mosques, shut up in similar enclosures, in those cases in which the galleries were not reserved for them. The *maqṣūra* of the Prince surrounded, in front of the *miḥrāb*, a space entered by a special door communicating with his palace, either directly or through a long gallery.

The pulpit (*minbar*) is placed to the right of the *miḥrāb*; it could be a wooden erection mounted on wheels, as was the antique *minbar* in the Ka'ba. Several fine parts of pulpits of the 12th to the 14th centuries are still in existence. Those movable pulpits were, during the week, pushed back against the wall of the *qibla*, and were pulled into place for the celebration of the ritual Prayer. There were also fixed wooden pulpits, or there might be an erection of stone or marble like the pulpits of the present day Orient. The pulpit-platform of the Prophet became a stool with three steps. Under the Umayyads it grew into a ladder of nine steps, the lowest of which was surmounted by an arch. The pulpit is for the sole use of the imām appointed to pronounce the *khuṭba*, either on Fridays or on fast days. In important mosques a fixed wooden platform is erected in one of the bays next to the *miḥrāb*; there it is that the reciters of the Qur'ān, the *ḥazzābīn*, take their place for the ceremonies during which, the whole Qur'ān having to be recited rapidly, each *ḥazzāb* recites a different portion (*ḥizb*) of it.

The anterior bay of the hall of prayer opens into the court of the mosque, the *ṣaḥn*, which is usually paved with enamelled bricks. Sometimes trees and bushes add the beauty of their foliage to the ornamentation of the building. A basin and fountain are in the centre of the *ṣaḥn.* This court is often surrounded, on the three sides exterior to the hall of prayer, by one or several open galleries which are screened to the outside by the wall that encloses the mosque. Side doors, in many cases, give direct entrance into the hall of prayer. But the principal entrance is usually that which admits to the court. Those gates or doors, which are made of carved wood and are often covered with sheets of worked copper, are sheltered by porches ornamented with stucco or porcelain tiles. Near the doors important mosques have dependencies, latrines with running water and special installations for the carrying out of the ritual ablutions.

The mosque is surmounted by a tower, the minaret (*manāra, ma'dhana, ṣauma'a*), crowned by a gallery from which the muezzin broadcasts over the city the five summonses to the daily Prayers. Large mosques have several minarets, usually placed at the corners of the building. Their shape, their decoration, and the materials used in their construction, brick or stone, vary with the resources and the traditions of the country. In Syria, Egypt, and in the West, the minarets were square towers containing rooms that could be used as dwellings. In Persia and Turkey, they are cylinders containing only the stair that gives access to the muezzin's chamber. Those two shapes, and a polygonal type, have been combined in certain oriental minarets having a square base, passing into an octagon, and ending in cylindrical form. The top, which, in the Maghrib, is capped by a lantern surmounted by a ball of yellow metal, is, in the East, of varying designs.

To the mosque there is often attached a room into which the dead are borne (*bayt al-janā'iz*); it is placed near the *miḥrāb.*

The mosque is the central edifice of Muslim life. At the hour of each Prayer a certain number of worshippers assemble there, finding in it the conditions of legal purification, of certain orientation and of quiet, that ensure the validity of their Prayers. Teachers gave, within its walls, and still give, instruction. There, the qāḍī was formerly accustomed to give his audiences. For the traveller it is a meeting place and, at times, a home.

Mosques were neither maintained by the State nor served

by public officials. The foundation of a mosque by a ruler, or by a wealthy private individual, was always accompanied by the setting up of an endowment, in the East *waqf*, plur. *wuqūf*, in the Maghrib *ḥabs*, plur. *ḥubūs*, pronounced *ḥabūs*, which provided funds for the repair and maintenance of the building, and also for the salaries of the staff attached to it. Those endowments, being usually squandered by the administrators (*nāẓir*), great personages, desirous of winning the divine favour and a reputation for generosity, would endow them anew: otherwise the mosque would become a ruin. The *nāẓir* of the *wuqūf* of the mosque had in his own hands the supply of materials and the appointment of the minor staff: porters, sweepers, lamp cleaners, etc. In the "cathedral" mosques (*jawāmiʿ*), a direct or delegated nomination by the sovereign selected the *imām khaṭīb* as well as the ordinary imāms and the muezzin. The Prophet had, indeed, been the first *imām* and the first *khaṭīb* of the Muslim community; and his successors, the caliphs, had preserved the custom of celebrating the Friday Prayer in the great mosque of Medina, Damascus, or Bagdad. They delegated this function, as we have already pointed out, to the provincial governors who, in their turn, passed it on to personages of note. This example was followed by lesser, more or less independent, sovereigns, into whose hands crumbs of the caliph's power had fallen. The imāms of the smaller mosques were chosen, on the authority of a general and remote delegation of the powers of the prince, by the governors, the qāḍīs, or the imāms of the large mosques, etc. Custom requires that the muezzin should have a sonorous voice and, if possible, that he should be blind, a so frequent occurrence among peoples who inhabit dusty lands: it is feared that he may cast his eyes on the balconies, the common resort of the women.

The ritual Prayer being the essential ceremony of the Muslim cult, it is usually celebrated when it is a question of begging the protection of Allāh from any present or threatening calamity.

The disappearance of the moon or of the sun as a result of an eclipse is averted by the "Prayer of the Eclipse" (*ṣalāt al-khusūf*, or *al-kusūf*, according as it is the moon or the sun that is involved); they differ from the Friday Prayer only in the wording of the *khuṭba*.

Everywhere the fruitful rains are necessary to the life of Nature, and nowhere more so than in the lands that saw the birth of Islam and throughout which it first spread. The "Rogations" for rain (*ṣalāt al-istisqā'*), drawn up by Islam, have therefore, like the Christian Rogations, taken the place of ancient local rites. But the Muslim rite has not, like that of Christianity, kept the poetical form of the old customs. It consists merely in a Prayer, analogous to that of Friday, but preceded by three days of pious exercises and fasting. A wooden board, on which are inscribed Qur'ānic verses suitable to the occasion, is erected on the summit of the minaret of the mosque. At the end of the *khuṭba* the worshippers undo their garments, turn them inside out, and put them on upside down: that is the only ancient rite that has been incorporated into the official ceremonies. The essential rites, in the eyes of the masses, are the practices of sympathetic magic that use water to summon the waters, such as the plunging of living beings or stones into watercourses, and those in which cows, the representatives on earth of the rain-filled clouds, take part. Such practices are followed by the common people in addition to any truly religious mediation.

The pilgrimage is an institution of peculiar interest to the Muslim religion. Firstly, because it is a revival and a syncretism of ancient rites common throughout the Semitic East; and also because, gathering together in a great annual assembly a throng of several tens of thousands of the faithful from all parts of the world, it is the only real bond that unites the different Muslim communities, and the only opportunity for a Pan-Islamic reunion. Geography, even allowing for the improved communications of the 20th century, has singularly isolated Mecca, and the climate is hardly conducive to its becoming a centre of intellectual life. But the city that possesses the House of Allāh is none the less a mighty centre of attraction. We shall dwell here a little on the ceremonies that take place within its walls.

The Mecca practice formerly made a clear distinction between two kinds of ceremony: those that took place around the Ka'ba and in its immediate neighbourhood, the *'umra*; and those of which localities near Mecca were the scene, 'Arafāt, Muzdalifa and Minā, that is, the *ḥajj*. The *'umra* is Qurayshite and belongs solely to Mecca; the *ḥajj* is of the Ḥijāz. The Mecca sūras of the Qur'ān do not mention the *ḥajj* but even the earliest of them testify to the veneration which Muḥammad felt for the Ka'ba, the protector of the Qurayshites, their caravans and their wealth. There is no reason to doubt that Muḥammad prayed to his God before the Ka'ba. It is true that, during the last period of his stay in Mecca, he turned his face towards Jerusalem; but it was not long before he once more faced the Ka'ba, at the same time working it into a cycle of Abrahamic traditions which he thought would prove attractive to Jews and Christians: Zamzam had sprung forth in order to give to drink to Agar and Ismael, the latter of whom had then helped Abraham to build the Ka'ba, the true House of God. Muḥammad's revised plans reverted to the memories of his youth in his desire to restore to Mecca its high place as holy ground. Head of a community that grew continuously as the Bedouin tribes came to adhere to it, Muḥammad fitted the ceremonies of the *ḥajj* also into the biblical legend and introduced into them the sacrifice of Abraham. The Medina sūras of the Qur'an imposed the pilgrimage as a duty upon all Muslims. Muḥammad, anxious to enter his native city as master, but peacefully, referred to the *'umra* and the *ḥajj* in his negotiations with the Qurayshites in seeking to persuade them to allow him to enter freely at the head of his followers. In the year which followed the fruitless attempt of Al-Ḥudaybiya, he carried out an *'umra* in empty Mecca, and then finally, in 630, after the conquest of the city, he celebrated an *'umra* and a *ḥajj* in which tradition claims to find the rules which have fixed the form of the Muslim pilgrimage, seeing in them a combination of the two earlier rites, brought together by the *fuqahā'*, and constituting the most important ceremony of Islam.

The *'umra,* that is to say, the rites that are performed at Mecca around the Ka'ba, has therefore been introduced into the group of ceremonies that constitute the Muslim pilgrimage (*ḥajj*). But, in 1184, it was still an independent Mecca festival, celebrated by the whole population of the town in the first month of *rajab*. However, the orthodox teaching has striven hard to destroy it as a separate ceremony, and tolerates it only as a supererogatory act which may be performed at any time during the year, except in the two *ḥajj* months, *dhū lqa'da* and *dhū lḥijja*, or one which can serve the newcomer to Mecca as a salutation to the mosque and the sacred territory.

A short description of the holy places will simplify our explanation of the ritual of this double ceremony which has become an integral part of the pilgrimage of the Muslim whom we shall accompany, from the day of his setting out until his return to his family.

In a harsh, sun-scorched region, a valley runs down between the red mountains on which no tree nor any grass grows. When the violent thunderstorms that bring to mind the deluge of old burst overhead, then, for several hours, the valley is swept by raging waters, which furrow and lay waste a soil that cannot absorb them. Here and there, however, there are cracks in the hard surface, and the waters find their way into them, and so form the subterranean pools that feed the few permanent springs that the valley holds. Zamzam is the most abundant and the most precious in spite of its hard chemical composition. Around it, and on the road that extends along the Red Sea from Syria to the Yaman, men have built Mecca. Muslim tradition, seeking to connect with the memory of Abraham the whole religious history of the Ḥijāz, has shown Agar, abandoned with Ismael in the desert, running from one hill to the other, calling for help, and the angel Gabriel causing the spring to leap from the soil beside the child who was to be the ancestor of the peoples of Central Arabia. It is to Zamzam, too, that, by the same tradition, Abraham came and rebuilt, with Ismael's help, the House of God (*bayt Allāh*), the Ka'ba, on the very spot on which it had been built by Adam, only to be swallowed up and destroyed by the Flood.

The Ka'ba, a square enclosure, bounded by a stone wall, roofed at a remote period with palm branches, later surrounded by a sloping terrace, suffered, according to Islamic tradition, from the irreligiousness of the Qurayshites who filled it with their idols, until the day when Muḥammad broke them, and made an empty place of the House of the invisible and far-off Allāh. Today it is a large cube (*ka'ba*) of undressed stone, without any definite ornamentation, twelves metres long, by ten broad and six metres high. A sloping terrace drains the rain waters into a gutter of wood covered with gold-gilt metal (*mi'zāb*), with its outlet beyond the north-west face of the structure. Its four faces are entirely covered by a material woven of cotton mixed with silk, green in colour, the "vesture" (*kiswa*), which is made in Cairo at the expense of the sovereign, and sent each year with processional pomp, at the period of the pilgrimage, together with the *maḥmal*, the symbolic palanquin that seems to represent the King's majesty. At two-thirds of its height the *kiswa* has inset a wide band of black material on which are embroidered verses of the Qur'ān relating to the Ka'ba. This is the "girdle" (*ḥizām*) of the temple. The vesture, which the Ka'ba casts off each year, is not lost: the Banū Shayba, an old Qurayshite family, which has the traditional duty of guarding the House of Allāh, present a few beautiful fragments of it to those great personages to whom they owe honour or thanks for gifts received, and carry on a lively trade in the remaining pieces, these being offered for sale in the small shops that surround the mosque.

At the south-east corner of the Ka'ba, the black stone (*alḥajar al-aswad*) is embedded in the wall at a height of a metre and a half above the present soil level. It is a piece of soft granite which has been broken, either by the Qarmaṭs when they carried it off to Lahsa, or as the result of a local accident. The pieces have been joined, and the whole thing (forty centimetres in diameter) is surrounded by a silver frame ten centimetres broad.

To the right of the corner at which the black stone is situated, at the beginning of that side of the Ka'ba which, in a northward direction, ends in the "angle of 'Irāq", is a door of the temple, raised two metres above the ground outside, and reached by a portable wooden stair of four steps. The Ka'ba is open to the faithful during the year on a few fixed dates, but, at any time, the Banū Shayba grant admittance to generous persons. The days of public entry to the Ka'ba are also, for this numerous family, days of blessing, seeing that they sell the right to pray on the spot on which the Prophet prayed, to participate in the sweeping and washing of the temple, to carry in the water of Zamzam used for washing it, and so on. This water drains into a kind of trough placed on the right of the door and on the outside of the wall, a position that had once been occupied by the *maqām Ibrāhīm*.

A very old sacred stone is also pointed out on which, according to Muslim tradition, Abraham climbed when laying the upper courses of the Ka'ba, and from which he summoned the future generations to the *ḥajj*. The prints of his feet are still to be seen. The *maqām* is today at some distance from the wall of the Ka'ba, inside a pavilion of stone and metal: people come to touch and kiss the outside of the *maqām*.

Between the 'Irāq corner and the Syrian corner (*al-rukn al-shāmī*) extends a kind of annex of the Ka'ba, enclosed within a semicircular wall which leaves an open passage in front of the two corners of the temple. This is the *ḥijr*, where tradition places the graves of Hagar, Ishmael and numerous prophets, and where it is said that Hagar's sheep were folded. Tradition adds that the *ḥijr* was once a part of the Ka'ba, the ground it encloses being looked upon as equally holy with that of the House itself.

On the face between the Syrian corner and the Yamanite, the fourth angle of the Ka'ba, and symmetrically placed with reference to the black stone and the temple door, tradition preserves the memory of a second sacred stone and the traces of a second door, constructed at the time of the rebuilding of the Ka'ba by 'Abd Allāh b. Zubayr, and walled up again by Al-Ḥajjāj.

The Ka'ba is surrounded by a sort of ellipsoidal roadway, paved with stone flags (the *maṭāf*), on which the pilgrims make the ritual circuits (*ṭawāf*). It lies below the level of the floor of the Ka'ba and also below that of the vast courtyard of the mosque, for it was on this level that the torrents, gushing down from the mountain, often passed and cut deep into the soil.

Outside the *maṭāf* and opposite the corner at which the black stone is fixed, there rises the domed pavilion, the *qubba* of Zamzam, which shelters the broad lip of the well in whose depths flows the sacred spring. On the great days of the pilgrimage it is hither that the crowd of pilgrims throngs, eager themselves to draw, as the Prophet did, the holy water in the buckets pendant from the cords which, by the friction of centuries, have filed and cut deep hollows in the stone parapet. Fortunate those pilgrims who succeed in fetching up water enough to drench their garments; nay, even to soak into their very souls!

Others come to dip their grave clothes in the well, drying them afterwards on the gravel of the great court. The water of the spring is sold, too, in flasks of burnt clay, the sale of which is a perquisite of the Corporation of the Servants of Zamzam (*al-Zamzamīyīn*). Attached to the qubba is a storehouse in which the articles belonging to the mosque are housed. A stair leads to the terrace from which the muezzin of Zamzam intones the first call to prayer. He used to fix the time for this after consulting various antiquated instruments, which had been replaced by a chronometer regulated at Greenwich.

Beside the qubba of Zamzam rises a witness to the gate giving entrance to the original precincts of the mosque, the arch of the Gate of Banū Shayba. Farther on, close to the qubba of the *maqām Ibrāhīm*, and outside the *maṭāf*, is to be seen the pulpit (*minbar*), from which the imām delivers the Friday *khuṭba*. This pulpit which, since the reign of the Osmanli sultan Sulaymān, towards the year 1560, is of stone and marble, and therefore a fixture, was, before that, made of wood and mounted on wheels. For the *khuṭba* it was pushed back against the wall of the Ka'ba. It is also outside the *maṭāf* that three small pavilions have been built for the use of the imāms of the Ḥanafite, Mālikite, and Ḥanbalite rites. By special privilege the Shāfi'te imām celebrates the Prayer behind the *maqām*.

The little temple and its dependencies are surrounded by a vast court, the soil of which is covered with small pebbles and intersected by flagged pathways. This is the *ṣaḥn* of the mosque, bounded by covered galleries of several tiers of arches, of irregular shape and size. The *ṣaḥn* measures approximately a hundred metres by a hundred and sixty, almost the dimensions of the inner court of the Louvre. The galleries are pierced by twenty-two doors, of which the chief are *Bāb al-salām*, the "Door of the Salutation", to the north-east, and *Bāb al-ṣafā'*, to the south, opposite to the corner of the black stone.

This door gives access to *al-ṣafā'*, the little elevation which, with al Marwa, to the north-east of the mosque, marks the limit of the *mas'a*, the track which, in imitation of Agar, or rather following an old ambulatory rite, the pilgrim must traverse seven times, increasing his pace between the two corners of the mosque. Stairways of a few steps lead to the tops of the sacred hillocks. The old track, once the bed of the torrent, which skirts the mosque on the eastern side, is today the street (*Shāri'*) of the *mas'ā*, a long line and then a lane of shops, in which those of the barbers stand out, being continuously besieged by the pilgrims who have adopted the rite of the pilgrimage in *tamattu'*.

Many sacred dwellings, and the cemetery tombs attract those pilgrims who are able to prolong their stay in Mecca; but such "pilgrimages" have no ritual character.

The pilgrims visit the cemetery of Mecca, as they do those of Medina, Bagdad, Damascus and Cairo, because they believe that they find in them the tombs of the Companions of the Prophet, as well as of other venerable personages. They reckon that the invocations they address to God in their favour will bring them in exchange a precious *baraka*. At one time pious visits were paid to the house of Khadīja, the Prophet's first wife, then to the house of his birth, the house in which he gathered together his disciples, the dwelling of 'Alī, etc. The Wahhābites, in the course of their invasion of Mecca in 1803, had claimed to have destroyed those idolatrous sanctuaries; today, peaceful masters of Central Arabia, they forbid all demonstrations that have the character of a personal worship of Muḥammad and of his family. They have also reacted against some of the money-making customs.

The district surrounding Mecca is holy ground. Its boundaries are marked, in accordance with the Muslim tradition, by the points at which the devils halted on seeing the fire lit by Abraham on Mount Abū Qubays, above the holy city. It is really, therefore, the space enclosed within the radius of the light of the sanctuary. At those points heaps of stones, now replaced, it seems, by pillars or columns, gave notice that one had entered the *ḥaram*. The conception of holy ground is not an Islamic novelty; it was current in ancient Arabia, where the holy places of the gods were surrounded by reserved lands on which the beasts that were consecrated to them grazed in peace. The *ḥaram* of Mecca is protected by interdictions, by tabus. Within it the native animals must not be interfered with, with the exception of a few harmful species, and vegetation of natural growth must not be cut. Even the soil must be respected, for no grain of it must be carried outside the *ḥaram*.

Those interdictions are of general application, must be obeyed by all, and are quite independent of the regulations that govern the ceremonies of the pilgrimage. They explain why entry to the territory of Mecca is strictly forbidden to non-Muslims.

It is the duty of every Muslim to undertake the pilgrimage to Mecca once in his lifetime, but there are conditions: he must be adult, in good health physically and mentally, and have means enough to meet the expenses of his journey while maintaining his family during his absence; the route he has to follow must be a safe one, etc. A woman may undertake the *ḥajj* only with the permission of her husband or of her guardian, and must either be accompanied by her husband or be under the protection of another. A Muslim may also delegate to another believer the accomplishment of the pilgrimage in his stead, and the deed will be put to his credit and not to that of his substitute; the latter must, in all cases, make it clear, when performing the rites, that what he does is not done for his own benefit, but for that of another. If a believer dies without having done the *ḥajj* and has omitted it without legal cause, he remains guilty of a sin that will be put in the balance on the Judgment Day. It is therefore essential to his eternal happiness that, after his death, the *ḥajj* should be undertaken in his name by a substitute. He may include in his will the clauses necessary to provide for the expenses involved, and, if he has omitted to do so, his heirs will be doing an act of piety if they make good his omission.

A number of important people have taken steps to arrange that their dead bodies should undertake the pilgrimage, followed by burial in Mecca or Medina in holy ground. The Shīʿites seek their last abode beside the saints of their sect, at Karbalā', or at Mashhad Ṭūs.

Every traveller who leaves his home and dares the mysterious dangers of the way, protects himself against them by propitiatory rites; for the pilgrim these are specially important. In crossing the threshold of his home he must do so with the right foot first. He goes to the mosque and celebrates a Prayer of two *rakaʿāt*; his friends follow him with their blessings, and, throughout the journey, he calls constantly to mind the sacred act that he is striving to accomplish. But it is only on the borders of the holy ground that his pilgrim rôle truly begins.

Indeed, before reaching the limits of the holy ground, he finds, on one or other of the tracks that end in Mecca, stations (*mīqāt*, plur. *mawāqīt*), the position of which has been determined by the post-prophetic traditions: one ḥadīth fixes, for example, the stopping place of the pilgrims from 'Irāq, a province that was conquered for Islam only after the death of Muḥammad. The present day names of the *mawāqīt* do not, however, correspond with those of the traditional texts. It is at such a stopping place that the pilgrim must accomplish the rites that make him fit for the sanctuary.

We have already said that the ceremonies of the Prayer are set within a ritual of sanctification (*iḥrām*), and of de-sanctification (*taḥlīl*); in an abstract form the worshipper enters into communion with the Divinity. In the *ḥajj* or the *'umra*, it is materially that the pilgrim approaches the "House of Allah", the Ka'ba. He introduces his real self into the presence of God. The rite of the passing over, the sanctification, the *iḥrām*, the change of personality, assumes thus a more concrete form than in the Prayer, and the mere utterance of a formula is not enough. The pilgrim must, or rather ought to, for the rule admits of some modification, don a holy costume of archaic garments: a band of stuff around the loins, reaching to just above the knees, the *izār*, and another about the shoulders, the *ridā'*; on the feet leather soles fastened with straps of the same material (*na'l*): that was the classic costume of Abraham, the "Father of Islam". It is still that of many of the inhabitants of the lands bordering on the Mediterranean, and of the deserts of Arabia and Syria. The *'umra* is first completed, followed by the de-sanctification at Mecca, and, on the seventh of the month of dhu l-ḥijja the *iḥrām* is renewed for the purposes of the *ḥajj*, without meanwhile going beyond the holy ground. In practice the *qirān* is the pilgrimage of the specially pious who arrive in Mecca a short time before the beginning of the *ḥajj*; the *ifrād* is that of the faithful who arrive at the last moment; the *tamattu'* that of the travelling Muslim or merchant who performs the *'umra* on reaching Mecca, some considerable time before the date of the *ḥajj*.

Wearing the *iḥrām*, the pilgrim dedicates to Allāh the

victim which he leads to the Minā sacrifice; he marks the consecration by a visible sign which is a survival from pre-Islamic Arabia. The modern Bedouin, like his ancestor, like many men in every country, marks the beasts of his flock with a special mark, called *wasm*. His ancestors made special marks on the hide or on the ear of the exceptional beasts that they offered to the gods, and which were thenceforth freed from the yoke of man. It is this ancient rite that the pilgrim follows when cleaving the hump of the camel that he is about to sacrifice to Allāh, and when he fastens about the neck of a bovine victim a neckband (*taqlīd*), made out of two sandals united by a leather thong or palm fibres, in memory, doubtless, of the time when he presented himself stark naked before the House of Allāh.

From then on, sanctified, the pilgrim is subject to various personal tabus which are a consequence of the ceremonies he has performed when assuming the *iḥrām*, and which have nothing to do with the territorial rules prohibiting hunting, etc., already described. He must abstain from sexual relations and everything that may lead up to, or give an opportunity for, such relations, such as perfumes, sweet-smelling oils, jewels, etc. He must neither cut nor pluck any hair from head or body, nor pare the nails of his hands or feet. This second prohibition is a preliminary to the sacrifice of the hair of the head and the nails, symbolic of that of the person himself. There would be no absurdity in thinking that the first of those two prohibitions was, at one time, a step preparatory to a solemn act of sexual intercourse, of holy prostitution.

The believer enters Mecca by a route that the example of the Prophet has marked out for him. Immediately on arrival, he proceeds to the mosque, where he makes the circuit prescribed for new arrivals (*ṭawāf al-qudūm*). He enters the mosque by Bāb al-Salām, taking his first step over the threshold with his right foot. Crossing the court, he goes towards the Ka'ba and the black stone; if not prevented by the crowd, he kisses it, "an act that will give him heavenly delight". If he is unable to do this, he will touch it with his right hand or with the end of his staff, which he will then carry to his lips. Then, moving from left to right, the worshipper makes seven circuits of the Ka'ba, the first three with a leaping gait which the Tradition, ever anxious to wipe out the memory of the most obvious pre-Islamic rites, attributes, foolishly enough, to a swaggering gait adopted by the Prophet. At the beginning of each circuit the worshipper touches the black stone. He also touches, near the Yaman corner, the spot to which we have referred as recalling the memory of an ancient stone. The Tradition says that the 'Irāq and Syria corners must be ignored, since they were not at the ends of the original Ka'ba, which extended as far as *ḥijr*. Having completed the seven circuits, the worshipper celebrates a Prayer of two *raka'āt* behind the *maqām Ibrāhīm*.

The pilgrim may reckon those circuits as part of the ceremonies of the *'umra* and the *ḥajj* which he proposes to perform; for the rite of the *tawāf* precedes each one of those solemn acts. They also include the *sa'y*, the race from one to the other of the little high places of al-Ṣafā, and al-Marwa, which must be run immediately after the *ṭawāf*. The pilgrim leaves the mosque by Bāb al-Ṣafā', goes up to the first sanctuary, then goes on to the second, keeping to the *mas'ā*, and advancing between the two boundary marks next to the corners of the mosque, with a swinging stride not unlike that adopted for the first three circuits of the *ṭawāf*, and which is derived from the same pre-Islamic rite. The worshipper has then accomplished one of the seven passages of the *sa'y*. He retraces his steps and repeats the course until the seventh time, when he ends up at al-Marwa. Verses of the Qur'ān and pious formulae are repeated during the *ṭawāf* and the *sa'y*, which it would be beyond the scope of this modest book to quote.

When he has come to the end of those two ceremonies, the pilgrim who does only the *'umra*, and he who does both the *'umra* and the *ḥajj* in *tamattu'*, desanctifies himself by having his head shaved. From that time he is released from all the personal tabus that the *iḥram* imposed, and can enjoy, in the Holy City, all the easy pleasures that are organised for his benefit. He is recommended to attend the mosque assiduously, to contemplate the House of Allāh, and to complete supererogatory circuits of the Ka'ba, as well as to visit the historic spots which recall the early days of Islam. The pilgrim in *qirān* remains in Mecca without desanctifying himself after the *'umra*.

The pilgrimage (*ḥajj*) is begun on the seventh day of the

month of *dhu l-ḥijja* with a *khuṭba*, preached in the mosque from the pulpit which is placed against the wall of the Ka'ba, by the Ḥanafite qāḍī or some person whom he appoints in his place. This *khuṭba*, which immediately follows the *ṣalāt al-ẓuhr*, gives counsel to the pilgrims and supplies a kind of programme of the ceremonies in which they are about to take part.

The following day, the eighth, is called the day of the slaking of thirst (*yaum al-tarwiya*), because, it is said, the pilgrim must lay in a supply of water for himself and his mount. The throng of pilgrims, on foot, on horseback, on camels, in motor-cars, a motley crowd, above whose heads rise the palanquins, and who are preceded by the official processions of the two *maḥmal*, the Syrian and the Egyptian, move on towards 'Arafa, about four hours camel ride distant, passing through Minā, a long street through a bare and sterile valley, and lined with structures that are used only during the period of the *ḥajj*. In imitation of the Prophet, the pilgrim performs, at Minā, the Prayer of the *ẓuhr* and remains there during the first hours of the night of the ninth. The length of this stay is, however, not determined by any rule.

The ceremony which takes place during the day of the ninth at 'Arafa is the culminating point of the *ḥajj*, and its essential moment. If the *wuqūf* of 'Arafa is omitted the pilgrimage is null and void. Religious practice, careful to save from this misfortune the pilgrim who may have been delayed by unforeseen obstacles, has agreed that the pilgrim who is present at 'Arafa at any moment whatever between sunset on the ninth and dawn on the tenth would be taken, by a convenient fiction, to have completed the *wuqūf* of 'Arafa. But such delay involves the obligation to sacrifice an expiatory victim.

'Arafa, where the ceremonies of the *wuqūf*, the "station" before Allāh, are celebrated, is a little plain, surrounded, on one side, by a semicircle of hills, in the centre of which, upon piled up barren rocks, rises the holy mount, the *jabal al-raḥma*, the "mount of mercy". Under the 'Abbāsid caliphs, plans had been made to bring drinking water to this stifling enclosure, where sometimes are to be found crowded together sixty to eighty thousand persons, with their animals, tents, food supplies, the necessities as well as the refuse of men already weakened by a long journey, and with nerves unstrung by religious emotion. But the administrative negligence that is one of the laws of the East brought to speedy decay works that seem once to have been first class. Educated Muslims have protested against a carelessness that threatens the public health and which the Wahhābite government is striving to overcome.

It is in the afternoon of the ninth, after the sun has passed the zenith, that the *wuqūf* of 'Arafa, the essential ceremony of the *ḥajj*, begins. The pilgrim stands erect (*waqafa*) before Allāh. Pious formulae are recited under the leadership of an imām who delivers a solemn *khuṭba*, one of the four ritual *khuṭba* of the *ḥajj*. As soon as the sun has set, a very interesting ceremony begins, the origin and meaning of which are uncertain. The pilgrims proceed to another valley, called Muzdalifa, situated between 'Arafa and Minā, overshadowed by a height called Quzaḥ, a high place already held in veneration in pre-Islamic days, where they must pass the night of the tenth and accomplish a quick *wuqūf* before the dawn of that day. But, although theologians try to resist this custom, the journey from 'Arafa to Muzdalifa, at sunset on the ninth, is a mad rush, a torrent that flows wildly (*ifāḍa*), in which, every year, there are fatal accidents. The *wuqūf* of Muzdalifa is followed, like that of 'Arafa, by a "flight" (*ifāḍa*) which brings the pilgrims back to Minā at sunrise. It is there that the final ceremonies of the *ḥajj* take place, on the tenth of *dhu l-ḥijja*.

When they arrive at the foot of the steep slope (*'aqaba*) which leads down to Minā, the pilgrims find themselves at the beginning of the road which runs between the buildings of the temporary city, and before a stone stele, having in front of it a kind of basin. This is the *jamrat al-'aqaba*, into which the pilgrims solemnly cast the seven little stones that they have picked up at Muzdalifa, an action which they accompany with the utterance of the formula of the *takbīr*: *Bismillāhi, Allāhu akbar!*—"In the name of Allāh: Allāh is great!" The meaning of this rite, which is observed, in varying forms, throughout all the Semitic East and in North Africa, and finds analogies in yet other places, is not so clear that we can deal with it in a few lines. The Muslim Tradition, moreover, does not burden itself with elaborate explanations: Abraham, tempted at this place by Satan, and pursued by him, escaped by throwing seven stones, and the present day rite is only an imitation of the pious gesture of the ancestor of Islam. The stele is called, in the popular language, "the Great Satan" (*al-Shayṭān al-kabīr*).

Now it is that the pilgrim sacrifices the victim which he has consecrated, either while taking the *iḥrām*, or during the *ḥajj*. The head of the victim is made to face the Ka'ba; its throat is cut by its owner or by one of them if, as frequently happens, it is common to several pilgrims. Part of the flesh is eaten by them, and the remainder distributed among the poor, who have come out from Mecca to receive it; a few pieces, after having been dried in the sun, are taken away by the pilgrims; but the greater part of the animal's body is left lying on the ground, imperfectly buried, and, from this heap of carrion, in spite of the dryness of the climate, there emanates a terrible and dangerous infection. Yet, for some more days, people continue to live in Minā. It is probable that, before Islam, the sacrifice took place at a specially appointed place in the valley; the Sunna has reacted against the ancient customs by declaring that it could take place on any part of the territory of Minā. From this sacrifice the tenth of the month of *Dhu l-ḥijja* is given the name of the "day of throat-cutting" (*yaum al-naḥr*).

Although this sacrifice is not the most important part of the *ḥajj*, and although the *wuqūf* of 'Arafa is theoretically the principal incident, it is the day of Minā that is commemorated throughout the Muslim world. Each head of a family sacrifices on the tenth of *dhu l-ḥijja* an animal, usually a sheep, which he slaughters after having placed it with its head pointing in the direction of Mecca, and whose flesh he divides among the poor. It is the "feast of the victims", *'īd al-aḍ ḥā*, or "of the offerings", *'id al-qurbān*, in Turkish, *büyük bayram*, called in the Maghrib the "Great Feast" (*al-'īd al-kabīr*).

After completing the sacrifice, the pilgrim puts himself into the hands of one of the numerous barbers, whether professional or temporary, who fill Minā on that day. He has his head shaved and his nails cut. This bodily waste is carefully buried. From that moment he is partially desanctified. He is in the *taḥallul al-ṣaghīr*; but the sexual tabu still remains with its consequential prohibitions, that of perfumes and the rest. And, as if this necessary consequence of sanctification had some unknown connection with the Ka'ba, it is not cancelled, the pilgrim is not entirely desanctified, does not enjoy the *tahallul al-kabīr*, until after he has completed, at the House of Allāh, the circuits called *ṭawāf al-ifāḍa*, because of the fact that they are completed after a "flight", a rapid journey from Minā to Mecca. They must be followed by a *sa'y* between al-Ṣafā' and al-Marwa, if this has not been done at the beginning of the *ḥajj*, that is, if the pilgrim has done the *'umra* and the *ḥajj* in *qirān*.

Modern usage considers that the pilgrim has then completed the ceremonies of the pilgrimage (*manāsik al-ḥajj*), and that he may either return home or remain in Mecca, where he has the choice of amusing himself, of indulging in pious exercises, or of engaging in trade. But this rule has not the unanimous support of all the learned men of Islam. The law lays down that the pilgrim should return to Minā and spend three days there, the eleventh, twelfth and thirteenth of *dhu l-ḥijja*, a period to which the Tradition gives the name of *ayyām al-tashrīq*, by allusion, doubtless, as people say, to the pieces of sacrificial flesh that the pilgrims dry in the sun. Each day the pilgrim must go to *jamrat al-a wusṭā*, and throw at each of them, and on each day, seven stones as ceremoniously as on the first day.

The pilgrim (*al ḥājj*, in Turkish pronunciation, *ḥājī*), has now completed all the compulsory rites. Custom recommends him to make, at the Ka'ba, some "farewell circuits", to drink, and to carry away, water of Zamzam, etc. The mass of the pilgrims disperses after a few days stay in Mecca.

Europeans have been present at the ceremonies of the *ḥajj* and have described them; we have Muslim accounts, and it is easy to discuss them with believers who have taken part in them. It is possible, therefore, to form a fairly accurate idea of the mental impression that remains. In the real life of the pilgrimage the *wuqūf* of 'Arafa keeps the leading place which Muslim law assigns to it. All witnesses agree in expressing, in more or less happy terms, the deep impression made on their hearts and senses by the prodigious throng of tens of thousands of men (Qā'id b. Sharīf says six hundred thousand!), each with his spirit reaching out as he turns his eyes to the *jabal al-raḥma*, listening with passionate attention to the *khaṭīb* who takes the place formerly occupied by the Prophet, and who is, for a moment, a living incarnation of him; a throng that intoxicates itself with the ever repeated cries of: *Labbayka yā Rabbī Labbayka!*; men pushed to the extreme limit of nervous exasperation by hunger, fatigue, emotion, the resplendent light and the burning sun. Certain ceremonies of the Ka'ba, the midday Prayer, or that of the evening in the mosque of Mecca, appear to have left lively impressions, but more fleeting and less pure. There is brutal and ugly jostling around the Ka'ba, and the atmosphere, too, is rather spoiled by the people of Mecca. The journey from 'Arafa to Minā in *ifāḍa* is mainly a memory of a struggle to pass, of crushing, of constant danger at the hands of men and Nature. The Bedouin are still the murderous robbers they were before Islam. We do not know to what extent the Wahhābite government has been able to remove the danger of disease from the slaughter of the sacrifices at Minā. The casting of the stones takes place amidst wild and dangerous pushing.

At Mecca, the splendour of the religious life is tarnished by the population, whose essential occupation is the exploitation of the holy places. Read Burckhardt, Burton, Snouck, Batanūnī, or Ibn Sharīf, and it will be found that the thing that remains in their memories is the ruthlessness of the people of Mecca, the smiles and the artfulness that they plentifully employ in their endeavour to earn, in a few days, their living for the whole year; guides to the *ḥajj*, (*ṭawwāfīn*), hirers of mounts, those who let houses and rooms, sellers of Zamzam water and of pieces of the *kiswa*, women of easy morals, barbers, keepers of historic houses, merchants of all standards and of all kinds of goods, quickly empty the purses of the pilgrims. Moreover, it would only be a strange ignorance of the character of the populations that live in the shadow of the great sanctuaries of the human race that would reproach the people of Mecca with their mercenary habits, and would see in them a fault peculiar to Islam. We should like to believe that the Wahhābites have reacted against such usages, but it would be a miracle if they had abolished them.

The pilgrim returns home, filled with the tremendous joy of having accomplished the crowning act of his religion, proud of the right to bear the designation *ḥājj* amidst those others of the faithful who have no claim to the title, and being, as it were, ennobled. He also experiences a dim, inward sense of the power of Islam that can bring together each year so many men of strange races and incomprehensible tongues. But, at the same time, he returns bearing deep within him a complete disillusionment regarding the infernal, scorching, blinding, waterless, shadeless, lifeless land in which Allāh has chosen to build His House. He bears, too, a fierce grudge against the fawning, greedy people of Mecca.

Failure to observe the rites of the *ḥajj* has consequences that vary with the importance of each of them. We have already said that the pilgrim who did not take part in the solemn *wuqūf* of 'Arafa, or who, in spite of being given every benefit of the doubt, appeared at 'Arafa neither during the evening of the ninth nor during the night of the tenth and before the dawn of that day, "missed" the *ḥajj*; he must begin again at the beginning. Breaking the sexual tabu is also a cause of nullity. In addition, in those two cases, and for all other violations of the rules that do not themselves involve nullity, expiation (*kaffāra*) must be made by an additional sacrifice, or by a distribution of alms to the poor, or by days of fasting. We must here merely point out the principle of those expiatory acts without giving their details.

The believer has ended his pilgrimage; he has gained, in the sight of Allāh, merit which will be accounted to him in the Judgment Day. But he has not paid the visit to that place which frequently attracts and moves him most deeply, that of the tomb of the Prophet at Medina. The organisation of the caravans which, after the *ḥajj*, accomplish the journey to that town in three, four, or ten days, is one of the principal preoccupations of the people of Mecca. The neighbouring tribes profit by the business too.

On entering Medina, the believer draws near, not to Allāh, but to the Prophet. He need not consecrate himself, but he honours him almost to the point of worship. Custom has long since created, around Medina, a holy site, a *ḥaram*, within which it has copied the tabus which, around the House of Allāh, protect animals, plants, and the ground itself.

The mosque of the Prophet is situated in the oldest quarter of the town. Several times burned down, devastated by floods, dishonoured by the restorations of Turkish architects, it seems to be, in spite of the luxury of its decorations, even more devoid of grandeur and beauty than the mosque of Mecca itself. None the less, it is with profound reverence that the traveller reaches its threshold, traverses the principal bays, and enters the "garden" (*ar rauḍa*) which, following the tradition, leads to the tomb of the Prophet and, near by, to those of Abū Bakr and 'Umar. The house of 'Ā'isha, in which the Prophet died, and where he was buried, is said to have been a quite tiny dwelling, close beside the original mosque. And the mosque, growing from age to age, arose around the holy tomb, overflowing the house of 'Ā'isha and those of Abū Bakr, 'Umar and others, until it became the vast edifice that today provides room for thousands of worshippers.

In the Prophet's *rauḍa*, beside the *miḥrāb*, where traces are to be found of his pulpit, the pillars against which he leaned, and a thousand sacred memories, the pilgrim makes an invocation which special regulations prevent him from turning into a Prayer (*ṣalāt*), since that would be to insult Allāh. The arrangement of the various sites does not permit of a circuit being made of the tomb. But no precaution could arrest the development of the cult of the Prophet, any more than it could that of the saints. The pilgrim who has not kissed the wooden screen (*shubbāk*) that surrounds the Prophet's tomb has not, in the minds of the people, completed his pilgrimage. As at Mecca, a thousand pious memories keep the visitor in Medina; in the cemetery he visits the graves of the chief personages of the early days of Islam: 'Ā'isha, Fāṭima, 'Uthmān, etc.

Pilgrims who are both devout and curious may further end the *ḥajj* by a journey to Jerusalem, a city sanctified by the presence of so many prophets, especially by that of 'Īsā (Jesus), from which, one night, tradition tells that Muḥammad ascended to heaven, led by Gabriel (*mi'rāj*); but this visit is in no way compulsory and is not so popular as that to Medina. The chief object of the visit is the mosque of 'Umar and the place that contains the sacred rock, the *ṣakhra*.

The return of the pilgrim to his home is marked by ceremonies similar to those of the departure. His friends come to congratulate him and to profit in some sort by the atmosphere of holiness which he brings with him. He distributes pious souvenirs, water of Zamzam, pieces of the *kiswa* and so on.

The pilgrimage is *the* great ceremony of Muslim life. It brings together, once a year, representatives of the various communities of the Muslim world. It is, therefore, so to speak, the plenary assembly as well as the fair of Islam. But the way to it is often long and full of peril. Ṣūfīs, no doubt, accustomed to the life of the roads and its accidents, went in leisurely fashion to Mecca, singly or in small groups. But the main body of pilgrims, more pressed for time and more timid, gathered at fixed dates in centres from which the caravans, officially organised, armed and provided with food, mounts and money, journeyed, growing constantly as they advanced, towards the Holy City. The caravan made up at Cairo for the transport of the *kiswa* destined for the Ka'ba, and accompanied by the sovereign's symbolic litter, the *maḥmal*, was a rallying centre for the African pilgrims, coming, some by way of the plateaux of Maghrib and the Saharan oases, others travelling the long routes from the Niger, Lake Chad, Tibesti, and the Egyptian oases. Of those last, some touched the Nile at Khartoum and reached Jedda, the port of Mecca, after crossing the Red Sea. The Damascus caravan which, from the 16th century, drew travellers from Constantinople, and was accompanied, after that period, by the *maḥmal* of the Sulṭān, followed a traditional route to the East of the Red Sea and through Arabia Petraea. Those two caravans, that of Cairo and that of Damascus, have always been led by a person of considerable importance, called *amīr al-ḥajj*, usually belonging to the family of the sovereign, and appointed by him.

Steamship navigation and railways have, since the second half of the 19th century, completely changed the system of transport. The railway from Damascus to Medina, which was to be extended to Mecca and so put an end to the caravans, was demolished during the 1914–1918 war. Only a small part of it has again been made fit for service. I am ignorant of its present condition.

The 'Irāq caravan, which gathered pilgrims from Central Asia and Iran, as well as those coming from India by the overland route, was, from the 8th to the 13th century, the official procession, headed many times by the Caliph in person. Usually, and each year, he delegated the duty to a great personage, the *amīr al-ḥajj*. The latter played a greater or smaller part in the ceremonies, corresponding to the authority which his master exercised in the Islamic world; when the 'Abbāsid caliphate began to decline, he found himself in competition with the amīrs of the other two caravans. Moreover, the place that each group of worshippers occupied in the various ceremonies, at 'Arafāt for example, and the rank that each should assume in the holy processions, such as the *ifāḍa*, gave occasion for quarrels and fights which the people of Mecca and the Bedouin seized on as a pretext for pillage, and during which lives were lost. One section of the Indian pilgrims and those from the East Indies come by sea and disembark at Jedda.

The Egyptian caravan continues to convey overland the *maḥmal* of the King; but the pilgrims who used to accompany it go by sea, some by Suez and Jedda, others by Alexandria and Kaiffa, from whence they take the railway connecting with Medina. Pilgrims from India, from the East Indies and those from the Maghrib reach Jedda in vessels chartered by the protecting governments. The ancient roads of the *ḥajj* are now only historic memories.

Modern transport conditions facilitate the application of the prophylactic measures which have been adopted by international agreement during the present century, with the object of preventing the spreading of epidemics by the returning pilgrims: provision has gradually been made for medical examination before and after, and for periods of quarantine, without, however, being rigorous enough. In fact, the gathering together in the holy places, at Mecca, 'Arafa, and Minā, of a throng of people from all parts of the world, bringing with them the germs of diseases, all the more dangerous for being foreign to the country into which they are introduced, constitutes a periodic danger to the health of the human race. The Ḥijāz has been the starting point of several serious epidemics of what has been described as cholera. European countries endeavour to ensure the transport and return of their Muslim subjects under satisfactory sanitary conditions. In Mecca official hostels are replacing the ancient living quarters provided by the rulers, and which, as is natural, had been allowed to fall into decay. Since 1919, French Africa maintains in Mecca a hostel run by the Society of the Ḥabūs of the Holy Places.

The pilgrimage has not lost its religious importance. It is hard to foresee whether it will play the Pan-Islamic rôle which has obsessed the minds of some; in any case it is of considerable political interest. At least it has lost a part of its economic value, which has not been, it would seem, sufficiently appreciated by historians. The ease of communication has diminished the importance of the commercial relations of which Mecca was, to a great extent, the centre. But trade does still retain a place in the international gathering which, each year, brings together Muslims from all countries.

The two holy cities of Islam (*al-ḥaramāni*), Mecca and Medina, have not been endowed by nature with the material means necessary to ensure to a great city and its environs an active social and economic life. Their isolation has protected them from the effects of the great invasions. But the thieving habits of the Bedouin have kept their inhabitants in a state of constant fear of famine. The descendants of the family of 'Alī, mutually hostile cousins, who have been their governors, have had but one care: to ensure the food supply of the populace and, more important still, of the pilgrims whose reception is the main business of the holy cities. With this object they intrigued at one and the same time with the Bedouin chiefs and with the rulers of 'Irāq, Syria and Egypt. Each of the latter, copying the caliphs, has been anxious to describe himself as the "Servant of the Holy Places" (*khādim al-ḥaramayn*). In exchange for their generous and frequent presents, they expected to be given homage and, above all, to have their names proclaimed in the *khuṭba*, from the very pulpit of the Ka'ba, as well as from that of the mosque of Medina, and to secure the leading rank for the amīr appointed by them to be the leader of their national pilgrims. The Osmanli sulṭān, illegitimate heir of the 'Abbāsids, later exercised a strict protection of the holy cities. The war against the Wahhābites, at the beginning of the 19th century, restored to Egypt a part of the authority which, during the period of the Fāṭimid caliphs of the 10th or 12th centuries the Ayyūbids and, later, the Mamlūks, it had enjoyed in the Ḥijāz by providing for the food supply of that region. The gift of the *kiswa* for the Ka'ba is a matter of great political moment. The Muslims of India and the East Indies, because of their numbers and wealth, have an important place in the life of the pilgrimage. The suppression of the Constantinople caliphate and its replacement by a very active authority, which is, however, rather on the fringe of the "Muslim community", have given rise to the notion of a possible Pan-Islamic union with its centre in Mecca. It would not appear that the nature of the country, in spite of the shortening of distances by modern methods, can qualify it to be a suitable place for such a purpose: the dryness of the region and the severity of the climate make it a difficult place to live in. However that may be, the Wahhābite conquest of 1930, which differed so greatly from the invasion of 1803, both in conduct and in results, has opened up a new era for Arabia, and also for the pilgrimage, the standard of which has been raised by the new masters of Mecca, from the material as well as from the religious point of view.

. . . . .

Pre-Islamic Arabia had no religion sufficiently organised to provide for any sort of ritual fasting. It knew only those abstentions from food or wine that were imposed by religious tabus, or adopted in consequence of individual vows. Muḥammad, at the beginning of his residence in Medina, that is to say, at the time when he counted on the conversion of the Jews, prescribed the fast of '*Ashūrā*', which copied the Jewish fast of *tishri*. When Muḥammad had broken with the Medina Jews, the Muslim fast, under the influence of the Christian Quadragesima, was turned into an abstinence of one lunar month's duration, that of *ramaḍān*, which, in the old Arab calendar with its solar corrections, fell in Summer, but which, by the time the fast came to be properly organised, had slowly moved back towards Winter. Muḥammad did not foresee that the Muslim calendar would continue to move ramaḍān through the whole course of the year, nor that the severe obligation of a complete daily fast (*ṣaum*) would coincide, by thirty year cycles, with the longest days of the year.

From sunrise till sunset, more precisely; taking as the limit the instant in which it is possible to distinguish a white thread from a black one, or, according to one interpretation, a line of light on the horizon against the darkness of the sky as a whole, the believer is required to abstain entirely from food, drink, tobacco, perfumes, etc., as well as from sexual relations. But, during the night, all prohibitions are removed, and the faithful, wearied by long abstinence, make the best possible use of their recovered liberty. Needless to insist on the depressing consequences of such a régime, especially when enforced on men who work during the day. All Europeans who have maintained regular relations with the Muslim world are aware of the physical and mental effects of the fast of Ramaḍān.

The opening of the month of Ramaḍān is fixed, as in the case of all other months, by the appearance of the new moon. The beginning of the fast, and also its end, are, therefore, dependent on an astronomical observation that no previous forecast can replace. The state of the atmosphere, not to speak of an astronomic delay that could be foreseen, sometimes makes impossible or difficult the direct observation of the event. It is permissible to accept the affirmation of two trustworthy witnesses. But, in the towns, it is the religious authority, usually the qāḍī, who gives a definite decision. Local circumstances can give rise to disputes on this point between personages of equal authority. The fast can thus last for twenty-eight, twenty-nine, or, at most, thirty days.

In the towns the exact instants of the beginning and end of the fast are announced each morning and evening by the appearance of a green flag on the tops of the minarets of the mosques, and by a cannon shot. After the evening signal, it is customary to break the fast by a light meal called *faṭūr*, and to end the night with a last collation, the "dawn meal" (*ṣaḥūr*). A special crier, called *muwaqqit* or *musaḥḥir*, announces, in the towns, the last hour at which this repast may be taken.

The fast is obligatory only on adults in full possession of their physical and mental faculties, *'āqil, bāligh.* Are exempt, therefore, the sick, feeble old men, pregnant or nursing women. For other reasons a dispensation is given to travellers. But such dispensations are not irrevocable and, as soon as material conditions permit, the believer must accomplish his fast throughout any other month, or give expiatory alms (*fidya*). The voluntary violation of the sexual tabu is paid for by the freeing of a slave, or by a fast of two months, or by feeding sixty poor persons.

In the accomplishment of the fast, as in every other duty of

Islam, it is the intention (*nīya*) of the faster that counts. The mosques are specially well attended during the month of Ramaḍān. In the evening, after the Prayer of the *'ishā'*, the faithful gather in groups and, led by an imām, say a Prayer of at least twenty *raka'āt*, of which each group of four is separated by a pause. Hence its name, *ṣalāt al-tarāwīh*. It is accompanied by recitations from the Qur'ān and pious conversation, which may last until dawn. Some writers, Ibn Jubayr for example, have described those ceremonies interspersed with meals, which the faithful return home to eat, or have brought to them in the mosques.

Tradition asserts that the fast was instituted in Ramaḍān because it is during this month that the Revelation (*tanzīl*, Q. 2.181) "came down" to the earth, more exactly in the night of fate, *laylat al-qadr* (Q. 97, 1–3), in which, in popular belief, human destiny is determined for the whole year. The date of the night of fate is not precisely indicated. Consequently, the nights of the days of odd numbers, from the 21st to the 27th of Ramaḍān and especially this last day, are honoured by invocations and Qur'ānic recitations.

The "breaking" of the fast, which occurs on the first of the month of *Shawwāl*, is the occasion of a feast, *'īd al-fiṭr*, called in the Maghrib the Little Feast, *al 'īd al-ṣaghīr*. Like the Great Feast of the tenth of *dhu l-ḥijja*, the feast of the breaking of the fast involves a solemn Prayer, called *ṣalāt al-'īd*, consisting of two *raka'āt* with numerous *takbīr* and two *khuṭba*.

It is on that day that the statutory alms that mark the breaking of the fast must be given (*zakāt al-fiṭr*), which must not be confounded with the *zakāt* properly so called, of which we shall speak in the next chapter. Each head of a family must, in respect of each individual for whom he is responsible, give to the poor a *ṣā'a* of four *mudd* of the customary food of the country.

The feast is the occasion of domestic rejoicings that continue for three days. New clothes are worn. People congratulate and embrace each other.

The feast of Ramaḍān is one of the most living institutions of Islam. Muslim towns observe it strictly, and public opinion judges severely any individuals who seek secretly to avoid it.

• • • • •

For the Arabs, as for the Jews, worldly possessions may be a gift of the spirit of evil and foreshadow the lasting sufferings of the other life. But there is a way of avoiding this danger. If a man voluntarily gives back to Allāh a part of the possessions that He has Himself given, by this act he "purifies" what he retains. That is the meaning of the words *zakāt* and *ṣadaqa* which denote in Arabic the alms, and especially the statutory alms, enjoined by the Qur'ān and organised by the Prophet and his successors.

The *zakāt* is a religious tax which is levied on the various categories of possessions according to definite rules, the revenue from which is applied to different headings of expenditure. It affects the productions of the soil, cattle, precious metals (gold and silver), and merchandise. Those things are liable to tax only if they reach a certain minimum value called *niṣāb* which varies for each item. The tax is paid in kind. On values exceeding the *niṣāb*, the believer must give, for the fruits of the soil (cereals and fruits) one-tenth of the annual harvest, but a twentieth only if he has secured it only as a result of costly irrigation. In the case of cattle, the number and kind of animals to be delivered up vary according to the number and kinds of animals composing the flocks and herds. It is important to note that the tax is imposed on those animals only that have passed a whole year on the grazing grounds without having been used for any labour; the tax is imposed, in fact, on increase of capital resulting from the increase of idle flocks.

Precious metals and merchandise are taxed only if, during any one year, they have remained in the hands of one and the same owner, and have not served as a means of exchange. This limitation exempts, therefore, all values that are not merely hoarded, and that includes the greater part of all merchandise and articles of gold and silver. We must remember here also that, on the other hand, Muslim law prohibits lending for interest, the renting of monetary capital. But, by exempting from the *zakāt* values which, during one year, have not remained in the hands of a single owner, the law opened the way to a fraud which has been widely practised: a famous jurist of Bagdad during the 'Abbāsid period, Qāḍī Yūsuf, who died in 910, as soon as the end of the year drew near, transferred the wnership of his wealth to his son, who gave it back before the end of the second year, and so on: he avoided in this way any payment of *zakāt* whatever. But what stories have *not* been told of the qāḍīs!

The tax was gathered in kind by a collector (*'āmil*) who fixed and collected it himself or through his agents, as regards the fruits of the soil, and who, in the case of other values, collected it on the basis of the declaration of the taxpayer. The administrators of the *ṣadaqa* had thus to ensure, not only the levying of the correct amount of tax, but also to arrange for its transport to the depots where they were responsible for its safe-keeping. Official enclosures, which had kept the names given to those of olden time (*ḥimā*), held the camels of the *ṣadaqa*, and from them sales were made to individuals. The grain was stored in the silos of the *zakāt*. When the distribution among the various classes of beneficiaries came to be made, it was only partially in kind. A portion had been turned into cash.

This distribution was made among the following categories: first, to the poor and needy (*fuqarā'* and *masākīn*); then to the tax collectors (*'amala*); then to "those whose hearts one desired to win" (*al-mu'allafu qulūbuhum*), a class that has disappeared, but which was important in the beginnings of Islam, at the time when Muḥammad had need of a special fund applied to buying over the hostility of the Qurayshites. A fourth fund was devoted to assisting slaves to purchase their freedom from their masters; a fifth paid debts contracted in a pious cause. The sixth was applied, in principle, to the arming of the volunteers of the Holy War and to other military expenses incurred in the fight against the infidel. Next, provision was made for the expense of maintaining all institutions that were useful to the Moslem community, and that had been founded "in the way of Allāh" (*fī sabīli llāh*). Lastly, there was a fund for giving aid to poor travellers.

A single tax, of which only a seventh was devoted to the expenses of the State, is a somewhat archaic form of taxation which, from the very beginnings of Islam, was due for reform. But, under various names and a diversity of forms, the *zakāt* has endured; it is one of the pillars of the edifice of Islam, and could be displaced only as a result of a secularisation of Muslim law.

We must not confuse the statutory alms (*zakāt*), of which

we have summarised the general principles, with the alms which Muslims must give at the breaking of the fast (*zakāt al-fiṭr*) with which we have already dealt.

. . . . .

Religious thought has slept soundly in Islam for several centuries, but religious practices have continued to be faithfully observed. The fast, which gives rise to a sort of mutual espionage, is, on the whole, strictly kept in the cities. The pilgrimage, organised and regulated by governments for sanitary and political reasons, keeps its attraction for all those who can afford to undertake it. The townspeople conform to a certain degree with the duty of the Prayer, and throng to the Friday ceremony. In the country places people are less attentive. Present-day Bedouin are strangers to the practices of their religion, and, if we except the occasion of the passing of a caravan composed of town dwellers, there is nothing more unreal than the romantic prayer in the desert.

SOURCES

Juynboll: "*Handbuch*" (S.88); Gaudefroy-Demombynes: "*Pèlerinage*" (S.107); Wensinck: Salāt, E.I. 4.99; Padersen: Masdjid, E.I. 3.362; Berg: Sawm, E.I. 4.200; Schacht: Zakāt, E.I. 4.1270.

CHAPTER SEVEN

THE CALIPHATE

The Caliph—The Central Government and the Provinces—The Jih ād: the Army—Taxes: Zakāt, Kharāj, dues—The Tributary Peoples—Foreigners.

THE essential function of the head of the Muslim community is to be its *imām*, he who leads the *ṣalāt*, the ritual Prayer. The Prophet omitted to fill this function only in cases of absolute necessity. Uniting all authority in himself, since he was the interpreter of the Divine Word, he delegated, if necessary, to one of his followers the right to lead the Prayer, to head the pilgrimage (*ḥajj* or *'umra*), to bear his standard, and to command the soldiers of Islam. At his death, as we have already pointed out, nothing had been done to ensure the succession. It was as the outcome of an eventful election that Abū Bakr became Imām of the Muslim community, with the title of *khalīfatu'l-nabī*, or *khalīfa rasūli llāh*, "Lieutenant of the Prophet". This title was maintained by the supreme imām, the Caliph; but it was soon exchanged for "Caliph of Allāh", *khalīfatu llāh*.

The first caliphs were Companions of the Prophet who had come to power according to no rule. Mu'āwiya combined the Bedouin custom of proclamation by the heads of families with the Byzantine tradition, that is to say, election with heredity. Not without opposition he had his son Yazīd declared heir presumptive (*walī al'-ahd*) by a gathering of tribal chiefs and high-placed persons representing the Muslim community. On his ascension the caliph was the centre of a new ceremony, in the course of which those present touched his hand; they kissed the hand of the 'Abbāsid caliph. The appointment of the heir presumptive and the partition of the Empire were, in the caliphate as elsewhere, the causes of grave disorders. We have already shown, in Chapter II, that the differing ideas that had arisen in the Muslim community touching the choice of a caliph had given rise to a division into Sunnites, Shī'ites, and Khārijites.

The power of the caliph is not exactly defined: it is the heritage left by Muḥammad. But Muḥammad, who owed his power to his personal authority, and to that conferred upon him by his status as the envoy of God, retained something of the character of the Shaykh of Arabia of old, of the arbiter (*ḥakam*), of the guardian of the Tradition. He is in no way the leader of the Holy War, commander of the forces of Allāh that go up against the infidel. He does no more than bestow upon them a sort of supernatural favour, a *baraka*. In imitation of the Prophet the first caliphs fix (*'aqada*) the standard (*liwā'*) for the commander of the troops. Neither Abū Bakr nor 'Umar nor 'Uthmān ever took an active part in the war. They were the trustees to whose care had been committed the canon law (*sharī'a*), that is, the Qur'ān and the Tradition, as their successors were guardians of that same law as it was systematised by the traditionalists and the jurists.

Even if the Umayyad caliph was not the king (*malik*), indifferent to the revealed truth and contemptuous of sound prophetic tradition whom the 'Abbāsid writers have depicted, he was none the less a strong ruler, careful to safeguard the temporal interests of the Muslim community, and to organise the State with the collaboration of the conquered peoples. He had the sense of the public good (*maṣlaḥa*). The 'Abbāsid caliph claimed that he was restoring the pure Tradition of the Prophet and giving anew to the *imāma* its full religious value. But he was also the heir of the Sāsānid King of Kings who proclaimed himself the equal of the Byzantine emperor. His subjects paid him, therefore, the honour of an almost divine pomp which contrasted strangely with the loudly boasted simplicity of 'Umar. He was no longer merely the imām who leads the community along the straight way. He was a sovereign ruler possessing subjects. His power was unlimited so long as he remained capable of exercising it. We could readily find amusement in building up, from sketches drawn by writers of history, the picture of Mu'āwiya, and contrasting it with that of Hārūn al-Rashīd; the first a chief of the Pre-Islamic sort, who receives visitors with simple familiarity, dominating them only by his knowledge of men and his smiling, ironic self-possession; the second a demi-god, gravely seated on his throne, surrounded by guards and courtiers, a monarch before whom men prostrate themselves, whose summons men obey only after having made their wills, for behind him stands the executioner with his ever-ready sword; one who wears the mantle and ring of the Prophet and displays to the world all the glory of religious tradition and a holy heritage.

The caliph delegated this limitless power in part to agents who themselves exercised it, or who, in turn, delegated it further: the leadership of the Friday Prayer and the khuṭba to an *imām*, Qur'anic justice to a *qāḍī*, the gathering of taxes to an *'āmil*, the command of the army and the administration in general to an *amīr*. The great 'Abbāsid caliphs have always had, like Louis XIV, the practice, more or less fortunate for their peoples, of punctually carrying on their kingly trade; they presided over councils and themselves signed or had read to them most important decisions. Secretaries of State (*kātib* plur. *Kuttāb al-sirr*), whose numbers were steadily increased, drew up and issued the decrees of the caliph, centralised and controlled the administration of the provinces and the revenues of the Empire. They were a caste, drawn at first from the tributary nations, then chosen from among new converts whose instruction was facilitated by the existence of many important literary works, and who, while maintaining the greatest discretion in their bearing, led, in their rich dwellings, a life much coveted by the mob. During the reigns of the first 'Abbāsid caliphs the Vizier received no special delegation of power; he is assistant to his master, his counsellor and his right hand, his companion at all hours, and it is not only within the covers of the "Thousand and One Nights" that he has to speed his master's sleepless hours. The well known Viziers of the period of 'Abbāsid greatness, the Barmakides, are Iranians. At certain times the title *ḥājib* which signifies the "chamberlain", the agent who serves as a screen and intermediary between the Prince and his subjects, has denoted a personage who is invested with the authority of an all-powerful minister.

From the 10th century onwards a foreign personality inserted himself between the exercise of power and the caliph whom he held in tutelage. He took the title of *amīr al-umarā'*, then that of *sulṭān*.

In the empire organised in this fashion, the unity of direction is maintained in theory, while, at the same time, very great freedom of action is allowed to the governors. In spite of the official postal service (*barīd*) set up or reorganised by the Umayyads, the provinces are very far from Damascus and Bagdad, and the freedom of decision enjoyed by the prince's lieutenants tends to become independence. The caliphate, at the time of its splendour, is too extensive and inhabited by peoples of too diverse tendencies and languages for cohesion to be maintained under a government that had no intimate contact with the common folk. The provincial governors become, therefore, one after the other, independent sovereign rulers (*malik, sulṭān*), administering freely a portion of the Muslim world, and transmitting their power according to the theoretical rules described above. But those sulṭāns do not detach themselves from the Muslim community. They take, it is true, the title of "Prince of the Muslims" (*amīr al-muslimīn*), but, in the Friday *khuṭba*, they cause to be proclaimed the name of the caliph, after but above their own. So there is no rupture of the bonds that united the different parts of the Muslim community, and it must be understood that it is not only religious bonds that remain: the faithful of the new State continue in theory in complete union with those of the rest of the empire of the caliphate. The local sulṭān remains, by a pure fiction, the representative of the caliph (*amīr al-mu'minīn*).

Muslim history offers some interesting examples of the persistence of this fiction, for example, in the sulṭānate of the Mamlūks of Egypt. Those sulṭāns have confiscated for their own profit the 'Abbāsid caliph who resides in Cairo, possessing no real authority, and, in practice, at the mercy of the Mamlūks. But he is still surrounded by all the outward veneration which his ancestors enjoyed in Bagdad. His presence gives to the Mamlūks a prestige with which they know how to adorn themselves in the eyes of other Muslim rulers and foreign kings. The chancellery and the diplomacy of the Mamlūks are sufficiently well known and, when we watch them at work, we have the impression that they are seeking to maintain for their own benefit, and over the heads of the caliphs, the haloed fiction of the unity of the Muslim community.

In the hands of the Ottoman sulṭān of Istanbūl the authority of the caliphate was fully restored, and the master secured obedience in the provinces. But Egypt is an example of the efforts at autonomy made by regions possessing a geographic and historic personality, and which resulted, in this case, as early as the 19th century, in a similitude of independence. Moreover, the Ottoman sulṭān had inherited only a small part of the Muslim empire of classic times, which had disintegrated from the moment when the Turks made their entry into the Islamic world. Not only Shī'ite Persia, but also Khārijite 'Umān, Sharīfian Morocco, India, etc., had rulers who gave no recognition whatever to the Ottoman caliph, granting to him not even the shadow of supremacy.

Of this great union under the rule of the caliphs, so soon shattered, and only partly renewed by the Ottomans, there remain nothing but a memory and a vague feeling of religious communion, defined by, and absorbed in, the new sense of nationality. In the last chapter we shall endeavour to give some idea of the new world into which Islam is entering.

The mechanisms of this grandiose machine were both simple and various: each region had its customs; each century was subject to external pressures. Seeking here to describe what is common to all the members of the Empire and not what differentiates them, what is Muslim and not what merely preserves local tradition, we cannot avoid returning, in spite of ourselves, to the early social institutions of Arabia, in which the Qur'ān saw the light and the prophetic Tradition was born.

During the first two centuries of Islam, as was the case before Muḥammad, the tribe was the normal social unit. The tribal organisation of the victorious bands remained, in the *jund* of Syria, as in the new cities of 'Irāq and Egypt; and those groups preserved traditions of kinship, of friendship, of hate and of ancient vengeance, which had an evil influence on the life of the Muslim community, especially in Syria and in Spain.

The tribes are groups made up of a larger or smaller number of families. Their origins are obscure, and the account of them that popular pride has produced are in great part fictitious. The original tribal framework has been generally broken: large tribes have disintegrated and their names are found today only as labels attached to small and feeble groups. Other formations have come together, sometimes composed of very diverse elements, and new tribes have arisen to occupy for a moment the stage of their world.

The Arab tribe has a chief, formerly called *sayyid* or *Shaykh,* today *Shaykh* and *qā'īd*. Historically the chief of the tribe is the head of one of the families who, by his courage in war, his coolness and eloquence in council, and by his generosity, imposes himself, at the *jamā'a,* on his assembled fellow tribesmen. One has only to reread the stories of Pre-Islamic Arabia to understand what a modern tribal chief is: they give us, without the need to change a line, the picture of the present day Berber or Turkish tribe.

Thus it was that, at the beginning of the caliphate, in settled communities, as among the nomads, in the new city camps, at Baṣra, Kūfa, Fusṭāṭ, as in the desert, the sovereign or his representative made his contact with the mass of the people through the chiefs of the tribes. He confirms the chief's appointment, invests him with military, administrative and financial powers, which he will then exercise with an independence that is tempered only by despotism and assassination. To certain Arab rulers, the exaction of a high price for the title of qā'īd, his deposition at the end of a few fat years, his imprisonment and the confiscation of his goods, seem but normal incidents of sound everyday policy. Sometimes, however, the appointment by the ruler of the chief of the tribe is a gesture of no significance: the shaykh owes his authority to personal prestige and the favour of his peers.

The conversion of the conquered peoples brought them within the tribal organisation, but this took place at a time when, over parts of the Empire, it was already losing something of its value, and when, through displacement and mixing of populations, its structure was becoming more and more artificial. The city communities, the new fiefs created for the caliph's favourites, the formation into groups, of individuals drawn together by their beliefs or their interests, were, in many places, taking the place of the former tribal divisions. It was, therefore, amidst a confusion of religious, social and economic rivalries, that the caliphs were called upon to administer the large territorial areas inscribed on the map of the Empire by geographical or political necessities.

In each of those areas the governor works with the aid of a staff of officials and a departmental organisation similar, but on a reduced scale, to those of the court of Bagdad. Their duties consist, chiefly, in maintaining order and in collecting revenue enough to satisfy the master, while being allowed to provide sufficiently for themselves.

Throughout this vast administration nothing is provided for productive expenditure, for such public works as roads, bridges, canals, irrigation schemes, etc. Just as in the Roman Empire in spite of its elaborate organisation, and in the western states of the Middle Ages, it is local associations, whether permanent or *ad hoc*, that see to the construction and repair of the works that are necessary to the ordered life of the community; although certain governors follow the tradition of Al-Ḥajjāj and themselves oversee and finance important public works; the caliph even gives his attention occasionally to an undertaking which affects his immediate interests.

Meanwhile, the hope of reward in the next world prompts rulers and great personages alike, with ever growing urgency, to return to the people, in the form of useful undertakings, a part of the possessions they have acquired by theoretically legal means; for Islam recognises works of piety. Those individuals found mosques, cause aqueducts and reservoirs to be built for the benefit of pilgrims to the holy cities, besides bridges, rest-houses, madrasas, monasteries for Ṣūfīs, and hospitals, seeking, at the same time, to ensure their continued existence by means of endowments (*waqf*).

The caliph supervises his agents and is kept sufficiently supplied with details of affairs great or small, not omitting society scandals, by a well-developed information service. The postal services of the caliphate, which carry rapidly across the empire the reports of the prince's agents and his commands, were organised by the Umayyad caliph 'Abd al-Malik, following, doubtless, a Byzantine model: they were called the *barīd*. The empire is crossed by numerous paths, along which posts are established at which horses are stabled and cared for by an experienced staff. The courier, after leaving the capital or the office of a provincial chief, finds, at each relay, a fresh horse to replace his spent mount, or even a substitute messenger if he himself should be unable to travel further. Those relays are made use of for the journeys of the ruler or of high functionaries. One of the oldest of Arab documents dealing with geography, the book of Ibn Khurdādhbih, is a description of the postal routes, a guide to the *barīd*. The management of the postal services, whose agents played an important part in the policing of the Empire, was entrusted to one of the confidential officers of the Prince.

At some uncertain date the Arabs had borrowed from the Persians the idea of the pigeon post, which was completely organised for the first time under the Mamlūks. Pigeon houses (*burj*, plur. *burūj*), erected on sites chosen and cared for by special agents, served as the points of departure and arrival of the pigeons which the riders of the *barīd* carried on their horses.

The caliph directs the *jihād*, the holy war on the infidels, waged for the purpose of compelling them to accept the Muslim faith, of reducing them to slavery, of exterminating them, or may be to enforce the payment of tribute. Islamic scholars, although they consider the *jihād* to be compulsory for all Muslims, are not agreed as to its religious value, nor do all of them make it one of the five pillars of the faith (*arkān al-dīn*). The explanation of this uncertainty is to be found in the origin of the *jihād*. During his preaching at Mecca, the Prophet was too weak for his Revelation to provide him with any weapon other than that of resignation and trust in God. After the Hegira, at Medina, it brought a message to Muslims urging them to resist by force of arms those who had driven them from their homes and who wished them evil (Q. 22.39 to 42). On the occasion of a raid carried out by Muslims in violation of the truce of the Pre-Islamic holy months, the Qur'ān (2.212) ordered them to fight. From the date of the conquest of Mecca (630), it repeats its enticements to battle against the enemies of the faith. But it is the *ḥadīth* that organises the holy war and which makes of it a formula for conquest. The warriors of Islam know that, as at Badr, the angels fight with them.

The *jihād* is not an individual obligation (*farḍ'ayn*), but a communal one (*farḍ kifāya*), which ceases to apply to the individual as soon as a sufficient number of warriors take it upon themselves. The independent nature of the Bedouin found satisfaction in the voluntary nature of this service. The rule was, moreover, that each combatant provided his own arms and his mount, except when he could obtain the latter from one of the enclosures of the *ṣadaqa*. He had the promise of great possessions in this world and the next. He could look forward to a glorious death which would make him *Shahīd* (plur. *Shuhadā*), "him who testifies" to his faith, and which would ensure to him, besides the joys of paradise, that immediate joy to be found at the gates of the everlasting garden, which popular belief taught him to see in the shape of a bird that fed on the ever ripe fruit of a tree that was always green. He could count on a booty which, in the first decades of the conquest, was enormous. Four-fifths of the spoil was divided among the warriors, a horseman receiving a threefold share. At Medina the remainder belonged "to God (Q. 8.42), to His messenger, to the messenger's family, to the orphan, the poor and the traveller", a provision which was in line with the old generous habits of chieftains in Arabia. Later, the Doctrine divided this fifth of the booty into five parts, with the same classes of recipients, but with the caliph taking the Prophet's place.

It was not a matter only of a probably fruitless series of excursions, but the object was rather a lasting conquest, that brought men to submission and secured the occupation of cultivated lands. A very clear conception of the realities, united to a certain innate sense of the value of human life, led the conquerors to respect the lives of the vanquished, and even to abstain from collecting mobs of slaves for whom they had no use at the time.

The essential was to treat with the natives and to exact from them a tribute which would be a permanent ransom of their persons and their possessions. This tribute, which was a delivery in kind, dates, textile materials, arms, perfumes, slaves, etc., or in gold or silver metal, was later fixed in the form of a tax on land (*kharāj*) and a personal tax (*jizya*). It seemed wiser to deal with the human material after the manner of the good parent and to set it to work for the good of the community. The conquest of Syria, also, brought under the rule of Islam peoples who were, for the most part, Christians or Jews, and who, consequently, profited by the exception laid down in favour of the "people of the Book". The Zoroastrians were classed with them, and the Sabaeans were invented. Finally, an even simpler formula was discovered by drawing a distinction between the infidels who submitted voluntarily and with whom the Muslims concluded a treaty (*ṣulḥan*) of protection, and those who were conquered by force (*'anwatan*) and who were dealt with by the sword and reduced to slavery. It was once more a mingling of practical sense and compassion that caused the *ḥadīth* to order that crops, trees and irrigation works were to be respected. This anxiety to preserve things, which was both generous and wise, is all the more interesting for being contrary to the habits of "primitive" races who think first of "eating up" the enemy.

The imām of the Muslim community has the duty of carrying on the *jihād* against the peoples of the "war territory" (*dār al-ḥarb*) which is immediately adjacent to the "territory of Islam" (*dār al-Islām*). The leaders of the army must make sure that those peoples know the doctrines of Islam and that they refuse to follow them; that being so, it is necessary to fight them. The holy war is therefore permanent on the frontiers of Islam. The 'Abbāsid caliph, who knew how to go through all the gestures suited to the part he had to play, organised each year the Byzantine raid. He encouraged the faithful who "obeyed" (*mutawwi'a*) the law with piety to establish themselves in the fortresses in distant provinces (*ribāṭ*), there to lead the lives of warrior monks. At one period, when the ranks of the armies of the caliphate were filled with mercenaries and chance levies, those volunteers of the holy war did in fact fill the classic rôle of defenders of the faith.

No true peace is possible between Muslims and infidels. This is an absolute and theoretical conception which could not resist the power of facts, so that a juridical expedient had to be found, a *ḥīla*, to make it possible to conform to it and yet escape its implications. The Doctrine granted that Muslim princes could conclude truces (*hudna, muhādana*) with the infidels for a maximum period of ten years, in the case of an insuperable weakness of the Muslim State, and in its interests. They could break such a truce when they pleased on making reparation (*kaffāra*) for their broken vow.

The *jihād* is an "effort", a "zeal" for the faith which has caused the Tradition to say that the pilgrimage is a *jihād*; it extends therefore to the struggle of the imām of the Muslim community against those Muslims who reject the sound doctrine. The Fāṭimids made war in Syria in the name of the *jihād* against the governors of the 'Abbāsid caliphs and against the Hamdānids. It was the *jihād* that legalised the pursuit of heretics.

The army of volunteers, the multitude of the *jihād*, who had been fired by the lust of conquest, soon became, for the Umayyad caliphs, a precarious and uncertain support, which they endeavoured to reinforce with regularly recruited troops. They therefore reconstituted the Byzantine military formations by the name of *jund*, and the Arabs who were landowners had to furnish a certain number of soldiers. The latter were entered on the registers at the *dīwān* of the army as entitled to a pension in addition to their share of the booty. In those armies composed of "Syrians" who were the loyal supporters of the Umayyads, the formation of the fighting corps was modified in imitation of the organisation of their enemies. The deployment of the warriors in long lines (*ṣufūf*), in front of which were fought the single combats so dear to the glory (*mufākhara*) of the older Arabs, was abandoned; battalions and squadrons (*karādīs*) were created, each of which had its own individuality. The new converts, the *mawālī*, were then admitted to the army. As early as the Umayyad period there were bodies of troops receiving pay (*murtaziqa*).

The Umayyads had found their main strength in the loyalty of the "Syrians", that is, of the Arabs quartered in Syria. The 'Abbāsids were protected at first by the troops that had raised them to the caliphate, by the Arabs established in the eastern provinces, who had come under Iranian influence, and by the Iranian *mawālī*, by those, in a word, who were called Khurāsānians. But they, like the Umayyad "Syrians" before them, soon exhausted their warlike qualities, and the caliphs were forced to rely on foreign mercenaries who became the real masters of the Empire. It was in this way that the Turks set up a military aristocracy whose members shared the provinces among themselves, down to the day when the Osmanli had rebuilt the Muslim State to their own liking and for their own use. Meanwhile the Mamlūks had organised, in Egypt, an army of an original kind, with bodies of slaves bought in the market place and levies of freed slaves who had become landowners, to whom were added native irregulars.

The former soldiers of the *jihād* are found again among the volunteers who fought on the frontiers. Among the troops organised by Hārūn al-Rashīd they are ready to undertake raids or to take part in the annual campaigns against the Byzantines. At all the weak points of the Muslim borders they fill the *ribāṭ*, the camps in which the horses always stand picketed, ready to be saddled for battle. Later on, the *ribāṭ* became a sort of monastery fortress inhabited by men in whom may be seen the warrior monks of the Crusades. The Marabout (*murābiṭ*) is the man of the *ribāṭ*.

From the start of the regular organisation of the army the men were grouped, Roman fashion, in tens, hundreds, thousands, and tens of thousands. This division was retained by the Turks, the Mamlūks, the Moroccan sulṭāns, etc. The older terms used to designate the commanders of those different bodies are, beginning with the lowest rank, *'arīf*, *naqīb* or *khalīfa*, *qā'id*, *amīr*.

In the classical period, beginning at the end of the 9th century, the Muslim army is composed of bodies of mercenaries and occasional troops raised among the natives according to various rules.

This is the kind of organisation which is everywhere made compulsory by such circumstances. In modern Morocco, immediately preceding the French protectorate, the sulṭān was still carrying on the Spring and Summer raids which gave him some remains of authority and provided him with material resources. For these he gathered occasional horsemen around a group of permanent troops. But this permanent core had not a single, lasting composition; at the beginning of each dynasty it was the tribe of the ruler himself and the chief personages of the allied tribes who formed the military kernel. The self interest of such elements would seem to ensure their loyalty, but their intrigues are always a danger to the peace of mind of their ruler, and he is not long in finding this out. He then creates a guard of mercenaries who cannot but be devoted to him, seeing that they are isolated from the social life that surrounds them. He finds them among Abyssinians, Turks, Negroes and even among those who form no part of the Muslim community, namely, Christians.

In a Muslim State in which the wild enthusiasm of the first conquest has declined, the essential core of the army consists entirely of those mercenaries who form the hard loyal nucleus around which gather the tribal horsemen, whom any murmur of intrigue or whisper of insurrection can scatter. Like the Pretorians of Rome, those foreign troops, during certain troubled hours in the history of Islam, seized power, and energetic rulers were compelled to resort to mass executions in order to free themselves from them. The massacre of the janissaries in 1826 is nothing more than a late example of this process.

Provision for the payment of the troops was, consequently, from the time of the 'Abbāsids, one of the first essential items of the Muslim budget. Historians cite, as being a grave indication of penury, the case of the 10th century caliph who had to meet the demands of his soldiers by reducing the cost of his table.

. . . . .

The history of Muslim taxation has still to be written. We give here only a short outline, which may not always be correct. In principle, the Muslim community is subject to a single tax, that of the legal alms, the *zakāt*, but the revenue obtained from it does not suffice to fill the public coffers (*bayt al-māl*), the more so because a considerable part of the produce of the *zakāt* remains, legally or illegally, in the hands of the treasury agents. From the beginning of the conquest a new kind of revenue began to come in, the plunder of war (*ghanīma, fay'*). First, portable booty, the spoil of the battlefield, the proceeds of pillage in camps and dwellings, etc., of which the Prince received one-fifth. Then the occupation of the country put into the hands of the victors an enormous amount of non-portable plunder, the lands of the vanquished. Muslim jurists later drew a distinction between the rules affecting lands taken by force (*'anwatan*), and those that were occupied by treaty (*ṣulḥan*). But the men who conquered the Byzantine or Persian provinces were neither governed by such definite principles nor hampered by such subtleties of the legal mind. They found before them two kinds of property: private property and the domains of the ruler. Some proprietors accepted Islam at once, and came, with their possessions, under the Muslim régime of the *zakāt*. But, in most cases, they kept their religion, their customs, and a precarious enjoyment of their lands, over which the Muslim community acquired, by right of conquest, a kind of overlordship. A tribute called *kharāj* was exacted from those precarious tenants.

The second kind of property was that of the estates of the Byzantine emperors and the Sāsānid kings, and included also lands that had been long ownerless or had been recently abandoned by the flight of their possessors before the invader. Acting with foresight, and careful to protect the interests of the public treasury, the provincial governors created, out of those lands, estates which were assigned to persons of high rank, and on which a tax was levied similar to the *kharāj* and known by the same name. Thus the cultivation of those lands was assured, at the same time as the communal revenue. In the towns, non-Muslim inhabitants with a certain competence were required to pay a poll tax (*jizya*), which, in country places, was assimilated to the *kharāj*.

This state of affairs which, after all, in the Byzantine provinces, merely continued the existing practices, and, in other cases, followed closely related customs, was disturbed after the 8th century by the conversion of the conquered inhabitants to the religion of their conquerors. It seemed as if the disappearance of "infidelity" necessarily involved the abolition of the *kharāj* and the *jizya*, but the caliph's treasury could not be satisfied with the much lower and much less certain income from the *zakāt*. So it was decided that the conquered lands should continue to pay the *kharāj*, whatever the religion of their owners, a law that was not enforced without difficulty.

The amount of the *kharāj* was determined by the caliph in accordance with customs in force before the conquest. 'Umar thought, it is told, that the Sāsānids had levied too low a rate of taxation on the lands of the Sawād, and that it was necessary to increase it. The collection of the tax was greatly facilitated by he existence of large estates, and the administration was careful to find, in each area, a notability who should be responsible for it. This collector (*'āmil*) was independent of the governor (*amīr*) and was usually nominated by the caliph. He sometimes gave a written undertaking to pay a fixed sum to the Treasury, while accepting all responsibility for the collection of the taxes. By the time of Hārūn al-Rashīd's caliphate the stage had been reached of farming out the taxes which, in Egypt, were regularly put up for auction. There, as elsewhere, this expedient was adopted in an attempt to replenish a needy exchequer in spite of an unsound economic system. There was no longer any distinction between the tithe (*'ushr*, or *zakāt*) and the *kharāj*; the same *'āmil* collected both.

The personal tax and the land tax were not the only things that the first administrators of the Muslim community were able to borrow from the well-developed financial organisation of the Byzantine Empire. They found there taxes on travellers on entering, on leaving, or in transit through their territory; on market rights, weights and measures, mills, irrigation rights, and so on, which the caliphs condemned with indignation as illegal dues (*mukūs*), but which, in their great need, they could not do without. Each ruler, on his accession, made the ritual gesture of abolishing the *mukūs*, but did not disdain to follow the custom of bequeathing them, with some increase, to his successor. Governors drew an additional revenue from voluntary gifts, made on festive occasions or on some other pretext.

Because of his representative character, the caliph's share seems to have been fixed in advance by law and custom: one-fifth of all war booty and of the produce of the mines and pearl fisheries, fugitive slaves, and unclaimed estates.

. . . . .

We have spoken of the subjects of the caliph as if they were all alike. It is necessary to make it clear that they fall into distinct categories. The Muslim community is made up of believers (*mu'minīn, muslimīn*), and includes free men, among whom freed slaves remain to some extent dependent on the family of their owner, slaves whose emancipation is recommended by the Qur'ān and the Sunna. Among the non-Muslims, the idolaters are, in principle, excluded from Muslim territory (*dār al-Islām*), and must be fought on their own soil (*dār al-ḥarb*); but practice must have allowed some relaxation of that rule. Non-Muslims, people of the Book (*ahl al-kitāb*), that is to say, Jews, Christians, Zoroastrians, and certain idolaters are tolerated on Muslim soil in a state of inferiority; they are tributary members, subject to the poll tax (*jizya*).

At the beginning of the conquest of the Byzantine and Persian provinces, the social and religious status of the communities of "People of the Book" had been respected. The bishop, the Rabbi, or some important personage belonging to the group, had assumed its direction and governed it according to their former special customs. In addition, the tributary could appear before the Muslim qāḍī, although his evidence was considered to have no legal force. In the application of the *lex talionis*, the price of the blood of a tributary was valued at half that of a Muslim. Tributaries suspected of conspiracy with the enemies of Islam were severely punished. The penalties which supported the prohibition of wine drinking did not apply to them. The status of the tributaries was therefore distinctly inferior to that of Muslims. They were made to feel it in a particularly brutal way under the caliphate of the 'Abbāsid, Al-Mutawakkil (847–861), and under that of the Fāṭimid, Al-Ḥākim (996–1020); various humiliations were put upon them, the invention of which was attributed to the caliph 'Umar, who had actually never thought of them: giving way to Muslims in the streets and meeting places, being prohibited from riding, bearing a special mark (*shi'ār, ghiyār*) on the shoulder, blue for Christians, yellow for Jews, black or red for Zoroastrians. Their houses could not be built to the height of Muslim dwellings. The churches and synagogues which they were allowed to keep were later the subject of bitter dispute, some were demolished, and the repair of others was forbidden, so that they became ruins. Their worship was tolerated only in so far as it did not disturb the life of the Muslim community, a reasonable formula, but an arbitrary one which sanctioned every abuse.

Although the majority of the tributaries had accepted

conversion to Islam, there remained, in the chief towns of the Empire, important communities of Jews and Christians who, without losing their tributary status, yet occupied a place of consideration in the life of the caliphate. The Master's medical man was a Jew or a Christian; tributaries filled the offices of the ministries; others practised banking or carried on trade; and the mob had ever a store of anger, constantly ready to be poured out on those people who, in their outward life, displayed a sufficient modesty, but whose intimate life was known to be easy, and who enjoyed authority in the State; and at the call of the *fuqahā'* it would burst upon the Jews and the Christians.

The presence of non-Muslim foreigners on Muslim soil could not be altogether avoided. Not to mention ambassadors charged with missions from foreign princes, who enjoyed special immunities and were thus exceptions, foreign merchants of all nationalities and of divers faiths were, after the 8th century, numerous within the bounds of the Empire. The Doctrine had found in the old Arab custom of protection (*jiwār*) a legal means (ḥila) of guaranteeing the safety of infidel merchants on Islamic soil, without relieving them of their *kāfir* character; the caliph or the provincial governor would give the foreigner a certificate of safety (*amān*) which made of the outlaw, whose murder was legal and whose goods were, as it were, ownerless property in Muslim eyes, a kind of protégé, on the same footing as a tributary (dhimmī). The Doctrine tried to make people believe that the *amān* was valid for three months only, or at most for a year; but there is evidence to prove that longer stays were common.

The infidel in possession of the *amān*, the *musta'min*, travelled and traded throughout the territory governed by the prince who had guaranteed his safety. Muslims, punctilious in matters of principle, continued to profess that contact with the infidel was unclean, and that it involved complete ablution (*ghusl*). In Chapter Thirteen we shall describe the importance of foreign trade in the Muslim community.

From the 9th century, circumstances placed certain Muslim communities in a similar situation with regard to a foreign authority to that which put the *dhimmī* under the protection of Islam; in Syria, in the regions occupied by the Crusaders, and in Spain, in the "re-conquered" provinces. In 1184, the Andalusī, Ibn Jubayr, after having taken note of the very bearable régime under which the Syrian Muslims lived, under the rule of the Frankish princes, compares what he has observed with Sicily, where the court of the Norman kings is full of sham converts, where the Muslim populace lives in safety, but where men of culture suffer from the humiliation of their condition. In the 20th century, the number of Muslims living under "infidel" dominion is considerable. They are not relegated, as in the Spain of the "*reconquista*" to the position of colonial peoples, very like that of the *dhimmī*; but they are yet deprived of a part of their civil and political rights. There are *fatwās* which authorise Muslims to reside in "war territory" (*dār al-ḥarb*), provided they are permitted to carry out the duties of their religion.

It would not be possible to trace the evolution of the institutions enumerated in this chapter throughout the last century and a half. So far as international relations are concerned, it is quite a thousand years since the Muslim princes first entered into treaties with Christian rulers, which have not been broken less frequently by one party than by the other, but which have, nevertheless, established a political and economic, régime of value to both. The agreements arrived at with the object of regulating the status of non-Muslim foreigners on Islamic soil, and known by the name of "capitulations" created islets of protected persons around the consuls of European powers. They had deeply affected international life in Turkey, Egypt, Persia, and the Berber states. They have been abolished recently as a logical result of the political evolution of the Muslim world. The latest treaties have maintained the rule which prohibits the access of infidels to the holy cities, Mecca and Medina, and their neighbourhood, except for the ports of Jidda and Hudayda. Non-Muslim Europeans who have really entered the holy cities and brought back descriptions of them, such as Burton, Snouck-Hurgronje, Wavell, etc., have done so at the risk of their lives. The increase of historical studies among Muslims leads us to hope that the archæological studies that are so much to be desired will be undertaken by them.

The *zakāt* has not been allowed to disappear altogether from the list of taxes imposed in Muslim territory, any more than the *jizya* of the tributaries. But both, in most Muslim countries, are combined in a unified fiscal system after the European fashion. The evolution of Turkey is complete in this respect as in all others.

SOURCES

E. J. Arnold: *Khalifa*, 2.953; Mez: *Renaissance* (S.128); Ibn Hodeil: *Traité du Djihād*, edited and translated by Louis Mercier, 1939; Heffening: *Islam, Fremdenrecht*, 1925.

CHAPTER EIGHT

THE FAMILY

Marriage: celebration: rupture—Slavery—Emancipation.

WHEN entering upon a rapid study of the conditions governing the juridical and traditional life of the Muslim, it must be said again that Muslim law, since it is derived from the Qur'ān and the Tradition, and so fails to separate the spiritual from the temporal, is a canon law; that it is in force throughout the whole Muslim world; and that it is completed, and sometimes contradicted, by the local customs which still occupy a considerable place in the actual lives of the peoples, customs which it is not possible to describe here. It must also be remembered that the Arab-Muslim mind knows nothing of the custom of embodying principles in a formula after the manner of classical Roman law: the Qur'ān and the Tradition have been called in to decide particular cases, and the Doctrine has, by analogy, extended to like cases the solutions which they offered. Muslim law is made up of specific cases.

The Muslim family was not a creation of Muḥammad's. It is the original Arab family, placed within the framework of a higher religion. For the ancient Bedouin-Arab family, nucleus of the tribe, the essential ingredient of a life of pillage and a constant fight to survive was the presence of many sons. This was ensured by the fertility of their marriages and by polygamy which, in itself, provided the family with abundant female labour. The allocation of the sons to this family or to that was therefore a highly important matter, which was governed by two ways of bringing about a union: that by which the woman and her children became members of her husband's clan, and that which kept the woman in her own clan and allocated the children to her. Traces of this second kind of marriage are frequently found in stories describing the older manner of life among the Bedouin, and it is represented today by the important position in the family which is held by the maternal uncle (*khāl*). But, during the life of Muḥammad, the first kind of union was by far the most frequent in Arabia, as well as generally prevailing in the Eastern countries which the conquests brought into the Muslim Empire, and which followed Romano-Byzantine or Semitic law. It is now the rule in the Muslim family.

Its historical beginnings are difficult to trace. Certain definite facts show that the customs of married life were different in Mecca and Medina, where they had doubtless come under Jewish influence, and early relations with the *muhājirīn* were marked by hesitation and dispute. But, here too, Muḥammad succeeded in bringing custom into harmony with the interests of the parties.

The Muslim family has remained patriarchal, and the head of it maintains his authority over his wives, over his children even when of age, and over his slaves, down to the last day of his life. The child of a married woman belongs to the husband, except when the latter raises objections, or it is proved that the child has another origin.

In pre-Islamic days marriage was looked upon as a kind of sale in which, after the consent of the parties had been given, the husband made to the wife's father a payment called *mahr*. Muslim marriage has kept this ancient form; but the dower is assigned to the wife and considered to be an indemnity for the sacrifice of her person.

The demand in marriage (*khiṭba*) is presented after discreet inquiries and parleys in which the women delight to take part. It is frequently a case of a marriage of cousins and of plans made long before. In order to avoid a refusal, the suitor obtains the co-operation of a person of importance whose prestige will carry the day. When financial matters have been arranged between the two families, the date of the contract is fixed (*'aqd al-nikāḥ*). This concludes the marriage, which consists in the declaration of the consent of the parties and the payment by the husband of the dowry

The consent of the parties is the first condition essential for the validity of the marriage. The man gives it himself, except when he has not reached puberty or is unfit: in those cases a tutor intervenes to give the consent. A woman is always unfit: scholars disagree as to whether she can, or should, give her consent. But the law lays down that her tutor for marriage (*walī al-nikāḥ*) must declare her consent: the woman is silent. This tutor is her father or her grandfather or, in default of such, a member of the family in accordance with a fixed order, or, lastly, a person appointed by the magistrate (*ḥākim*). The father or grandfather have special powers, the effects of which are serious, and against which modern legislation has been actively directed. As in Old Arabia, he has the right to force his daughter into marriage (*jabr*); he is said to be *walī mujbir*. This compulsory power lapses when the woman is not a virgin and is of full age.

The dowry (*mahr*, *ṣadāq*) paid by the husband is assigned by the Qur'ān to the wife, and no longer to her father, but various arrangements put it, after all, at his disposal. It is usual for a half only, or possibly two-thirds, to be paid at the time of the contract; the balance may not be exacted till after the consummation of the marriage, and is still payable after a marriage has been broken. If the husband breaks the marriage before its consummation, he must leave half the dowry in the possession of the wife. The amount of the dowry is fixed by the parties, and may be exceedingly small; on that subject the *ḥadīth* is rich in anecdotes. If the amount is not specified in the contract it is fixed by resort to the *mahr al-mithl*, a dowry of a value corresponding to the social rank of the wife.

The marriage contract has, among people who confuse the spiritual and the temporal, no specifically religious character. It may be celebrated in the mosque, but also in the home of the parties. The ceremony begins with the recitation of the *Fātiḥa*, the first sūra of the Qur'ān, which is, of course, the introduction to every act in a Muslim's life. An exhortation (*khuṭba*) is, as a rule, delivered by the *walī* of the bride, or by a pious and learned person. When the families of the contracting parties are uneducated, it is well that an educated man should make certain that the laws are observed, and that efficacious formulas are pronounced. It is necessary also that the terms of a contract which will have grave moral and material consequences should be known to two persons, who will, in future, be able to bear witness to them; they are two *'udūl* (sing. *'adl*) who have the name and qualifications which all witnesses to deeds must possess who are acceptable to the qāḍī.

The marriage contract may be made between two persons under the age of puberty through the agency of their *walī*. Puberty is roughly fixed at fifteen and twelve years, but it may be established earlier; jurists are, moreover, of the opinion that, at the age of seven years, a child can give valid consent. The *walī* resolve such uncertainties in arbitrary fashion, and determine the consummation of the marriage as soon as both spouses have been recognised as having attained the age of puberty. An insane person may marry provided his *walī* assists with his presence.

Muslim law has maintained the laws forbidding the marriage of near relatives, down to, and including, uncle and niece. A union between first cousins is sanctioned by custom. No more than four wives are permitted at any one time, and it is forbidden to bring two sisters as wives into the same household. But, after the dissolution of the marriage, especially by the death of the wife, union with a sister-in-law is customary, although not having the force of law, as it is with the Jews, and as it would appear to have been in Pre-Islamic Arabia.

Relationship through a foster-mother is still, by Muslim law, an impediment to marriage, as it was in Arabia of old. Jurists have extended the prohibition to numerous relatives of the foster-mother and of the child.

Marriage between non-Muslims is forbidden. The Qur'ān had made an exception for the women of the tributaries (*ahl al-kitāb*), whom Muslims were permitted to marry; but the Doctrine, under the Shāfi'ites in particular, made such unions practically impossible. Along the same line of ideas, the Qur'ān permitted a woman to marry a man of a rank beneath her own only in exceptional circumstances; the status of the husband is determined by his rank in society, as well as by his fortune, which must be sufficient to ensure to his wife the continuation, materially, of her accustomed way of life. The husband is free to marry even a slave; the princes have always contracted unions with shepherdesses.

Such are the principal rules governing marriage, loosely arranged by contract and made binding by consummation. But, in actual social life, they are lost in a complication of interlaced ceremonies and practices, which are foreign to Islam, ancient mystic customs that exist among all peoples, with variations according to the beliefs of each. A step of such moment to the parties and the social group to which they belong, is of interest to every member, and is one to which the company of génies who, although invisible, live in intimate relationship with the world of men, cannot be indifferent. The spouses pass from the class of single persons into that of married people. There are rites to be observed in the passing.

In the Muslim world it is necessary to distinguish between the customs of nomads, of settled peasants, and of town dwellers. But, without being able to go into details which would be without end, we shall indicate only the principal practices that are to be found everywhere. The whole body of ceremonies is called *'urs*, and the spouses are *'arūs* and *'arūsa*, from the time of the signature of the marriage contract, an act which is followed by a feast (*walīma*), which celebrates the treaty of friendship between the men of the two families. All the members of their own social group are invited. The Doctrine makes it compulsory as being the essential public proclamation of the marriage. A refusal of the invitation is looked upon as an insult; the qāḍī, however, may not accept it.

The most important customs are connected with the consummation of the marriage (*dukhla*). Among the rural populations there is a very evident survival of the rite of pursuit and flight. In the towns the bathing of the bride is the occasion of great rejoicing among the women, who assemble in a *ḥammām*, specially hired for the day. The adorning of the bride, the night in which her hands and feet are dyed with henna (*laylat al-ḥinnā'*), and her face made up, gives occasion for another feast which is held, in this case, in her parents' house. On the following day, the bride is led in procession to the husband's home, where she is ceremoniously placed on a "throne", and the presents are set out—a third feast for the women. Meanwhile, the husband, he too having previously gone to the bathing place, accompanied by his friends, pays a visit to the mosque or, more commonly, to the *qubba* of a saint, finally returning home in a procession with music, dancing and singing. There he is brought into the presence of his wife.

During those ceremonies, the bride and bridegroom are

particularly exposed to the attacks of the jinns and to the danger of the evil eye. It is the duty of the groomsmen, the viziers of their sulṭān of a day, (*wuzarā', waqqāfīn*) to protect him from them during the retreat which he observes before the consummation of the marriage. Various rites, in which ears of barley or of rice, pomegranates, almonds, fish and eggs play a part save him from impotence, and help to ensure the fertility of the bride. The public demonstration of her virginity is important, since it makes impossible an immediate rupture of the marriage. The coarseness of this formality has led to its being modified or suppressed altogether. Consummation is followed by a feast which, in certain countries, takes the place of that which accompanies the making of the contract. The period of seven days immediately following imposes on both parties certain prohibitions which are scrupulously observed.

The marriage of a widow or divorced woman is marked by a contract as in the case of a virgin; but it is no longer of interest to the invisible powers, and the ceremonies are confined to the traditional meals and a few discreet rejoicings.

Law and custom give the husband absolute authority over his wife and children. But Qur'ānic law, very favourable to the wife, has given her a status which is, in some ways, more advantageous than that bestowed by modern European law. Financially, she retains her own separate estate; she remains mistress of her dowry and of any goods she may acquire by inheritance, by gift, or as the fruit of her own labour. In practice it is difficult for her to exercise those rights; but she is certain of maintenance, lodging, and service, according to her rank.

The husband is superior to his wife: "men have a degree above them", says the Qur'ān (2.228); a woman is worth half a man in matters concerning ransom for a murder, inheritance, and the giving of evidence. The Qur'ān grants to the husband the right of severe correction, that is to say, the right to beat his wife and to put her in quarantine. On the other hand, it counsels moderation. The position of the wife in conjugal life depends, as it does elsewhere, on her individual ability to act consistently, and to ensure that her opinions are listened to. Many mothers exercise, over the members of their households, an authority almost equal to that of the husband. But Muslim law, as we shall explain, exposes the wife to the continual threat of repudiation, with no need to justify it, or of the marriage of the husband to a new, additional, wife, whose presence can greatly modify the nature of the family life. The Ḥanafite rite, followed by modern jurists, consequently approves the *ta'līq al-ṭalāq*, that is, the introduction into the marriage contract of clauses requiring the husband to repudiate his wife, and so to give her her freedom, if certain circumstances should arise, if, for example, he marries another wife, if he absents himself for too long periods from the conjugal domicile, if he does not permit his wife to pay frequent visits to her family, or to stay with them, and so on. Those provisions, excellent in themselves, give rise to abuses and much quarrelling.

Consequently, the Doctrine provides for the prolonged absences of the husband which the pilgrimage and the demands of business make possible. An ancient custom allowed the man, when resident away from home, to contract a temporary marriage called "enjoyment" (*muta'*); the Qur'ān seems to authorise such an arrangement, and Muḥammad makes it legal for his warriors. But it would appear that 'Umar called it debauchery. The Shī'ites maintained its legality. With a little subtlety of interpretation, it can be made legal even for the Sunnites. It was for long accepted in Mecca as applicable to pilgrims, who thus resumed, as a sort of rite, the sexual relations that were forbidden during the period of their sanctification (*iḥrām*).

Modern society has kept, except in certain social classes, and that only within the last few years, the ancient conception of the separation of men and women into two "clans". The married woman must show her face only to men between whom and herself there is a matrimonial impediment. The wearing of the veil is the external manifestation of this principle.

In Old Arabia a marriage was dissolved by the unilateral will of the husband, and by the utterance of a formula of repudiation, or by the retreat of the wife to the protection of her own family. Muslim life barely recognises, however, this second method of dissolution. Thus the husband can repudiate his wife at his own pleasure, she then regaining her liberty, and receiving the balance of the dowry which remained unpaid at the time of the contract. To make the dissolution legal he only needs to pronounce, at any place or on any occasion, a form of words embodying his repudiation. If he is a minor his tutor intervenes. Jurists decided that drunkenness did not annul the repudiation. It was very dangerous to give the force of irrevocability to words which might have been lightly uttered. The Revelation, always ready to find a way out of embarrassing situations, has intervened in several passages in the Qur'ān. The first necessity was that the repudiated wife should be kept under observation, and, if she was found to be pregnant, that the paternity of the child should be assigned to the husband, and that the wife should receive proper maintenance until her confinement. The law therefore decreed a waiting time (*'idda*) of three menstrual periods (*qurū'*), during which the wife continues to be maintained by the husband, and at the expiry of which, in the absence of any indications of pregnancy, the repudiation becomes final. This waiting time has been used to modify the effects of a hasty repudiation; so long as it has not expired, the husband can take his wife back without any formality. A second repudiation may be annulled in the same way; the third is final. The Doctrine has, after some controversy, allowed that, if the husband utters such a formula as "thou art repudiated three times", the repudiation is final. When the silence of the husband has given finality to a first or a second repudiation, he may contract a new marriage with the same wife after the first has been liquidated; after a third repudiation the woman is forbidden to him (*ḥarām*). But the Qur'ān has decided that, if the wife contracted marriage with a third party, and that marriage was dissolved, she again became lawful (*ḥalāl*) for her first husband. This decision allows the use of an expedient by which a third repudiation may be cancelled; an accommodating man agrees, for honourable payment, to contract an unconsummated marriage with the woman, repudiating her immediately, thus permitting the remarriage. Strict interpreters of the law require that this *muḥallil* should be a real husband; here, however, we get involved in the subterfuges (*ḥiyal*) of Muslim law which are the subject of the amusing tales told in the compilations of '*adab*. This practice was condemned in Deuteronomy xxiv, 3 and 4), and in the Gospel (Matthew v, 30 and xix, 9).

Repudiation involves, for the husband, the obligation to pay to the wife the whole amount of her dowry. He will, therefore, be tempted to subject her to treatment calculated to make her life unbearable, and which will drive her to buy his repudiation by abandoning her dowry, or even by payment of an indemnity. This, with the acknowledged impotence of the husband, is one of the cases in which the law permits the wife to have recourse to the authority of the qāḍī, who may then force the husband to repudiate her, and to pay her her dowry.

The situations we have described, and all those that proceed from them, have been regulated by the four schools of *fiqh*, with important variations which are all equally valid. A Mālikite Muslim, for example, may undertake in his marriage contract that he will be governed, in whole or in part, by the provisions of Ḥanafite law, supposing he finds them to be to his advantage. In modern Muslim states, moral habits and the development of the economic life tend to create new rules, which get rid of the abuses of the law of repudiation, such as the *jabr* and the marriage of young children. There is a general tendency in favour of European legislation on the subject. In 1926 Turkey adopted the Swiss civil code and abolished repudiation.

It would be childish to try to comprise within a general formula the status of the Arab woman. The poor and the peasants lead an existence of constant labour which, because of the indolence of the male, often weighs heavily upon them. In well-to-do families the young women used to be, and often are still, occupied solely with their personal adornment and the care of their children. Their empty lives find no variation except in pilgrimages to the tombs of the saints, sundry feasts and ceremonies, visiting, or gatherings in the cemetery on Fridays. Those are years during which the cares of the toilet and the retailing of society gossip fill the same place as in the apparently more fully occupied lives of Western women. When they grow older they take an active interest in the care of the home. Illiterate for the most part, they can no longer supply the social needs of a young generation of men whose cultural advance has been rapid. Consequently, many Muslim families, in the urban middle and upper classes, cause their daughters to be given an education which, by profoundly changing the mentality of the mothers, has already produced a generation differing greatly from the preceding one.

The Qur'ān has maintained the polygamy which was

customary among the Bedouin, but it has limited to four the number of wives a man may have at one time. It has also kept the serial polygamy of the repudiation, not to mention concubinage and prostitution. It has also agreed that it could be a good thing to have only one wife, and monogamy is, in fact, forced upon those who live a settled life, and especially upon town dwellers, by present-day economic conditions and customs. There is, therefore, no serious obstacle in the way of approximating more closely to the standards of those countries whose legal system admits of divorce. There has been much loose talk about the exception made by the Qur'ān in favour of Muḥammad in the matter of the number of his wives. But it should be recognised that the history of the wives and children of the Prophet is a confused succession of improbabilities, in which it is not possible to discern the truth. It can at least be remarked that it was in accordance with custom that the Chief should have more wives than the other members of the clan. Moreover, Muḥammad's marriages were for the most part political alliances: Ḥafṣa is the daughter of 'Umar, Umm Ḥabība the child of Abū Sufyān, 'Ā'isha of Abū Bakr; Ṣafiya, the Jewess, is the daughter of a conquered chief, and therefore was assigned as legal booty to the victor.

The children born of the husband's wives constitute his family, provided they were born six months after the consummation of the marriage, or up to four years after its dissolution. The family receives, and gives equal rights to, the child born of a concubine. As for the chance child, the law tries to ignore its existence. The husband may dispute, by the special procedure of the oath of malediction (*li'ān*) the paternity of his wife's child. An opposite course of law permits the child to be attributed to a father other than the actual husband. By this roundabout means it has been possible to recognise an illegitimate child, and also to practice adoption in spite of its abolition by the Qur'ān.

The Arab family, in the wider sense of the word, was completed by the inclusion of the slaves, whether white or black. The Qur'ān retained slavery, while recommending that they should be well treated and set free. In order to appreciate the moral value of the institution, it is necessary to know the conditions under which they lived.

The slave (*'abd*, plur. *'abīd*; fem. *ama*, *jāriya*) is not a complete person; he is a chattel of the master's, having been acquired like all other possessions by purchase, gift, or inheritance, and the rights of property in him may be transferred by the same legal process; without, however, being allowed to separate from his mother a child under seven years of age. The slave, if he is over age and fitted for it, may be invested with a share in the personality of his master for the purpose of carrying on a trade in his name, and, although, in principle, all he earns belongs to the master, he can still acquire a small competence. A slave may marry a slave, and a female slave may marry either a free man or a slave; their children are slaves of the woman's master. A slave may announce the repudiation of his wife, this being of full effect after the second time. The waiting time of a widowed, repudiated, or pregnant slave is half that applicable to a free woman. A master may not marry a slave unless he first gives her her freedom; otherwise she is a concubine, and her status is recognised by Muslim law: such an association ought always to have been preceded by a period of "liberation" (*istibrā'*), but this was rarely observed. The slave who gives a child to her master is called "child's mother" (*umm walad*); the child is free and is treated like a legitimate child, the mother gaining her freedom with the death of her master.

The Qur'ān and the Sunna look upon the emancipation of a slave as an act of piety which will be rewarded in the future life. The master, acting on his own discretion, announces the emancipation in terms that permit of no ambiguity. It may be done with certain reservations, such as, for example, that the emancipation will come into force only with the death of the master, and that it may be revoked at any time previous to that event; if the master should sell the slave in question, the act is a kind of tacit revocation. A slave may also be *mukātab*, a state well known to Roman law: it is announced that he shall have gained his freedom when he has paid a certain sum of money to his master, a condition which presupposes that he is practising a trade and is saving money. It is enjoined on the master not to exact the whole amount, and the Qur'ān has provided for a part of the tax called legal alms (*zakāt*) to be set aside for the benefit of slaves desiring to purchase their freedom.

The freed slave (*maulā*) remains bound to his master, not only by the bonds of affection and social necessity which keep him a member of the tribe, but also by legal obligation. The master is entitled to collect the estate of a freed slave who dies without legal heirs, an event of frequent occurrence. The master is the natural guardian of the freed slave and his descendants.

Slavery has held an important place in the life of the Muslim world. Slaves and freedmen are encountered at every point in its history. If we wish to form a sober judgment regarding the moral value of the institution, we must make a distinction between family slavery and great masses of slaves. In this, Muslim history repeats that of Roman society. Muslim slavery has been evil only in certain particular cases. The trade in negroes destined to supply the markets of the East, especially that of Bagdad, with human flesh, and the manufacture of African eunuchs, or slaves (*ṣaqāliba*) of Abyssinian or European origin during the heyday of the 'Abbāsid dynasty, were practices contrary to all civilised standards. The wretched condition of the slaves that were crowded together on the great landed estates of Lower Mesopotamia in the 9th century caused the terrible slave war of the Zanj. The abundant missionary literature of the time gave rise to great popular indignation over the sufferings of Christian slaves in the Berber prisons and hulks. But it should not be forgotten that the Europe of that period had also its prisons and galleys, where life was by no means enviable. The history of the slave trade in the American colonies is a blot on the reputation of Christian Europe. Slavery must be looked upon, without sympathy as without disgust, as an obsolete institution and a violation of the dignity of man.

SOURCES

Juynboll: *Handbuch* (S.88);—Schacht: *Nikāh*, E.I. 3.975; *'urs*, E.I. 4.1094; *talāq*, E.I. 4.667;—W. Marçais: *Takruna*, 355 and 381 (with bibliography), to be completed by Reich: *Villages Araméens de l'Antiliban*, 80–126.

CHAPTER NINE

PROPERTY

Intestate Estates—Wills—Habūs.

THE laws of succession are a much greater obstacle to the evolution of Muslim law than are those that govern marriage. The law of inheritance was laid down by the Qur'ān; it forms an important chapter of the canon law, in which the temporal and the spiritual are inextricably tangled together. Juridical practice was indeed prepared to give way to local custom, but has not been able to ignore completely the requirements of the Holy Book.

Just as it kept, in their essential features, the marriage laws of Old Arabia, so the Qur'ān has kept those governing inheritance; but, in both cases, it improved the position of women. The patriarchal régime of Arabia, being adapted to a tribal organisation in which each group looked distrustfully on its neighbour, or was actually at war with it, and in which he is most prosperous who can muster the greatest number of fighting men, adopted, logically, a law of succession through the father, which favoured the male line; the maternal line and all women were excluded. The Qur'ān, on the contrary, gave to women their legitimate share.

In Muslim law the succession accrues, in principle, and in accordance with old Arab law, to the paternal line, the *'aṣaba*, who have been likened to the *agnati* of Roman law. The allocation of the estate among them is made following the same order as that which applies to matrimonial guardianship, that is, roughly in the following order: descendants, ascendants, collaterals. The women of the paternal line are, like the men, *'aṣabāt*, but are entitled to no more than a half of the share of the male heirs. This principle, simple in its application, has been complicated by verses of the Qur'ān which created privileged heirs who, in every case, must receive a fixed share in the estate (*farīḍa*). Their rivalry with the normal heirs gives rise to complications which give to the "science of privileged shares" the chief place in legal studies. In claiming their fixed share they break up the order of the '*aṣaba* to whom they generally belong. They are, after the sons: (*a*) the daughter or daughters with one-half or two-thirds of the estate and, by extension, the daughter or daughters of the son; (*b*) the father or the mother with a sixth and, by extension, the grandfather or grandmother; (*c*) the sister or sisters-german for half or two-thirds and, by extension, the half sisters through the father; (*d*) brothers or sisters through the mother for one-sixth each, or one-half in all, according to their number; (*e*) the widower for a half or a quarter; (*f*) the widow for one-half of the widower's share. Those Qur'ānic provisions appear to have been introduced immediately after the bloody battle of Uḥud (624), for the purpose of settling particular cases of which we have no details. We shall content ourselves with a few examples of the complications that ensue.

The son is the first heir; he cannot be ousted by the daughter, whose right to a fixed share disappears, and who participates only to the extent of half a male share. If there is one son, she therefore receives one-third; if two sons, one-fifth, and so on. The sister-german is ousted by the sons and daughters, by the sons and daughters of the son, and by the father and the mother; it is only in the absence of any of those that she gets her *farīḍa*, or shares the estate with her brothers. The widower receives one-half of his wife's estate, but a quarter only, if she should leave one or more children, etc.

When the allocation of the fixed shares has been made to the heirs who present themselves, two cases may arise:

1. The whole estate is absorbed; in this case it frequently happens that the allocation of the fixed shares is arithmetically impossible, as shown in this classic example:

Two daughters, each $\frac{1}{3}$, in all $\frac{2}{3}$ . .	$\frac{16}{24}$
The father and mother, each $\frac{1}{6}$, in all $\frac{2}{6}$.	$\frac{8}{24}$
The widow, $\frac{1}{8}$	$\frac{3}{24}$
Total	$\frac{27}{24}$

The solution lies in making the division in 27ths.

2. In the absence of descendants and heirs entitled to fixed shares, or after these are provided for, the balance of the estate is allocated to the relatives in the paternal line, in the following order: (*a*) ascendants, if there are any beyond the grandfather; (*b*) to the collaterals of any degree; (*c*) to the master, if the deceased is a freed slave; (*d*) if there are none of those categories of heirs, or if none comes forward, the estate is allocated, in whole or in part, to the Public Treasury (*bayt al-māl*), if it is administered according to the law. This default of heirs is more frequent than one would expect: if, for example, the sons, who have a preference over all other classes of heirs, absorb the whole estate or share it with their sisters; if the father and mother and the grandparents can, besides their fixed share, claim the balance of the estate as *'aṣaba*, the other heirs with fixed shares have no right to anything more, and the balance of the estate, if there is no *'aṣaba*, has no legal claimant. It has been agreed, however, that, if the Public Treasury is considered not to have a clear title, then heirs whose share is fixed, whoever they may be, divide the estate. In default of any such again, the maternal line may be allowed to inherit, or even any Muslim who can seize the estate.

The four orthodox cults have different solutions of each of the cases we have described. They do not agree as to the estates of infidels, in which, in the opinion of most legal authorities, no Muslim may participate, and which cannot be claimed even by fellow infidels. They are disagreed on the subject of the succession of an apostate (*murtadd*), whose estate, according to the most widely accepted opinion, is allocated to his Muslim heirs or to the Public Treasury. Khārijite law differs hardly at all from the Sunnite, except that it does not permit the master to receive the estate of a freed slave, and prescribes the giving of an unclaimed estate as alms.

Shī'ite law is very different, being based on the equal right of the two lines, the paternal and the maternal; it should be recalled that Fāṭima transmitted to the 'Alids the estate of the Prophet. Thus Shī'ism has divided the natural heirs into categories, of which each takes precedence over the next in order, adding to the list the class of "heirs for special reasons": the husband or wife, the *maulā*, that is, the master who has freed the slave or has obtained the conversion of the infidel, and, lastly, the *imām* of the Shīʿite community as representing the public exchequer. In addition, it recognised the right of succession of infidels, apostates, and murderers, and the right of the *mukātab* slave to purchase his freedom out of the proceeds of the estate.

The heirs have no right of sasine on any part of the estate since it is not held to form part of their own fortune as it does in French law. Their claim may be validly made only after the debts due by the estate have been paid. There is, therefore, in Muslim law, nothing resembling succession under *beneficium inventorii*. The debts, which are immediately deducted, include not only those resulting from expenditure on the funeral and liabilities contracted by the deceased, but also those that represent religious duties unfulfilled, such as the *zakāt*, the fast, or the pilgrimage; the expenses required for the engagement of a third party to undertake the pilgrimage on behalf of the deceased are a charge on the estate.

The canon law has thus laid down in great detail the rules of succession. It also permits inheritance by the will of the deceased, while limiting the discretion of the testator.

The Qur'ān has not confirmed the importance assigned, in Old Arabia, to a person's last wishes, which certain verses appear to turn into mere religious or moral recommendations. Other passages have expressed approval of the tendency to use the last testament as a means of reforming certain provisions in the customs regulating succession *ab intestat*, and advise the granting of preferences in favour of the father, the mother and other relatives, together with the widow, in addition to those whose title to fixed shares is otherwise recognised. But the Doctrine, basing its decision on the very existence of such shares, declares that no testamentary disposition may be made in favour of any particular heir. The canon law, too, has insisted on securing for the legal heirs the main part of the estate, and has decided that a will (*waṣīya*) may dispose of no more than one-third of it. It has even protected the estate from any verbal arrangements which the testator might make during his last illness, or since the last occasion on which he might have ventured into regions which war or epidemic had made dangerous. Consequently, all donations, cancellations of debts, and emancipations of slaves effected during that period are null and void. The law requires that the legatee, of sound mind, like the testator, be alive at the time of the latter's death except in the case of the children born up to six months after that event.

Such provisions limiting the freedom of the testator have not gained the approval of public opinion. The business is therefore fruitful in *ḥiyal*, legal tricks aimed at getting the better of the law: transmission by gift (*hiba*) and the foundation of an endowment (*waqf*) are often used for that purpose.

The name given to a will (*waṣīya*) derives from the fact that it includes the nomination of the testamentary executor (*waṣī*) whose duty it is to supervise the division of the estate. He also names the tutor (*walī al-māl*) who is to administer the inheritance of minor children, an appointment which usually falls to the mother, acting under the supervision of the qāḍī. The latter, if the deceased fails to do so, appoints this *walī*, or himself carries out his duties. The last wishes of the deceased are generally expressed verbally in the presence of two witnesses (*'udūl*) who will subsequently be able to testify to them before the qāḍī.

The presence of numerous foreigners, merchants mostly, has raised the question of their succession. The Doctrine began by refusing all rights of inheritance between foreigners, and by obtaining, by this means, a large number of vacant estates for the benefit of the exchequer. Then, in the 12th century, although still refusing to recognise inheritance between foreigners and Muslims or tributaries, allowed the transmission to a foreigner's heirs of any property left within the territory of Islam, after payment of all creditors, and even went so far as to admit the validity of legacies made by the foreigner in favour of a Muslim or a tributary.

Endowments have played, and still play, an important part in the economy of Muslim countries. The name given to them is *ḥubūs* (sing. *ḥubs*, plur. *aḥbās*), transcribed by the French as ḥabous. In the East it is called *waqf*, plur. *auqāf*, which has given the Turkish *vakûf*; both roots signify "retaining", or "shutting up".

The feature that is common to all kinds of *hubūs* is that the property cannot be alienated; the income which accrues is devoted to a pious foundation or to the descendants of the founder, and the property passes, according to the varying opinions expressed by the Doctrine, either to the heirs of the founder, or to God, which means that the property becomes ownerless. The origin of the *ḥubūs* is obscure, and legends have grown up around it. It would appear that the earliest of them were founded by the caliphs out of the vast domains left masterless as a result of the conquests, and which it was important to have cultivated if loss to the exchequer of the tax payable on them was to be avoided. It is not known whether this *kharāj* was at that time an actual tax, or whether it was levied as a lump sum. Whatever may be the origin, dating, like that of other institutions, from the so little known period of the Umayyads, the custom of the *ḥubūs*, under two very different influences and in two separate forms, spread rapidly.

The first is that of the pious foundation. We have already remarked that the budget of the caliphate made no provision for public works: the mosques, aqueducts, works for the conservation of water supplies, the madrasas, the hospitals, were all the personal creations of rulers, eager to acquire fame in this world, and a reward in the next. There was no assurance that such works or buildings would be preserved or maintained, or that the means would continue to be provided for the retention of the staff that saw to their continued usefulness. So the founders endeavoured to protect their works from decay by creating, out of properties abandoned to God or the community, according as conflicting doctrines provided, estates the revenues of which would be applied in perpetuity to the maintenance of the foundation. Such estates were preferably made up out of city properties, dwelling houses that could be let, the shops of the *sūq*, or *ḥammām* from which a regular income could be collected, provided the expenses of their maintenance were met out of revenue. Or they might be rural domains; or, if the founder was a prince, a charge on the tax revenue of a village or district. Those properties had to be managed by one or more *nāẓir*, the founder choosing the first, who, in turn, appointed the second, and so on, or else he was nominated by the qāḍī who, in every case, exercised a general supervision over the *ḥubūs*.

The second type of *ḥubūs* supplied a very economic need. We have seen that the canon law set up a rule of succession which provided for a complete and complicated division of a heritage, without the person concerned being permitted to provide by will against the infinite subdivision of his property. A building, a house or a landed estate, after a few successions, ends by being divided into an infinity of parts, of which none can be profitably exploited. The institution of the *ḥubūs* becomes a remedy for this evil. The owner turns his property into an endowment fund for the benefit of his descendants, among whom the revenue can be divided *ad infinitum*. But the trust estate is kept intact and the possibility of its exploitation assured. Great personages, fearing their confiscation, protected their ill-gotten gains by this means. It is one of those ways of evading the law which the law's rigidity brought into general use. The administration of *ḥubūs* of this kind is arranged for in the same way as the others, under the supervision of the qāḍī.

Of those two classes of *ḥubūs*, the first alone figures in Muslim history, whose pages are full of accounts of pious *ḥubūs*, the works of generous founders. Ibn Jubayr, in 1183 and 1184, expresses his admiration at finding them everywhere in the East, and the deeds constituting *ḥubūs* occupy much space in the collections of Muslim epigraphy. The family *ḥabs*, although more modest, has none the less its part to play. Unfortunately the institution has been, in both cases, spoiled by the carelessness and bad faith of those charged with the duty of administration, and pious *ḥubūs* have frequently had to be renewed. This has been done with such zeal that, in Turkey, inquiries undertaken in the 19th century have estimated the property held by *ḥubūs* at three-quarters of the total amount of land under cultivation. Their total value appeared to be fifty million pounds Turkish in 1925, with a revenue amounting to three and a half million pounds in 1928. In Algeria, too, the *ḥubūs* absorbed half of the cultivated land; in Tunisia a third; in Egypt, an eighth. It is probable that the same conditions prevail in other areas.

However useful the institution of the *ḥubūs* may have been, it has the serious drawback of withdrawing a great deal of wealth from circulation, besides depriving it of active and disinterested management. Arbitrary confiscations, illicit sales, and the exchanges that administrators have been able to effect, have not availed to remove this grave cause of the impoverishment of Muslim countries. Wide domains have continued to be cultivated in the most primitive way. More than that: it suffices to have read the deed of foundation of the *ḥubūs* of a mosque in order to question the possibility of administering efficiently, and of keeping in repair, a long list of shops or parts of shops in various city streets, of patches of land scattered over the countryside, of bits of orchards. Governments, since Turkish days in the 16th century, and especially since the 19th century, have given their attention to improving the condition of the *ḥubūs*, and to correcting their ill effects, by putting the property, by some means or other, into circulation once more, without changing the purpose of the endowment. The first attempt to this end took the form of letting the property on a perpetual lease in return for a lump sum paid immediately, and based on the value of the property at the beginning of the tenancy, plus a perpetual rent, thus retaining the principle of the *hubūs*. The tenant's enjoyment of the property became hereditary. In default of an heir, it returned to the foundation. Arrangements of this nature were made in Tunisia (*enzel*), in Algeria (*anā*), and in Morocco (*guelza*) where they took the form of life interests.

The present day governments of Muslim countries have created machinery for control and centralisation, and have sought to lessen the importance of the *ḥubūs* by putting the properties back into circulation, and getting rid of the abuses that reduced their value, without injuring the institution itself, which may, in certain cases, still be useful, and which is defended on religious grounds by the conservative parties. In 1924, Turkey put an end to the administration of the *auqāf* and, in 1926, authorised the sale of the property of endowments to communes and to public institutions. Egypt is slowly following the example of Turkey. Russia, under the Czars, had confiscated the *ḥubūs*, and Soviet Russia has abolished them. France has followed a hesitating, and sometimes contradictory, policy in Algeria, and has consequently accomplished nothing definite. In Tunisia and Morocco, the property of *ḥubūs*, which have been reorganised under the control of the two governments and the protectorate, either contribute usefully to the purposes for which they were created, or become subject to the ordinary law of property.

. . . . .

Muslim law recognises the various methods of conveying and holding property which Roman law had devised: sales, leases, partnerships, wages, etc. The rights attached to landed property, such as irrigation rights, have been minutely regulated. The law of easements is treated separately and independently of property rights, being looked upon as constituting a property of a special kind.

In a general way the provisions of Muslim law are such as derive from the Qur'ān and the Sunna which, originating in the customs of Mecca, has been influenced by Romano-Byzantine law in a manner and to an extent which are still undefined. It is a body of legislation which developed rapidly during the Middle Ages by the incorporation of customary law created daily by the practice of commerce. It has become the law governing commercial transactions in the Eastern Mediterranean; it has been one of the sources of European law. Thus, apart from its practical interest to the Muslim world, it is of considerable historical importance.

In its broad lines the law of contract in Muslim jurisprudence does not greatly differ from European legislation. We shall return to this subject in Chapter XII.

SOURCES

Juynboll (S.88); Schacht: *Mirāth,* E.I., 3.577; *wasīya,* E.I. 4.1193; Heffening: *waqf,* E.I., 4.1154.

CHAPTER TEN

JUSTICE

The Qāḍī—Talio and Ransom—The Mufti—Crimes punished by the Qur'ān—Theft, Brigandage, Apostasy, Adultery, Wine—The Chief of Police—The *Muhtasib*—Present-day Organisation.

MUSLIM rulers have mostly considered it to be their absolute duty to do justice personally. It was formerly their custom to hold audiences every week, on Mondays and Thursdays. They then played the part of supreme arbiter, that of the Arab *ḥakam*, which, with them as with the Prophet before them, was that of an interpreter of the Word of God. But the first caliphs had already been forced to delegate their judicial powers to a judge, a person who, in the armies and the junds of Syria, supervised the application of the laws governing war booty, successions, the talio, etc. The post of qāḍī was created by the Umayyad caliphs together with other judicial appointments, probably as a result of Syro-Byzantine influence. We can give only a short outline of the very complicated history of the functions of a qāḍī.

The qāḍī is an arbiter who settles disputes between persons who appeal to him, and who pronounces sentence of the law on delinquents against whom charges are brought by private persons. He is assisted neither by a representative of the Public Prosecutor, nor by an executive officer, and he has personally no power to carry out a sentence. He is competent to decide any of the questions affecting the life of the community that may have been dealt with by the canon law, the *sharī'a*, that is, marriage, dissolution of marriage, the care of orphans, successions, contracts of various kinds, and the punishment of criminals. The qāḍī gives his decisions unassisted, and, even if the Doctrine requires him to gather counsellors (*shūrā*) around him, he is notin any way obliged to give heed to their opinion.

In the time of the Umayyads the caliph appointed a qāḍī for each province. The Arabs retained their patriarchal practice of domestic and tribal justice, and the tributaries had their own special courts. But circumstances removed the easement of the qāḍī's duties that those two institutions provided, and he was soon driven to delegate all or part of his powers to subordinate magistrates. Later, the provincial capital, becoming the capital of an independent amīrate, had, like Bagdad, its supreme qāḍī (*qāḍī al-quḍāt*, in Spain, *qāḍī al jamā'a*), with a whole hierarchy of subordinate judges.

So he came to appoint delegates while preserving his own power intact and exercising it at will. And, as he held, not only the power of judgment, but also that of administration, and as the qāḍī was, at various periods, keeper of the public treasury, imām for the Friday *Khuṭba*, administrator of the estates of orphans and of *ḥubūs*, and tutor to those who were incapable of managing their own affairs, he had delegates for the performance of all those duties. He is, therefore, a chief justice, sitting on the high seat of judgment.

The understanding is that only verbal testimony may be given before him, but supporting documentary evidence is not disdained. Two witnesses are required to testify to the real existence of a disputed undertaking, or to the accuracy of any statement of fact. Whether it be what we call a civil case, or a criminal prosecution, the judge must give unlimited credence to their evidence. Since, however, it would be impossible, in every case and for every witness, to inquire into the latter's trustworthiness, the qāḍī draws up a list of men whose perfect probity in the legal sense (*'adāla*) has, after investigation, been vouched for by a person whom he trusts. The persons so chosen, whose number may vary from ten to thousands, are then alone qualified to give evidence officially before the qāḍī, and to supply him with the materials on which his decision will be based. They are the persons, in fact, who study the facts of the case, and the evidence they give, while it may be gathered from the study of the documents or from personal and accidental observation of the facts, is more frequently the sum of convictions formed after an inquiry into which public gossip enters to an alarming extent. The two legal witnesses have come to fill the rôle of assessors to the qāḍī. They occupy the position of counsellors and, in their relations with the public, that of registrars of contracts and drawers of writs, in fact of notaries and clerks of court. In certain circumstances, in criminal cases for example, the qāḍī may be compelled to accept the evidence ot eyewitnesses, and even of women, although their evidence has only half the value of that given by a man.

The qāḍī was appointed by the caliph or his representative in the province, the sulṭān, governor, or grand qāḍī. The qāḍī, in his turn, nominated deputies (*ḥākim*, plur. *ḥukkām*) to act for him in his several capacities. All those people had to have the complex qualities that constitute the *'adāla*, worthiness to be a judge. The Doctrine told that the qāḍīs of ancient times had a perfect knowledge of the canon law, but that, later on, it was not possible to find a sufficient number of men possessing an adequate knowledge of the fine points of detail which the four orthodox cults had decided in different ways: and so it came about that it was accepted that, after all, knowledge of the law by a qāḍī was a matter of secondary importance, and that, in addition to a few sound principles, his essential qualifications were honesty and good sense. He could make up for want of knowledge of the law by choosing learned counsellors, or by delaying judgment until he was provided with the reasoned opinion of an acknowledged juridical expert. Cervantes, who had such a profound knowledge of Muslim life, created in Sancho Panza what is only partially a caricature of the Andalusian judge, and the cases of which he made him judge are drawn from Arab folklore. The virtues of the qāḍī must manifest themselves by a perfection of behaviour which forbids him to take part in over-sumptuous feasts, to attend gatherings for singing or gambling, and to frequent circles of doubtful reputation. The popular opinion is that his duties tempt him to error, and therefore expose him to the risk of hell-fire, and the saying of Saḥnūn is current: "to perform his duties is to have one's throat cut without the use of a knife". This is given as the explanation of the customary stubborn refusal to accept the post of qāḍī.

The qāḍī was not paid for his work, but the instruction not to accept gifts, which is repeated on each appointment, is a proof that the custom was a common one. Later, he was permitted to receive a salary charged on the funds of the *ḥubūs*, and to take a share of the fees paid by litigants.

In olden days no special building was set aside for the court of the qāḍī. His sittings were held at first in the mosque or in his house, and he could even hold court on the public highway. The hall which was later reserved for his audiences, the *mahkama* (magh. *mahakma*), is usually an annex to the mosque. The qāḍī has assistants (*'awn*), "sergeants", "ushers", who summon the parties and keep order in court.

His decisions are of the nature of an arbitration and merely entitle the winning party to take redress as he may. Even in criminal matters they are only a judgment between parties. It is the injured person or the legal representative of the person who has been murdered or injured who presents the case to the judge.

When the crime is a voluntary act, murder, or wounding which is of such a nature that the same treatment can be practised on the assailant, the right of vengeance may be exercised. It is the victim or his authorised representative who, after trial by the judge, takes his revenge under the judge's supervision. But it is necessary that the criminal be capable of exercising his civil rights, and that he have the same social status as the victim. There is no *qiṣāṣ* if one of the parties is, for example, a Christian, and the other a Muslim, or if one is the father of the other.

When the legal conditions necessary to render the *qiṣāṣ* possible are not present, or when the victim relinquishes his right, a pecuniary indemnity (*dīya*) must be allocated, the amount of which varies with the gravity of the circumstances surrounding the crime. The indemnity for the murder of a man was fixed by the Sunna at a hundred camels or something equivalent. For wounds, the judge decides the amount of the indemnity by calculating the depreciation of the mercantile value of the victim caused by the crime supposing he had been a slave. The *dīya* for a crime committed against a woman is half that given for a man; the *dīya* of a Jew or Christian is one-third that of a Muslim.

In the Umayyad period, in Egypt, the payment of the *dīya* was imposed by the administration. The qāḍī, having heard the complaint, remitted the case to an expert who determined the gravity of the wound, fixed the amount to be paid accordingly, and informed the *dīwān* of the army. A reduction of the relevant amount was made from the pension of the guilty person and applied for the benefit of the injured man's family (*'ashīra*). In certain circumstances the qāḍī may put the plaintiff as well as the defendant on oath.

The tributary and the *musta'min* foreigner normally seek justice from their special magistrates, but they may in all cases have recourse to the qāḍī who, in the opinion of most authorities, may refuse to hear them. But he alone is competent if a Muslim has an interest in the case. The qāḍī judges by Muslim law alone, and cannot accept pleas concerning an unlawful thing, such as pork or wine for example. The criminal law is valid against the foreigner as well as in his favour, except for the crime of using wine.

No matter to which of the four Sunnite rites the qāḍī may belong, he must judge the case according to the decisions of jurists of the rite which the parties profess. In large towns it became necessary to give to each rite a special qāḍī, provided it had a sufficient number of adherents. It is inadmissible for a Sunnite to receive justice from a heretical judge, Shī'ite or Khārijite. The question arose in an acute form in Egypt under the Fāṭimid caliphs, who, although they appointed Shī'ite qāḍīs and organised an active propaganda in favour of their doctrines, were compelled to retain Ḥanafite qāḍīs.

We must not forget either that the qāḍī is a delegate of the power of the caliphate, and that, in his person, the spiritual and the temporal are combined, that he is at once a religious personage and a layman, and that he must, because of those facts, conform fully to the doctrine professed by the imām of the Muslim community.

The grave religious crisis which stirred Islam during the second half of the 8th century and the greater part of the 9th, had serious effects on the careers of the qāḍīs. The charge of Dualism, of Manichaeism, and, vaguely, of impiety, which was contained in the word *zindīq*, and which was brought against so many important personalities belonging to 'Abbāsid circles, does not appear to have been levelled at the heads of the qāḍīs. But, when Mu'tazilism, which had abandoned the traditional position of the *fiqh*, became, under Al-Ma'mūn, the doctrine of the Muslim community, a great number of qāḍīs refused to accept it and the caliph commanded that they should be made to swear an oath of conformity that took the popular form of an adhesion to the principle of a created Qur'ān. This inquisition (*miḥna*), which operated in the contrary sense in the period of Al-Mutawakkil (847–861), was pursued with great brutality against numerous qāḍīs whom their enemies hastened to denounce to the agents of the caliphate. Everything about the qāḍī, even his dress, is designed to mark the fact that he is the delegate of the caliph: he wears his colours. Under the 'Abbāsids he was clothed in black with the official embroidery, but he appears to have worn those garments only on great occasions. But it was white that was generally adopted for the clothing of jurists (*fuqahā'*). For the celebration of the Friday Prayer in the name of the Prince, the qāḍī donned his official garments. Many pages of Muslim history show qāḍīs occupying the highest positions in the State, as viziers, generals in the army of Sicily, princes in Seville.

The complexity of the canon law, which had become much more involved in the course of time, had produced a multiplication of works of jurisprudence with which the judges found it more and more difficult to become acquainted. As their usual counsellors were inefficient, the qāḍīs, and most Muslims with them, had recourse to a few men who enjoyed a reputation for learning, and who gave legal consultations (*fatwā*); important personages in Spain were seen to ask for *fatwā* of a *faqīh* from Qairūwān, the stronghold of Mālikite law. Those givers of *fatwā*, those *muftī*, became, by princely decision, official interpreters of the canon law. There was, in Constantinople, a great *muftī* who became chief justice. The title and the function, although with greatly weakened authority, still exist in the Muslim world. In Algeria, at Tlemcen, fifty years ago, the qāḍī represented the Hadri clan, that of the Arabo-Berbers, and the *muftī* the Coulongli clan, that of the Turco-Berbers. The former was a Mālikite, the latter a Ḥanafite; altogether influential rivals.

The patriarchal and narrowly canonical manner of the qāḍī's jurisdiction led, in course of time, to a restriction of his field of action. Custom, followed by the Doctrine, allowed the qāḍī, as we have pointed out, to apply arbitrary penalties to crimes of less gravity than those mentioned in the Qur'ān, penalties that were more lenient than those inflicted by law, and which were called, for that reason, *ta'zīr*, or reprimands. But social life had been too profoundly changed for the ruler not to insist on having permanent and direct control of the means of preserving law and order among the people. As early as the time of the Umayyads we note the emergence of a chief of police (*ṣāḥib al-shurṭa*), who was, at one and the same time, the person who executed the judgments of the qāḍī in matters of Qur'ānic criminal law, and the judge of an indeterminate number of minor offences which he punished summarily. He also kept a watch on criminals, whom he sought out and eventually brought before the qāḍī. This new jurisdiction passed, in the course of a history that has not yet been written, into the hands of the local governor, the *ṣāḥib al-madīna*, the qā'id, the *pasha* of the Turkish administration. Its "lay" character must not be exaggerated; in Islam we never find the temporal clearly distinguished from the spiritual, but it covers matters that do not come into the province of the *sharī'a*, that is, within the competence of the qāḍī.

Whereas minor offences were, for the most part, brought within the competence of the chief of police, other offences, and certain specified infractions of the law, were dealt with by a special magistrate, the *muḥtasib*. He appears for the first time in the 8th century with very extensive but well-defined powers: offences involving weights and measures, markets and workshops, the quality of foodstuffs, that of manufactured goods, trade corporations, prostitutes of both sexes, taverns and the drinking of wine, games of chance, the freedom of, and the maintenance of good order on, the public highway, the condition of buildings from the point of view of preventing interference with the life of the community, and, in a general way, public morals and behaviour. They were the same as the powers of the Roman Curule Aedile, and it cannot be doubted that the *muḥtasib* inherited that official's functions indirectly through his Byzantine counterpart, the agoranome. He fitted admirably into the Muslim framework, since the Qur'ān condemned all kinds of fraud, and instructed each of the faithful to "command the good and forbid the evil" (*al-amr bil ma'rūf wal-nahy 'an al-munkar*), a formula which became, in the 11th century, the accepted definition of the *muḥtasib's* function, which was the *ḥisba*, that is to say, the upholding of public honesty and decency. The jurisdiction of the *muḥtasib* is clearly based on the canon law (*sharī'a*); he is an assistant to the qāḍī.

Muslim law recognises two categories of crime. The first are of human and private nature; they are subject to the law of the talio and of ransom. The second class includes theft, brigandage, extra-marital sexual relations, apostasy, wine drinking. In neither class does the penalty wipe out the offence, for that will receive its punishment in the next world; it may be expiated, however, by a course of conduct (*kaffāra*) which no earthly authority can enforce, and the fruits of which can be gathered only in a future life.

The crimes dealt with by the Qur'ān carry definite penalties (*ḥadd*, plur. *ḥudūd*). It is interesting to note that, in Islam, as in most of the communities of antiquity, theft (*sirqa*) is severely punished. Ordinary theft consists in seizing by surprise something that is in the possession of another and has a certain value. It used to be punished by cutting off the right hand; in case of any repetition of the offence, the left foot was removed, after that the left hand, and lastly the right foot. Anecdotes found here and there in Arab literature seem to prove that the police of the larger towns carried out those penalties in brutal fashion, although the Doctrine had attached to them conditions which ought to have made them the exception rather than the rule. Armed robbery or brigandage was punished with death, but here again the Doctrine subjected the strict enforcement of the penalty to various conditions. Since 1858 the Turkish penal code has dealt with theft on the lines of European legislation. The Qur'ānic law on theft and brigandage has been almost completely forgotten by the Muslim world of today. It had been gradually displaced by the decisions of successive police chiefs or pashas, as well as by the "reprimand" (*ta'zīr*) of the qāḍī as applied to minor offences. The *ta'zīr*, according to one writer, varied with the social status of the accused: in the case of great men and notabilities it was a discreet warning uttered by a delegate of the qāḍī; *fuqahā'* and suchlike were called into his presence and admonished; merchants went to prison, and the common people received the lash.

Female adultery, in pre-Islamic society, was punishable by summary patriarchal justice only in so far as it was tortious. The Qur'ān adopted a Judaeo-Christian view in declaring all extra-marital sexual relations to be criminal. The man, as well as the woman, may be given a hundred strokes of the whip, and the reintroduction of the Jewish penalty of stoning is attributed to 'Umar. The Doctrine provided for stoning in the case of persons who are *muḥṣan*, who have lived, that is, in the bonds of legal matrimony, and applies it to sodomy as well. But, in practice, the law on *zinā'* is inoperative; the Qur'ān requires the evidence of four persons who were present when the act charged was committed and, in addition, it condemns to a hundred strokes of the whip the informer who cannot prove the truth of his accusation. The offender must accuse himself and do it with insistence. It should not be forgotten that all this is inscribed in the holy book when describing the adventure of 'Ā'isha lost in the desert, then found and brought back to Medina by a Bedouin. In Muslim life in the past, as in that of today, when a woman commits adultery, the husband or the head of the family does away with her. This is a common cause of murders that the courts punish only in so far as such punishment is sanctioned by the moral code of the people.

Apostasy (*ridda*), besides the pains of eternity, is punished by death. Although no Qur'ānic punishment (*ḥadd*) is provided for it, it is a crime against the "law of God" (*fī ḥaqqi llāh*). *Murtadd* may be excused only if it has been violently forced on the delinquent, and provided he has kept his faith in his heart. The culprit must be exhorted during three days to return to Islam. The abandonment of this penalty in doctrinal teaching is, in practice, compensated for by assassination.

The prohibition of wine drinking was decreed by the Qur'ān only after a period of wavering. Pre-Islamic Arabs drank wine and got drunk on it. It was the favourite drink at the 'Abbāsid court and in the city. The populace drank chiefly date wine (*nabīdh*). In principle, the prohibition applies to all fermented and intoxicating beverages (*sakar*). The offender is punished with eighty strokes of the whip according to the Sunnites, with forty according to the Shī'ites. In the history of Muslim social life the campaign against wine is one of the repeated themes of reformers who, in the name of the *ḥisba*, seek out the drinkers and break their wine jars.

There exists a considerable *ḥisba* literature, the publication and study of which have already begun, and which includes two kinds of treatise. One consists of the works of jurists having a purely dogmatic character, and are only of minor interest. The other group is made up of edicts of a sort which were handed on from *muḥtasib* to *muḥtasib* and contain a minute regulation of social and economic life in conformity with local customs; they are documents which will be of the greatest possible value for a future history of the trade and industry of the Muslim countries.

A certain confusion prevailed between those different jurisdictions, their respective scope not being clearly defined. In the absence of courts of appeal a litigant who was dissatisfied with one magistrate's decision could take his case to another magistrate, provided the decision of the first had not been carried out. It was also possible to claim damages for an unjust decision by application to a special magistrate called *nāẓir al-maẓālim*. A final appeal to the caliph was always possible.

During the 19th century most of the Muslim states abandoned the complicated judicial organisation of the classical period. For the *sharī'a* Turkey had, in each administrative division (*liva*), a qāḍī, acting under the supervision of the supreme muftī, the *shaykh al-islām*. The two principal magistrates were the *qāḍī 'askar* of Rumelia and Anatolia; criminal justice was the business of the *sūbāshī* and the *muḥtasib*. In 1874, courts of general jurisdiction and commercial courts left only the pure *sharī'a* to be dealt with by the qāḍīs, who were suppressed in 1924. To Egypt, under Mehemet Ali, the Sulṭān of Istānbūl sent each year a qāḍī and an assistant (*nā'ib*). Minor cases were judged by the latter or by a witness (*'adl*); important cases came before the qāḍī sitting with the *nā'ib* and the *muftī*, who gave a *fatwā* to the plaintiff. Criminal jurisdiction was dealt with by the *dīwān*, the chief of police and the *muḥtasib*. In the last quarter of the 19th century, a general reform set up civil and criminal courts with a bench of three judges, the *muftī* having supreme authority. Iran also knew the dual system of *sharī'a* and "lay" courts; the competence of the former was restricted in 1928 and, since 1931, there remains only the court of the *mujtahid*, to which the ordinary courts refer cases of a peculiarly canonical kind. In North Africa the jurisdiction of the qāḍī is confined to purely "Qur'ānic" cases, marriage, succession, etc. Appeal courts have everywhere been set up. Similar developments have taken place in other parts of the Muslim world.

SOURCES

Tyan: *Organisation Judiciaire* Chapters I and II (S.90); Gaudefroy-Demombynes: *Notes sur l'Organisation Judiciaire* (Rev. Et. Islam, 1939), (S.90); *Journal Asiatique* and *Journal des Savants*, 1947 and 1948.

CHAPTER ELEVEN

SOCIAL LIFE

Childhood; Circumcision; Education; Teaching—Housing—Games—The Hammām—Feasts—Costume—Sickness: Hospitals—Death: Burial, Tombs—Morals.

THE life of the Muslim peoples, varying so greatly from one period to another and from one country to another, has always been, and is still, enlivened by a series of ceremonies and practices which are common to all Islam. They will be the subject of this chapter.

Popular credulity still encourages belief in the caprices of Nature, and accepts the legend that the child sleeps in his mother's womb for four years after her husband has parted from her. The Doctrine has rejected such things.

The birth of a son is, for the Arab family, a joyful event; a daughter is not so well received. In pursuance of a pre-Islamic custom, the meaning of which is not clear, and which is condemned by the Qur'ān, daughters were sometimes buried alive immediately after birth. Prophetic Tradition sanctioned the ancient usage by which a birth was celebrated by the shaving of the head and the offering of a living sacrifice. On the seventh day after the birth, two sheep or goats were sacrificed and their flesh given to the poor. At the same time alms were given in the form of a quantity of silver equal to the weight of the infant's hair which was ceremoniously removed. The ceremony as a whole has kept its old name: *'aqīqa*. Immediately after the child is born it is considered to be a good thing to repeat the words of the call to prayer (*adhān*) into the child's right ear, and those of the *iqāma* into his left ear, so as to accustom him to the Muslim confession of faith.

It is recommended that a name should be given to the child on the seventh day, but this ceremony may take place either sooner or later. The name (*ism*) varies in different parts of the

Muslim world, for, alongside of the specially Islamic—that is, Arabic—stock, old local Persian, Turkish or Berber names, are still in use, not to mention the names of saints, whose influence extends over a wide area: Shu'ayb and Bū Medien are current in Orania, around the sanctuary of Sīdī Bū Medien at El-Eubbad near Tlemcen; Jilālī and Jalūl are as common as the qubbas of Sīdī 'Abd al-Qādir al-Jilālī. The principal truly Muslim names are those of the Prophet: Aḥmad, Muḥammad (also pronounced Mehemet and Mahammed), Muṣṭafā (Mostfa); of members of his family: 'Alī, Ḥasan, Ḥusayn; of the prophets and high personalities of Muslim tradition: Ibrāhīm (Brahim), Mūsā, Ismā'īl, Sulaymān, Dā'ūd, Isḥāq, Abū Bakr, 'Umar, 'Uthmān; finally 'Abd Allāh, (*'Abdu llāhi*). "Servant of God", and the variants in which the name of God is replaced by one of his ninety-nine appellations: al-Qādir, al-Raḥmān, al-Salām, al-Razzāq, al-Ḥamīd, al-'Azīz, al-Ḥaqq, etc.

The name of the child is completed by the addition of that of the father, Aḥmad ibn Muḥammad, and by other elements as well: first by a *kunya* which reproduces the name of the first son after the word "father of": Abu l-Qāsim (Muḥammed), Abū-Uthmān, Abū Tāshfīn, etc.; the whole may be a name famous in history which is given to the child *en bloc*: Abu l-Ḥasan 'Alī. It may also be a nickname, *laqab*: Nūr al-dīn (light of the faith), Bū Baghla (the mule man), Bū 'Amāma (the man with the turban), al-Aswad (the black), etc. ; or else an attribute, *nisba*: al-Ṣabbāgh (the dyer), al-Baghdādī (the man of Bagdad), al-Madanī (the man of Medina), etc. Daughters receive the names of the women of the family of the Prophet, Khadīja, Fāṭima, 'Ā'isha, Zaynab, etc., either in their original form or as diminutives; or they may be names of attributes or of flowers, etc.: Mabrūka (blessed), Maḥbūba (beloved), Sharīfa (noble), Māmīya, Zīna, etc.

The young child belongs entirely to the women: when able to do so the mother feeds it for two years. In all classes the child is the object of much love and tender care. The mother's chief anxiety is to protect it from the evil eye: it is with a view to protecting it from the glance of an evil jinn that many well-to-do families keep the child dirty and ill clad. A laudatory phrase which boasts imprudently of the child's good health or beauty is most dangerous and, as soon as it is uttered, the evil effect of it must be conjured away by a propitiatory gesture or expression.

Circumcision is a rite which is very strictly observed throughout the whole Muslim world, although it is not prescribed by the Qur'ān. It is practised, either on the seventh day, or on the fortieth, or in the seventh year, that is, at the beginning of the second period of life. The accompanying ceremonies vary from country to country. It may be remarked that they often show a similarity with marriage ceremonies: both are "transitionary rites". They used to be celebrated, like marriages, at a favourable time of year; it was the custom for the Prince to give presents.

Little boys are brought up by the women until the age of seven years. At that date he begins his life as a man, either by helping his father with his work as a herdsman, a farmer or an artisan, or by beginning the study of the Qur'ān at school (*maktab*, *kuttāb*, *msid*); but the latter is the lot only of a very few. At school he used to learn, and still learns today in many Muslim countries, to read and then to write down the Holy Book by a mechanical effort of the memory. On a small wooden board (*lauḥa*), covered with white clay or chalk slaked in water, he tries to reproduce a passage from the Qur'ān which has been given him as a model, and which he afterwards learns by heart, without any attempt being made by anyone to give him an understanding of its meaning, which would, in any case, be beyond his childish understanding: at least he acquires the rhythm and intonation of it. When the text that has filled a single board is fixed in his memory it is wiped out and a new one takes its place. When the pupil has learned a part of the Qur'ān, *ḥizb* or *juz'*, his family gives a feast for the master and the pupils. A more important ceremony (*khatma*) is celebrated when the young man has put the seal on his knowledge of the Qur'ān and has therefore become a *ḥāfiẓ*. Ibn Jubayr reproduces for our benefit the *khuṭba* that the young *ḥāfiẓ* preached on the evenings of Ramaḍan in the 13th century in the mosque of Medina, and which were followed by a banquet given by the father.

Already in the 14th century, Ibn Khaldūn was protesting against this method of teaching, then prevalent in the Muslim West, and was boasting of the superiority of Oriental methods by which the teaching of the art of writing was separated from instruction in the Qur'ān. Depending on the learning and good will of masters, self-trained and self-appointed, and whose claims to efficiency might or might not be supported by public opinion, some notions of grammar and arithmetic were added to the programme. With many children a natural gift for understanding the mechanics of the language, it could almost be called a philological sense, enabled them to achieve a satisfactory education in spite of the very rudimentary nature of its beginnings.

Furnished with this knowledge, the young man enters upon his initiation into the "Arab sciences" (*'ilm*, plur. *'ulūm*): the commentaries on the Qur'ān (*tafsīr*), the Tradition (*ḥadīth*), law (*fiqh*), the principles (*uṣūl al-dīn'* and *uṣūl al-fiqh*), grammar (*naḥw*), lexicography (*lugha*), rhetoric (*bayān*), literature (*adab*).

Here once more it was the memory that was chiefly developed; the young scholar was already well prepared to absorb learning in its most impersonal form. The teaching took place in the master's house or, preferably, in the mosque; the young man seated himself in his place in the circle (*ḥalqa*) of pupils who surrounded the master, who sat with his back to a pillar, or squatted on a little platform (*kursī*). A passage from a classical book was read and the master explained it; a few notes were taken; but it was above all the memory that was required to retain the text and the commentary. The curriculum was arranged as the teacher thought best: assiduous and capable listeners received his authority to repeat his lessons in another city, a *licencia docendi* (*ijāza*). In this way some of the books of distinguished masters were circulated, and their teachings diffused throughout the Muslim world.

This organisation, well known to our western Middle Ages, and not without merit, had, in the East, been extended and given a wider scope. 'Abbāsid caliphs opened "Houses of the Tradition" (*dār al-ḥadīth*); Al-Ma'mūn founded a "House of Knowledge" (*dār al-'ilm*), which the Fāṭimites subsequently imitated in Egypt, and of which the Mosque of Al-Azhar is an illustrious survival. This "University" of Cairo has been copied in the West, in the Zaītūna of Tunis and the Qarawīyān of Fez.

In the 11th and 12th centuries certain rulers, Niẓām

al-Mulk, Nūr al-dīn Zangī, Saladin, and others besides, founded schools of canon law (*fiqh*), which were seminaries for the study of the practice of religion and the orthodox Sunnite doctrine, which was then in process of replacing the prevailing Shī'ism. These *madrasa* (*medresse, medersa* in the Maghrib) gave to the already so influential corporation of the *fuqahā'* an organised doctrine and a coherent origin. The first founders of *madrasa* made certain of their permanence by setting up *ḥubūs*, and fixed the number of teachers as well as the nature of their teaching; and, as they were Shāfi'ites, the canon law was taught at first in conformity with the tenets of that cult. Later on, the other rites had their own *madrasa*. The Mamlūk sulṭān Baybars appears to have been the first to create the pattern of *madrasa* that included within its walls all four rites; the buildings were given the shape of a four-leafed clover. The *madrasa* marked a distinct progress in organisation, but a retrogression in the development of a general culture: it confirmed the contraction of Muslim thought.

Parallel with this State education, initiative groups, Ikhwān al-Ṣafā', Qarmaṭs, Ismā'īlians, had had their own schools. Ṣūfism developed its schools in conformity with the several tendencies that gave it its strength. The extension of the houses of the Ṣūfī (*ribāṭ, khānaqāh, takya, zāwia*) from the 11th century onwards, popularised their teachings, while preserving their monastic character. Certain *zāwias* of North Africa are fairly good models of those pious dwellings, in which was maintained, along with the special practices of the rite, a body of teaching intended to promote the interests of general Muslim culture. They also gave guidance in political and social matters.

. . . . .

The little girl is the natural assistant to the mistress of the house; as soon as she is fit for it, she shares, in the country, the rude labours of the women; in the cities, she runs errands for so long as she is not veiled, and, in the families in which the women are artisans, she learns their trade. But, on the whole, there is a reluctance to teach girls trades; their great business is marriage. In the classical period of Muslim society we find cultured women in the upper classes of the 'Abbāsid world. But, as was the case in ancient Greece, it was slaves and freed women who, in addition to their charms, were skilled in the arts of song, music, and the dance; they were sometimes even given an extensive education. The "Book of Songs" (*Aghānī*) gives examples of such, and "Tawaddud the Learned Woman" is one of the tales of the Arabian Nights. Women in general were not even allowed to study the Qur'ān.

. . . . .

In the Islamic world of today there is a striking contrast between the traditional institutions and those of quite modern origin that exist alongside them. This contrast is particularly sharp in education. The Qur'ānic schools are still there, and children, their board in hand, still swing their bodies in time to their chanting; teachers still give lessons in the mosques; the old universities still attract studious crowds, and, although modernised in some respects, still preserve their ancient traditional appearance and manners; even the medersas of the Maghrib, however completely they may have changed, remain schools of the canon law. And, fronting those houses of learning that are ten centuries behind the times, rise "houses of knowledge" as modern as any that can be found in Europe. In North Africa all classes of French schools are open to Muslims. Turkey has given itself a completely modernised educational system in three grades; Egypt, Syria, Iraq, have not only good primary schools, but have made an excellent beginning in secondary education; the University of Cairo, before the war, was making brilliant progress. In Muslim India the universities of Aligarh and Haiderabad are active centres of culture, supported by a well-organised system of elementary and secondary education. The existence alongside each other of such contrasting environments causes, among the different classes of the nation concerned, a disequilibrium that is not without its effect on social life.

A widespread woman's movement is leading women to take a share in the development of education. The younger generation of men have been feeling the disadvantages of the traditional upbringing of their wives. During the past century some of the latter had been able to get a useful education in Christian schools, where they had sat on the same benches with Catholic and Protestant girls. In the last few years national schools for girls have been founded in more than one country; in Turkey and elsewhere secondary education is making progress; and, both in the East and in the West, higher education is being made available to Muslim students.

A young man marries when almost twenty years of age. The nature of his married life varies endlessly, from that of the patriarchal family, all the members of which remain united during the life of the family head, to that of the completely modern couple with their own household. Housing conditions reflect this diversity: an ultra-modern mansion or flat with electricity installed, the sprawling palace sheltering several branches of one family, the classical Mediterranean dwelling, a tent, a hut, a troglodyte cave.

Of the palaces of the caliphs and other great men there remains only the memory that literature preserves for us. At the two ends of Islam, both of space and of time, there remain the castles of the Umayyads in Syria, and the palace of the Naṣrids, the Alhambra (*al-ḥamrā'*, the red) at Granada. The fragments which still stand at Mshatta, at Quṣayr 'Amra, at Quṣayr al-Ḥāir, etc., witness to the past existence of buildings so perfect and so grandiose, that archaeologists have difficulty in believing that they are not of Sāsānid origin. The real heirs of the kings of kings, the 'Abbāsids, have left of the edifices which they built of fragile materials, and which were doubtless more charming than imposing, nothing but the vast and tall pavilion in which they had the room for their official receptions (*īwān*), and the traditional architecture of which is Iranian. The residences of the caliphs consisted of isolated pavilions, placed here and there in gardens, among lakes that reflected the trees, and brooks fringed with banks that were beds of flowers; belvederes on the Tigris, frail edifices whose splendour lay in their decorations in the shape of mosaics, pierced stucco, frescoes, emphasised by the brilliance of the hangings that adorned the walls, and the carpets underfoot; all short-lived things. Each prince, too, erected his own pavilions, leaving those of his predecessor to their fate. In them he sought the pleasures of a day; in Summer the walls of his room were of felt moistened with water, or maybe they were covered with melting snow.

Arabia (The Ḥijāz, Yaman), even before Islam, knew houses of several floors, citadels that it was easy to defend against the simple weapons of the Bedouin. Underground rooms gave shelter from extremes of temperature. Among several types of dwelling inhabited by the average Muslim, the Mediterranean house on a single floor is still the commonest. A small hall, open to the entrance door, presents to the visitor a bench on which to rest while waiting till a man belonging to the household, or an ancient serving-maid, leads him through a winding passage into the rectangular court, of which a water pool occupies the centre, and in which a few bushes grow. Cloisters, with their clinging vines, surround it: on to it open the doors and narrow windows of the rooms; one of them, wider and deeper than the others, extends, in the dwellings of the rich, two arms in the shape of a T, forming a *līwān*. Everywhere recesses in the walls form alcoves, are made into cupboards, or fitted with shelves. In one corner a stairway leads up to the terraces on which is sometimes found an upper room; the terrace is the women's domain and a place of refuge on summer nights. Externally the walls are bare, pierced at most by a few windows that are not made to open. The interior is well screened from the eyes of passers-by, and defended against inopportune intrusions. The furniture is sketchy: a few boxes that the carpenter and the painter have covered with naïve designs, some mattresses, mats and carpets; occasional hangings on walls and doors; articles of everyday use, metal ewers, earthenware vases, all of which, whether of fine quality or commonplace, have retained their ancient nobility of form.

The menfolk are hardly ever at home in the day-time; they seek the day's supplies, go to their shops or workshops, attend to their business affairs, gossip in the streets, the sūq, or the tavern. Much card playing is indulged in today around the shores of the Mediterranean; in earlier days, and in spite of the prohibition of the ḥadīth that supplemented the Qur'ān, games of chance of many kinds were played on a draught board; a few authorities tolerate chess because of the absence of the element of chance and the royal tradition that India and Persia have given it. No legal prohibition has been able, down the centuries, to suppress the taste for horse racing and for betting, any more than that for pigeon racing and cock-fighting. Many great men have taken pride in their menageries.

Physical sports have their place in the life, not only of the child, but of the youth. Wrestling is much practised. The game of football with two opposing teams retains its popularity and its magic character. We see the sling employed in the childish battles which are also traditional ceremonies. During the great feasts there are games of skill at the *'Umra* in Mecca as well as at marriages, circumcisions, etc.

The ancient texts recommend the learning of the art of swimming, a surprising thing, perhaps, in a country like Arabia, where there are only irrigation tanks. There are, however, sudden and terrible floods. The hot bath is not of Arab invention; the conquering armies found it in Syria and adopted the custom, a course which, in addition to its sanitary merits, fell in admirably with the obligation of legal purity (*ṭahāra*) imposed on Muslims. But true believers at first manifested their disapproval of those buildings, the entrance to which was guarded by unchaste statues, and whose walls were adorned with pictures of still greater immodesty; none the less, statues and paintings continued to exist through several centuries of Islam. The lay-out of the baths varies only in detail, and the very needs that they supply ensure their practical identity with the baths of Rome. Out of the entrance hall opens a cool chamber, in which stone benches covered with mattresses or carpets await customers, as they issue from the bath. The owner (*mu'allim*) is there, behind his counter covered with coffee cups; then comes a second room, warmed for undressing and for rest in winter, and used specially as intermediate between the cold room and the *tepidarium*, the *ḥarāra*, which is the sweating room, and is surrounded by several small subsidiary rooms in which the bathers find hot and cold water. The customer is massaged and soaped by a bath attendant in the *ḥarāra* or in one of the small rooms. Passing back through the intermediate chamber, he stays there to rest in Winter, or, if it be Summer, he goes straight to the cool room (*maslakh*). The women of a household take great pleasure in hiring a bath for the afternoon and there making festival with their female relatives and friends. Rich people used to have a *ḥammām* in the house.

The celebration of feast days occupies a great place in Muslim life. The two principal feasts are the anniversary of the sacrifice of the pilgrimage, and that of the breaking of the fast. The Great Feast (*'īd al-aḍḥā, 'īd al-qurbān, al-'īd al-kabīr,* in Turkish, *büyük bayram*) commemorates the 10th of *dhu l-ḥijja,* the day of the *naḥr* which, at Minā, marks the end of the ceremonies of the pilgrimage; each family offers up, in accordance with the ritual, a camel or a sheep, which then becomes the basis of a banquet in which the poor have their share. The Little Feast (*'īd al-fiṭr, al 'īd al-ṣaghīr, kübük bayram*) celebrates the first day of the month of *shawwāl.* For both, the faithful, if they have the means, put on new clothes in order to take part in a solemn prayer with *khuṭba,* held in the *muṣallā* outside the town; they exchange presents and congratulations with handshaking, as the *ḥadīth* advises. The feast of the birth of the Prophet (*mīlād, maulūd* in the Maghrib) is celebrated throughout the whole Muslim world on the 10th of *rabī'* I; it seems to date only from the 10th century and to have become official only in the 12th. 'Āshūrā', which succeeded the Jewish feast of *tishri,* was raised to the status of a feast, and has acquired carnivalesque rites, especially in the Berber country. On the same date, the Shī'ites celebrated the anniversary of the death of Ḥusayn at Karbalā' (672) by the performance of a Passion (*ta'ziya*) and with processions, in the course of which fanatical worshippers beat their bodies and faces until the blood flowed. Other feasts are peculiar to the Shī'ites: the proclamation of the pool (*ghadīr al-khumm*); the death of Salmān, the 15th of sha'bān, etc., and ancient solar feasts in Persia, the Naurūz (1st January), and the Mihrjān (Autumn). In all parts of the Muslim world there are added to the official celebrations, rites, often more enthusiastically observed than they themselves are, associated with the anniversaries of saints (*mūsem* in the Maghrib), and which are usually survivals of ancient religions and seasonal rites. The qubbas of the saints are the objects of frequent excursions by the women, who carry thither their offerings.

The feasts provide an opportunity for demonstrating the resources of a cuisine that is governed by local custom. The *ḥadīth* attempted to enforce the observance of Muslim rules by noting the likes and dislikes of the Prophet; at least it gave the force of law to the customs that fix the standard of conduct during meals. Around low wooden tables or heavy trays or salvers made of earthenware or copper, the guests seat themselves, and help themselves with spoon or hand from the hand of the host, without the use of plates. The rich begin to show a liking for European crockery. Cooking resists outside influence more vigorously than is the case with dress. If the clothing of the Bedouin and the peasant (*fallāḥ*) preserves its ancient appearance, shirt or tunic (*qamīṣ*), drawers (*sirwāl*), a cloak enveloping the shoulders and body (*ridā'*, *haīk*); if legal officials, qāḍīs, muftīs, imāms, fuqahā', still wear the classic garments, over which are thrown elegant white draperies; if a part of the town population still remains faithful to the baggy trousers, waistcoats, jackets, and embroidered caftans of fine, delicately coloured cloth beneath a grey mantle; if manual workers still, and especially in the Maghrib, don those convenient "overcoats", the *burnus* and the *jallāba*, the generality, whether rich or poor, are more and more adopting European costume, which is doubtless more practical, less costly, and less durable; and most unfortunate from the point of view of the beauty of the silhouettes and colours of a Muslim street.

The majority of city women adhere to the classic costume, the heaviness of which is relieved by harmony of colour and charm of carriage: it is understood that they show it only to their quite close male relatives and to other women. Outside the home a heavy enveloping wrap conceals all trace of personality. European fashions, with the suppression or diminution of the veil, are invading the Orient and destroying its originality.

Jewels are, according to place and time, of great variety of form: ear-rings, diadems, necklaces, pendants, bracelets and rings. The materials used vary greatly: for the rich, gold, silver, precious stones, pearls; copper tinsel and iron for the poor. During the feasts and at a marriage a great show of jewels is demanded; from early days the hiring of jewelry was a very profitable business.

Fashions in hairdressing and in headdresses have varied greatly. The Bedouin still wear their hair long, with locks on the temples like the Jews; they wear a light turban of twisted cloth. In the cities the turban grew more complicated after the 9th century, and the *fuqahā'* increased its size until it attained truly comical proportions. The fashion of the enormous turban spread at the same time as that of the shaven head and felt cap or *shāshīya*. But, at the end of the 12th century, for example, the people of Bagdad still affect the pendant locks which they piously offer as a sacrifice to the scissors of some persuasive maker of sermons. The beard was often dyed; sometimes the hair also. The reddish-fair colour of henna was recommended in imitation of the Prophet. Today, the adoption of Western fashions is leading to an expanding use of the razor; certain surviving local rites recall the practice of shaving the head and beard of the vanquished.

The story of the early battles cannot be understood unless we remember that the weapons used were very simple: the sabre, the javelin and the lance were the three essential weapons, with the added protection of the shield and the coat of mail. 18th century Arabia had its archers, and archery has survived in some districts as a noble and traditional sport. The period of the Crusades saw the development of mechanical weapons and Greek fire. In its time the crossbow became one of the arms of the Muslim forces; then firearms.

Popular belief has kept, through the centuries, the certainty that illness is a result of the wiles of Satan, of the jinns, of wizards and witches, and that one must cure oneself by the use of magical counter-measures. But medical science, on the inspiration of the more realistic Greeks, had spread over the Orient before the conquests, and the 'Abbāsid caliphs had Christian doctors trained in the school at Gundēshāpūr. In the days of their greatness, Muslims collected, and added to, the observations of Greek medicine, and it was they who first introduced them to Europe. With them medicine was put alongside philosophy. The Orient of the 9th century (Bagdad, 794) had its hospitals, called in the beginning *bīmāristān*, "house of the insane". In the 10th century there were established in the cities hospitals founded by prominent men who provided for the payment of doctors and pharmacists and the maintenance of the sick by the creation of *ḥubūs*; the 12th century brought the *mustashfā*, "place of healing". In the

10th century an Iranian doctor tried to regulate the profession of medicine.

Death is also surrounded by rites, of which some are prescribed by the canon, and others, survivals of ancient customs, are inconsistent with the Sunna. When a sick person's family foresees his approaching end, they turn his head to face the *qibla*, and recite the *shahāda* in his name. The body is washed in accordance with the requirements of the greater ablution (*ghusl*) by two persons of the same sex as the deceased, and possessing a knowledge of the rites; the *ghassāl* or *mughassil* performs for him an act of piety which will be credited to him on the Judgment Day. For that reason the Doctrine looks upon any salary he may receive as an undesirable innovation (*bid'a*); the practice is to give him the deceased's clothing. The orifices of the body are closed with plugs of perfumed cotton wool, and the body itself wrapped in one or two pieces of seamless cloth; certain traditions tell that it is in this garment that the dead person will appear before God. We have already related how pilgrims take their grave clothes with them to Mecca, there to dip them in the waters of Zamzam.

Down to the moment of burial, which takes place on the same day if the death occurred in the morning, otherwise on the following morning, the women of the family maintain the traditional lamentations, *walwāl* (*wilwāl*, cf. Lat. *hululare*), in course of which they beat themselves on the face and breast, make gestures that symbolise the tearing out of the hair, scratch their cheeks and tear their clothes. The women of the neighbourhood assemble in order to take part in this rite, which includes also words in praise of the deceased. Such praise takes the form of the chanting of short rhythmical phrases of rhymed prose or verse, accompanied by the beating of a tambourine. The woman who is charged with the duty of making the funeral oration (*nādiba, naddāba*) is often endowed with real poetic talent: as in the case of the washing of the body, the pious fulfilment of the rite has come to be entrusted to professionals. Both the lamentations and the praising of the dead, of which pre-Islamic Arabia provides, in the poems of Al-Khansā', brilliant examples, are condemned by certain apparently genuine ḥadīths of the Prophet.

The body is carried to the cemetery on the trestle on which

it was washed, covered only by a cloth. Constantly changing relays of four men carry it on their shoulders, for this is a pious act which will be rewarded in the next life. At the head of the procession walk "learned" and pious persons (*fuqahā'*, *ṭulabā'*, *ikhwān* of brotherhoods, etc.), who chant the Muslim confession of faith and fragments of religious poems, the Burda of al-Būṣīrī for example. In certain countries women, contrary to the prescriptions of the Sunna, join the procession and continue the ritual lamentations.

It is generally believed that certain persons—usually important people—have difficulty in accepting the tomb that has been prepared for them. Their bearers must have recourse to a ruse in order to overcome the resistance of the dead man, which may be strong enough to bring them to a standstill, or even to force them to return.

The majority of the learned authorities disapprove of the bringing of a dead body into the mosque, although the custom persists in many parts of the Muslim world. When this is done, the rites that constitute the "Prayer for the dead" (*ṣalāt al-janāza*) are performed in the middle of the hall of prayer. In all places where the dead are excluded from the mosque, this prayer is said either in the cemetery or in a special room called *Bayt al-janā'iz*, attached to the mosque and situated behind the *miḥrāb*.

The tomb is a chamber so fashioned as to permit the body to lie on the right side, with the head pointing to Mecca and the feet pointing in the opposite direction: this *laḥd* is preceded, either on its long or its broad side, by a kind of ante-room which allows of the corpse being placed in the position required by the law.

Certain ḥadīths express disapproval of the rounded mounds which cover the tombs, and disapprove even more strongly of the monuments that crown them; both features are everywhere to be found. The custom of constructing buildings on them began to spread during the 10th century; the tombs of the Mamlūk sulṭāns in Cairo are fine examples of the numerous funerary mosques that are to be found throughout the Orient. Tombs in the cemeteries of all large towns are covered by a kind of domed chapel, a *qubba*; others are covered by a stone or brick pavement, from which rise one or more stone pillars, surmounted, in Turkey especially, by a stone turban. The tomb has generally, at head and foot, a stele of marble or stone, one having graven on it the funerary inscription, the other, verses from the Qur'ān.

All peoples have believed that their dead survived in another life in which their earthly needs would continue, and they have further believed that the articles that had been used in their households had been soiled by some evil spell. It is often difficult to know which of those two ideas survives in the custom of destroying all that had belonged to the dead. In Bagdad, in the 10th century, this practice was extended even to the boat which had borne him on the river. It is the first idea, complicated by that of the efficacy of the prayer for the dead, which preserves among Muslims certain customs that are also well known to other peoples: the funeral banquet repeated on various dates, visits paid to the cemetery accompanied by the performance of certain rites, animal sacrifices, almsgiving, etc. Mourning dress is not usually worn, but one occasionally comes across the practice of staining with blue dye certain parts of the body or articles of clothing, or that of not changing clothes for a certain period of time.

The cemetery is much frequented by Muslims, and especially by women. Although many graveyards are placed in arid spots, others grow up around the tomb of a saint and near a spring or a holy tree. Muslim settlements have frequently, in this way, cemeteries lying in the shade of dark foliage, pierced by rays of vivid light illumining the whiteness of the tombs. The women go there on Fridays and retail the gossip of the town. They bring their children with them, and one may often see the gay tones of their light-coloured garments moving towards the meeting place, while the many-coloured kites soar above the trees. Death is accepted with resignation, and the living who, apart from the compulsory rites, do not pretend to a grief that the joy of living quickly dissipates, frequent without sorrow the places of the dead, to whom they bring the tender tribute of memory.

It would be possible to attempt to give an estimate of the moral standards of Arab society in the past. A critical study of morals at various periods in Muslim history might be made, using as sources the chronicles of the historians or works of literature, such as the *maqāmāt* of Hamadhānī, the author of which poked fun at the customs of his time. The conclusion to be drawn from a study of the sort would be that, between the 8th and the 15th centuries, Muslim society was neither better nor worse than any European society at the same stage of development, a result which would be of very little interest to us. We may, however, try to take note of one or two peculiarities. Slavery, although never of a particularly odious character in the Muslim world, was the cause of the evil reputation it acquired in matters of sexual morality. The presence of young slaves and eunuchs in rich families encouraged sodomy, which was, and still is, one of the vices of Muslim society; it was so common among all classes that the Doctrine hesitated to condemn it. Meanwhile, female slavery, by providing the owner with concubines, accentuated the disorders that polygamy could not fail to provoke within the family, and yet did not rid Muslim society of prostitution. It must not be thought that prostitution was organised, on the Byzantine model, solely in the interests of foreigners, who had, moreover, at their disposal the convenient institution of the temporary marriage (*muta'*). In the 10th century the moral desirability of monogamy was being preached, but it was just then that indecency in literature was most prevalent; doubtless the East has usages and susceptibilities of its own, but, at that period, it was a matter of systematic verbal indecency.

By gradual stages the Qur'ān came to decide against the use of wine. After the conquests wine was still drunk everywhere, as had been the case before Islam. The *ḥisba* pronounced against the practice, and it was in the name of the *ḥisba* that reformers broke the wine jars in the shops. European industry, by importing its poisonous products, has transformed drunkenness into alcoholism.

The rule prohibiting men from going into the streets in the company of women or young boys, which was promulgated by the Ḥanbalites, or the command put upon women not to leave their houses, which was issued by the Fāṭimid caliph Ḥākim, do not fill the place of a moral principle. We must endeavour to explain that which guided Islam.

The society of Old Arabia had been inspired by a veiy strong feeling of *muruwwa*, "virility", that is, of the qualities that make a man fit to defend his honour (*'ird*) and that of the tribe. Islam substituted for *'ird* the *dīn*, faith, and invited the faithful "to do good and forbid evil", that is, to obey the divine commands and to abstain from, and to prevent others from doing, what God forbids. Morality and piety became one. Doubtless, the law insists on the importance of the intention (*nīya*) which leads the believer to act "for the face of God"; but it was Ṣūfism that appreciated to the full the driving force of love, and declared that love was the essential ingredient of merit in human action. The Doctrine on the other hand, has taken the secular and modern point of view, that of the public welfare, the *maṣlaḥa*, a kind of solidarity.

The maintenance of the family tie, from which is derived the force that binds together the members of the tribe, is another of the foundations of the Muslim community, one, however, which shook when Muḥammad, through the Qur'ān, enticed sons away from the faith of their fathers, just as the Christian gospel had done before him. The respect in which children hold their parents is as much a fact of Muslim life as it is a provision of the law. The Qur'ān and the Tradition have alike given attention to the proper behaviour of women (Q. 24.31). The Qur'ān prescribes justice and honesty towards all men, respect for weights and measures, fidelity to engagements and oaths, the delivery to the rightful owner of that which is received in trust, etc. No doubt historians have exaggerated the "socialism" of Muḥammad; none the less he sought the improvement of the lot of the weak and the captives, of slaves and wives, and of the widows and the orphans of the Muslim wars. There is, in Muslim society, in spite of the classes created by wealth and authority, a feeling of equality, which is curiously expressed by a certain attitude or tone that is common to all. The legal obligation of almsgiving is not an attack on the rich, it is a means of purification, a guarantee against a compensatory reaction in the life to come, in which excessive enjoyment of the things of this life will find its retribution. Moderation is one of the virtues which the Doctrine has held for merit to the Prophet, the pattern of the true believer. It is the serious disturbance of this balance which gives rise to the vice of vices, pride (*takabbur*), the vice which prevented Iblīs from bowing down before Adam as God had commanded him, and by which he was lost. The believer must avoid contempt and arrogance, and show, in all his actions, and even in his gait, humility sustained by gravity. The pride which the father feels in the number of his children is a vice of the former days. Islam condemns greed and avarice, but also the prodigality which was once a point of honour for the Arab. The Tradition insists on certain details of decorum and courtesy which have some relation to morality. All that hardly goes more than skin deep, and Muslim morality has happily been helped by the Ṣūfis and the philosophers to rise to higher things than the day to day practice of their religion, supplemented by a few modest virtues.

SOURCES

Lane: *Modern Egyptians* (S.93); Bourrily: *Ethnographie Marocaine* (S.92); Mez: *Renaissance* (S.128); W. Marçais: *Tanger, Takruna*; Bonjean and Ahmad Dyef: *Mahmoud, Enfant du Caire, Al Azhar*; Bonjean; *Une Fille de la Nuit.*

CHAPTER TWELVE

ECONOMIC LIFE

Agriculture: Farming Contracts, Irrigation Contracts—The Calendar—Commerce: Sūq, Roads, Merchants—The Working Classes: Production—Commercial Transactions: Sales, Sureties, Goods deposited on Trust—Lending to Interest.

THE economy of the Muslim countries can be dealt with here only in so far as it is dependent on the institutions of Islam. We shall have to omit, not only all that is of the present day, and that owes its existence to the changes that the past century has wrought in the material life of the world, but also those local conditions that arise out of the geographical and historical circumstances that have influenced the lives of the inhabitants of countries which, like India, the East Indies, Central Asia and Black Africa, have never really formed part of the Muslim community and were conquered for Islam at a late period. We shall, therefore, confine ourselves to brief details of the older, classical Muslim economy, within the limits of the Near East and the Mediterranean.

In a general way, the economy of those countries is pastoral and agricultural. Muslim law, which concerns itself in the first place with Arabia, deals with the ownership of domestic animals, the camels of the wealthy nomads, the sheep of the lesser folk, with asses, buffaloes, and the cultivation of palm groves and orchards, among whose trees grow patches of barley, wheat, durra, or vegetables, with the grazings of the open lands and the cultivation of oases or irrigated places. The country lives on itself as well as it can. The valley of the Nile and the Mesopotamian Sawad, with their soil enriched by floods or irrigation, are of a different sort; there we find, beside small scale intensive farming, the cultivation, by the use of colonies of slaves or half-free workers, of large estates producing abundant harvests of grain, while not neglecting the palm groves and orchards. Those lands are situated along the banks of the only navigable rivers that existed in the old territory of Islam, and the transport of produce to the numerous cities that lie on their shores is easy. The surplus is carried on camel back to the lands of the have-nots, although this trade in foodstuffs is confined to a few cereals, dates, dried fruits, and exotic spices. The provisioning of Mecca for the needs of the pilgrims necessitates the conveyance from Egypt of important quantities of barley and wheat, brought by sea to Jidda, or by caravans travelling by way of Sinaī.

The commerce of the Orient, which, from the 9th century onwards, is considerable, consists, therefore, in the exchange of the produce of foreign countries for that of local industry. The labour of the working classes of the larger Muslim cities does not supply local needs alone; local specialities provide goods for export. Goods carried by caravan in this way are small in quantity; whether produced by natives or foreigners, they are made use of by a wealthy society that is no stranger to the refinements of luxury, or else they are exchanged in the markets of Europe or of Central and Southern Asia.

The institutions of the territory reflect those two aspects of Muslim activity: the primary importance of agriculture and cattle raising, and of trade in distant lands. Muslim law concerns itself so actively with the products of the soil that it is they that have to bear the chief burden of taxation. Taxes are imposed in the first place on animals. The camel and sheep flourish everywhere on the steppes. The former, indispensable as a means of communication, is, like the latter, the principal source of food for both greater and lesser nomads, as they are indeed for the settled communities. Well watered regions have small, but very hardy, buffaloes. The ass is the popular mount of the settled people and the townsfolk. Spain and the Maghrib have mules. The horse is a luxury animal in 'Abbāsid society, as it was in Old Arabia; its use spreads as the Turks issue from Central Asia. The multitudes of the poultry kind are rarely well grown. Dogs, despised and necessary, mount guard over the farm and camping ground.

After the conquests, the system of Muslim taxation inherited from the Byzantine State the tax on harvests, later called the *kharāj*. The Treasury had therefore a direct interest in promoting the cultivation of cereals and in suppressing fallow lands. The large estates which, after the conquest, remained vacant, either because they were imperial property, or because their owners had abandoned them, were granted by the caliphs to men of importance who, frequently dispossessed, cultivated them very badly by the help of slave labour, or by giving out local contracts in the old style—exceedingly burdensome to those who accepted them. In this way much land fell out of cultivation. Although it raised the question of the illegality of usurpation, yet the Doctrine favoured the occupation and exploitation of vacant land, considering it to be justified in most cases, even without the authority of the Prince. Ownership was attained by the digging of a well or by the diversion of a stream, since it is the presence of water that brings life to the land by making sowing and building possible; in order to avoid usurpation, the Doctrine establishes, around the site of already existing water, a more or less extensive zone which may not be occupied.

In general, the Doctrine has provided only for the exploitation of land by its owner, or by a tenant in return for a payment in money or in food. It did not recognise, in the case of land watered only by rain, the contracts sanctioned by custom which provide for the land being sown by the owner, and then entrusted to a farmer (*muzāra'a*), or being sown, tended and harvested (*mukhābara*) by the farmer, who, in either case, retains an agreed part of the crop. These are, however, the covenants which do, in fact, govern agriculture in both East and West; in the Maghrib the farmer with a fifth share (*khammās*) is well known. The Doctrine has none the less insisted on assimilating the obligations created by those contracts to those of a tenant towards a lessor, and on so taking up a position which is contrary to the facts.

Such contracts are at present in general use. The same is the case as regards the *mughārasa*, which consists in the owner of the land giving it to a peasant to be planted with trees, of which he will have the proceeds for several years, and which will be shared equally at the expiry of the contract. This arrangement has not received the approval of the Doctrine. Being very unfavourable to the cultivator, it has been greatly modified in practice.

The only irrigation contract which the Doctrine recognises is that by which the owner of a grove of palms gives it out to be irrigated, fertilised, maintained, and protected from the ravages of birds or robbers, in return for a share of the fruit when it has been gathered and dried. The same system is applicable to vineyards, but not, in the opinion of most jurists, to orchards composed of trees of other kinds. The owner supplies tools, beasts of burden, etc. The contract of *muzāra'a*, referred to above, is then allowed by the Doctrine in the case of "white" land, that is, the uncultivated soil between the trees, which is usually planted with cereals or vegetables. This is the current practice in the case of plantations of olives, oranges, lemons, etc. The Doctrine insists, rightly, that both contracts the *muzāra'a* and the *musāqāt*, be held by the same person.

The question of water rights is of capital importance. The ownership and use of springs, streams and wells is governed by principles that are said to go back to the agreements arrived at between Hagar and Ishmael and the Jurhum respecting Zamzam. They are, in fact, usages imposed by the wisdom of experience on the peasants of the Near East and the shores of the Mediterranean. One owes to one's neighbour any surplus of water, so that he may drink and water his beasts, but not necessarily for the purpose of irrigation.

The Doctrine, which can be seen to be desirous of assimilating the contract of *muzāra'a* to that of an ordinary tenancy, does not, however, really favour the letting of the soil. It lays down, in principle, that the owner who does not sow his land must permit its cultivation by his Muslim brother. This is an extension of the idea of collective ownership; it is only when planted with trees, and consequently irrigated, that the soil may become private property and the subject of contracts. Collective ownership has survived in the form of tribal property, and the constitution of privately owned lands is still a serious economic and legal question. If the institution of the family *ḥubūs* came so easily into general use, it is because it satisfied an instinctive tendency to collective ownership.

In the Muslim world, as elsewhere, agriculture has seen hard times. The conquering Arabs, contrary to what might have been expected, judging by their practice of Bedouin banditry, had a respect for cultivated land, and were wisely anxious to spare the harvest in order not to lose tax revenue. They kept in good order the irrigation works of Syro-Palestine, the canals, the drainage of the valleys of the two rivers, and maintained the custom of making use of the Nile floods. The mistake of the caliphs was to found great estates as gifts to their favourites, only to confiscate them later, and so to cause, through bad methods of cultivation, a certain disequilibrium in production and in the distribution of the population. In the period of splendour in the 8th and 9th centuries, the people flocked from the country into the large towns, where they hoped to pick up the crumbs of the wealth that trade was amassing in them. They added to the numbers of the mob that had no economic value, and was ready for disorder of all kinds. In North Africa, the ravages of the Arab invasion of the 11th century and Turkish inefficiency brought to ruin the Romano-Berber irrigation works; in Spain the long wars of the *reconquista* prepared the way for the decadence of agriculture, which became complete as a result of the fatal richness of the American colonies.

We are compelled to omit details of the regulations controlling weights and measures; as in all nations, they have varied greatly with the passing of time and in different places. We shall only say that the measures of length were the "finger" (*iṣba'*) of six grains of barley (*ḥabba*) placed in line, the "fist" (*qabḍa*, of 6 *iṣba'*), the ell (*dhirā'*, of 8 *qabḍa*, which is in Egypt 58 cm.), etc. The current unit of measure for cultivated soil was the surface which a team could work in a day (*faddān*, *zwīja*, etc.); it varies greatly in size with the kind of crop, varying, for example, in present day Lebanon, from a quarter to two-thirds of a hectare: in Egypt today, 4,200 square metres. The measures of volume were the *'ashīr*, the *qafīz* and the *jarīb*: the *irdab* is 198 litres in Egypt. The *mudd* is the current measure for cereals; the Doctrine attempted to give it a definite value by declaring it to be equal to the *mudd* of the Prophet; a standard measure was kept in the house of the *muḥtasib*. The *mudd* of wheat in Lebanon today weighs from 12 to 18 kilos.

The unit of weight was the *raṭl* which, in Syria in the Middle Ages, varied from 600 to 720 *dirham*. Today the Egyptian *dirham* is 3.12 grammes, and the *qinṭār* is 140 kilos. The measures for weighing fine goods are the *mithqāl* of 4.25 grammes and its twenty-fourth part, the *qirāṭ* (carat).

Among the very old "customs" which rule agricultural life, there is one that even the Revelation has been unable to destroy, that of the seasons. The Qur'ānic lunar calendar is too deliberately inconsistent with physical realities for it to have been able to rule the order of administrative and agricultural life. The peasants have preserved, in a form that varies regionally, an ancient division of the year into twenty-four lunar mansions, which, governed by the position of stars on the horizon at moonrise and moonset, combine with the movement of the sun so as to provide, after certain corrections taught by experience, a very satisfactory agricultural calendar. People were satisfied, too, with the ancient Persian, Syrian and Roman solar calendars, which they endeavoured to bring into harmony with the Muslim calendar. In the 12th century, Ibn Jubayr, for example, takes careful note of the correspondence of its dates with the Christian year (*'ajamī*). Beginning with the government of the caliphs, people were made to understand that the tax on the fruits of the soil (*zakāt, kharāj*) could be collected only after the harvest, therefore at a date that varied in accordance with the lunar calendar, and that it was inadmissible that the vagaries of this calendar should permit of its being exacted twice in respect of the same harvest.

This calendar was established by the Prophet on the occasion of the "farewell pilgrimage" in 631. The year has twelve lunar months, which have 29 and 30 days alternately, 354 days in all. This alternation is not absolute, for the beginning of each month is not fixed in advance; it is determined by the fact that two trustworthy witnesses have seen the moon of the new month; so it is, for example, that the beginning of the fast (Ramaḍān) is not officially fixed beforehand, and that the fasting time may last 28, 29, or 30 days. Thus two months of 29 or 30 days may come in succession. Moreover, the system of lunar months does not produce complete numbers of days; it has been necessary to use the system of intercalations that was known to Old Arabia, and one day was added to the last month of the year eleven times in a thirty year period.

The months are called: Muḥarram, Ṣafar, Rabī' al-Awwal (Rabi the First), Rabī' al Thānī (Rabi the Second), Jumāda I,

Jumāda II, Rajab, Sha'bān, Ramaḍān, Shawwāl, Dhu 'l-Qa'da, and Dhu 'l-Ḥijja.

The day begins and ends at sunset; the night of Friday is, consequently, in the Muslim calendar, that which, in ours, falls between sunset on Thursday and sunrise on Friday.

The week appears to have been borrowed from the Jews and Christians: from Sunday to Thursday the days have names which are derived from those of the first four numbers; Friday is called *jum'a* (meeting) because of the gathering of the faithful that occurs on that day; Saturday (*sabt*) is, like the Jewish Sabbath, the sixth day.

The divisions of the day are regulated by the times for prayer, especially by the three essential astronomical moments, sunrise, apogee and sunset. The Arabs made use of the sundial, and they even made, by following Greek models and traditions, water clocks, which want of attention and the general decadence that overtook the arts soon rendered useless; only the ruins of them are left. Being attached to religious establishments, mosques or *madrasas*, those clocks made possible the exact determination of the times of religious ceremonies. The use of European clocks (for which the peoples of North Africa continue to have a somewhat excessive fancy) and that of watches has spread to all parts of Islam: we have already pointed out that the muezzin of Zamzam is provided with a chronometer regulated at Greenwich.

This modernism in details does not change the fact that the Muslim calendar is in sharp disagreement with the course of the sun, and consequently with the order of the seasons by which, in every country, the dates of the principal festivals and religious ceremonies have been regulated. It follows from this divergence that the pilgrimage and the fast, for example, take place at seasons which vary each year, whereas their origin assigned them to a fixed date. Pre-Islamic Arabia knew both a solar and a lunar calendar, the working details of which are not yet clearly understood; the names of the months, where their meaning has been discovered, correspond to seasonal divisions; for example, *jumāda* is the cold, *ramaḍān*, heat, *rabī'*, the time when the soil is covered with fresh grass. The inconveniences of an entirely lunar calendar are very evident, and it has been retained only because it is imposed by the divine texts (Q. 9.361), which must be understood as the Prophet interpreted them. In practice, however, the solar calendar has been kept or restored. In fact, the agricultural populations retain the observance of inaccurately determined seasonal ceremonies and rites. On the other hand, administrative and economic life, in Egypt and Syria for example, continued, after the Muslim conquest, to be regulated by the old Greek or Coptic solar calendars. In the 14th century we find them generally employed by the government of the Mamlūks for the keeping of public and private accounts. In the modern period the Gregorian calendar is being everywhere generally adopted in Islam, and the lunar calendar is tending to become no more than a religious framework.

The Muslim era, the Hegira (*hijra*), does not begin exactly on the date of Muḥammad's leaving Mecca in order to emigrate to Medina; its beginning was fixed by 'Umar in such a way that the year begins in Muḥarram, and that the first of that month keeps the date which it had in the year in which the Caliph put into force the new computation. The Muslim era begins on the 15th (or the 16th) of July, 622. A simple formula determines roughly the correspondence of the Muslim with the Christian year. If H is the year of the Hegira and G the Gregorian year, we have:

$$\left(H - \frac{3\,H}{100}\right) + 622 = G.$$

The market (*sūq*) plays a considerable part in the life of the city, being an essential element of its greatness; but we must understand the exact meaning of the word. Pre-Islamic Mecca had a place in which goods from the Yaman and Syria were warehoused for purposes of exchange, and in preparation for a further journey. On the other hand, markets were held on fixed days in various parts of Arabia, and the fairs of the Ḥijāz are famous. The toponymy of the Muslim world is full of the names of Monday Markets, Wednesday Markets, and so on (*sūq al-aḥad, sūq al-arba'*). But the word *sūq* in the sense in which it is used in the towns, while applicable to a simple market, means more precisely an assemblage of shops and workshops in which the industrial and commercial life of the city is concentrated. In Syria it was inherited from the economic system of Byzantium. The workshops and shops were built, in the Grecian type of town, along the triumphal way, between the principal gate of the town and the temple of the chief god, later replaced by a cathedral church, which was itself subsequently converted into a mosque. Later, artisans and merchants formed groups in a number of spacious parts of the town, which constitute, properly speaking, the *sūq* (plur. *aswâq*) or *bāzār* (Turkish). One still finds, in all Muslim towns, those districts which, during the day, are places of cool shade pierced by splashes of fierce light, and full of movement and colour, which, at night, are deserted and dead, guarded only by watchmen charged with preventing the depredations of the "piercers of walls". All the *sūqs* were not necessarily situated together in one part of the town; each trade could have its *sūq* apart from the others, and it is thus that, in many a city, the names of gates or buildings mark the position of the *sūq* of perfumiers (*al-'aṭṭārīn*), scourers of wool (*al-qaṣṣârīn*), etc.

Foreign merchants warehoused their goods and could find lodgment for themselves and their beasts in great rectangular buildings, in which, around a vast courtyard, stables and storehouses were surmounted by an upper floor, containing rooms opening only on the courtyard, and communicating with each other by means of a circular gallery. This was the *qaīṣarīya* (*e qaīsareya agora*), the imperial market in the terminology of Syro-Palestine and the Maghrib. Those caravanserais, *funduq* or *khān*, are to be found, not only in the towns, but at halting places on the commercial highways of the East. In addition, markets in the ordinary sense of the word are to be found in the town, as in the provinces, either daily or on certain days only, for the sale of the produce of the locality, beasts, vegetables and fruit. We have seen that the life of the market, of whatever kind, is controlled by a special magistrate, the *muḥtasib*.

The activities of the *sūq* were not limited to the sale of native productions; goods from abroad were plentiful. The Far East was accessible by a land route known to European travellers also; but it was by sea that most of the trade was carried on. The first years of the caliphate had not been favourable to navigation by sea; the Arab conquerors were not sailors, and the inhabitants of the Syrian coast had lost the ancient courage with which they at one time braved the fury of the waves. To 'Umar is attributed the tradition that advised Muslims to abstain from journeys by sea. It needed the enterprise of the Umayyads to build up again the Phoenician and Egyptian fleets, and to attempt naval expeditions against Byzantium. At a later period it was European mariners who brought about an increase of traffic with the Muslim East. In the Indian Ocean, Iranian tradition was preserved, and Basra was connected with Bagdad by canals, and the River Tigris attracted Persian and Arab vessels which had ventured as far as China.

A captain (*nākhudā*) and a pilot (*mu'allim*) steered great ships, driven by sail or oar aided by the astrolabe and the magnetic needle. In the 15th century they had at their disposal nautical instructions in verse, which gave them information regarding perils and shoals, the appearance of coasts, and the approaches to harbours. Vasco da Gama, on his arrival in East Africa, ventured into the Indian Ocean only after securing the services of an Arab *mu'allim*.

The roads out of Europe also led to Bagdad; to the Mediterranean by way of the Euphrates, Aleppo and Antioch, where there arrived, as early as the 9th century, Jewish merchants who knew also the direct route to India, passing by Alexandria, Farama, and the Red Sea; to Europe went hides and slaves. The chosen route of the Northmen ran to Russia and Prague. In the Mediterranean the navigation of the high seas was monopolised by Christian ships. In 1065 a Genoese fleet anchored at Jaffa, and the Crusades gave an impetus to commerce that was to be permanent. The endemic wars that disturbed the Near East interfered hardly at all with the journeys of traders: the only thing that had been able to stop them was the devastations of the Zotts, the Zenjs, and the Qarmaṭs. During the Crusades caravans circulated in Syria, through the ranks of the combatants, who found greater profit in holding them periodically to ransom than in plundering them.

The Muslim princes gave a hearty welcome to foreign merchants who, according to the Doctrine, got no protection in Islam for their goods or their lives. They could purchase security (*amān*) guaranteed by a passport on payment of a tithe (*'ushr*). The Doctrine limits the validity of the *amān* to one year, after which the *musta'min* foreigner should be treated as a tributary (*dhimmī*); in practice, foreigners prolonged their stay for several years. Then treaties were signed containing regulations applicable to their case. In the 13th century, according to one author, the fifth (*khums*) imposed on merchants varied between 20% and 36%. There were custom-houses (*dīwān*) in the chief seaports, Alexandria, Basra, etc. The princes reserved their right to restrict the liberty of foreign merchants who, according to the Doctrine, could not trade in forbidden goods, nor export articles, such as arms, the absence of which would weaken the Muslim State.

During the 9th and 10th centuries, to which we must turn if we wish to study the Muslim State at the height of its prosperity, merchants were important people. Those of Bagdad and Alexandria controlled prices, the former for trade in the Indian Ocean, the latter for that of the Mediterranean. The tales of their sea-going adventures, which fill literature with wonders, shed a poetic light on the activities of commercial speculation.

From the 8th century onwards the artisans of the Near East were scattering, throughout the Muslim world and abroad, articles cf their manufacture, of which magnificent specimens are to be found today in monasteries and church treasure houses. The recollection of the names damask and muslin (*Mosul*) is enough to make us realise the estimation in which the West held Oriental textiles. Fine linens, brocades, velvets, delicate materials in embroidered or plain silk, flowed out of the workshops of Persia, Bagdad, Damascus and Asia Minor. In Egypt, Coptic artisans, in return for a miserable reward, preserved, in the silk industry, the traditions of the days of the Pharaohs. The chief centres of production were Tinnis, Damietta, Alexandria, Dabib, etc. *Ṭirāz* was manufactured in those places; this word, which signifies embroidery, was applied specially to the materials with embroidered stripes which covered the court robes of princes. Those embroideries, as edgings or strips over the shoulders and in other places, outlined the sovereign's name. If it is remembered that the greatest mark of esteem that a prince could bestow on one of his subjects was to undo his own robe (*khal'*) and put it on the shoulders of him whom he desired to honour, it will be understood that the robes of honour (*khal'a*) distributed as rewards or decorations to their subjects were adorned with this embroidery. The custom was adopted by all representatives of the caliphs' power who, during the 'Abbāsid period, were required to wear official garments more or less adorned with embroidered bands. Their manufacture, consequently, became a considerable industry, but one having an official character, for those embroidered robes were not articles of commerce. Made in the caliph's workshops, or under the supervision of the prince's agents, they were collected by those officials and carried to court. Persia had placed embroidered medallions on the robes of her kings; the senators and knights of Rome had had the purple *clavi* of their togas; they were to appear again in Byzantium, and they still survive in certain features of modern Western dress. Other materials, the products of family workshops, had also to pass through the hands of an official inspector; the bales of cloth were sealed by him, and often passed from one middleman to another without being opened, although frequent fraud finally put an end to this trusting attitude. Artisans were miserably paid, but very high duties added greatly to the price of the materials.

In all branches of manufacture, day to day production, of the results of which we know little, turned out ever and again masterpieces, some of which have survived. We know what carpet making was throughout the East, and what it might still be. Public collections contain numerous specimens of objects of domestic utility in porcelain, copper, or glass, little luxury articles, writing desks, and caskets of all kinds, in onyx, silver, or ivory. The leather workers' art, cushions, saddlery, etc., was actively practised. Cabinet making, which has given us the infinitely adorned mosque pulpits, might be revived. Papyrus which, in the 9th century had everywhere displaced parchment, was itself replaced, a century later, by paper which, coming first from China by way of Samarkand, was produced in Syria as early as the 10th century. At the same period, Persia and Mesopotamia were making perfumes which merchants had previously imported from abroad. They were everywhere sought after, and the Doctrine, remembering that the Prophet had loved them, encouraged the faithful in their use.

The transactions which resulted from this industrial and commercial activity were regulated by Muslim law, but in a manner that was, at one and the same time, too rigid and incomplete: local customs added what it lacked. The Qur'ān had not had to concern itself with contracts concerning the land, but only with those that were entered into duly in the economic life of the "merchant republic of Mecca: sale, hiring, warehousing, wages, interest and exchange".

The Doctrine occupied itself in a special way with conditions governing sales, considering a sales contract to be typical. Questions of detail are solved in many different ways, varying with different schools of law, even in such important matters as the nature and exact classification of the thing sold. The value to be attached to written documents is disputed, while the essential character of verbal evidence is maintained. The consent of the parties must be made explicit by the utterance of a formula which is a survival of an ancient form of exorcism: and such utterance is the first condition for the validity of the contract. The sale is concluded, while buyer and seller grasp each other by the right hand, by the exchange of an offer (*ījāb*) and an acceptance (*qabūl*): "Do you buy this from me? I buy it from you." Or else: "Do you sell me this?" "I sell it to you." The second condition of the contract is that the subject of it should be a useful thing; it is unlawful to sell a thing that one may not be able to deliver, such as a bird on the wing; nor may one sell a wild beast which is of no use; nor things without social value, such as musical instruments or the materials of games; nor an unclean thing like a pig or wine; but this last prohibition does not apply to a *dhimmī* or a *musta'min* foreigner. There is disagreement as to the value of the ownership, and therefore the sale, of a watchdog or a heap of manure. It is generally allowed that the Qur'ān may be sold, for what the purchaser buys is the paper on which it is written and the skin which binds the leaves together. A sale is completed by the delivery of the object and the payment of the price, with a right of option to the buyer.

The giving of sureties and warehousing are the subjects of important contracts in a world in which merchants make lengthy stays away from home. The surety guarantees the debt of a traveller of whom the creditor may remain long without news. The contract of deposit or warehousing protects goods that the depositor cannot carry with him, or which may not be safe in his own store, and the person who receives them, by keeping them faithfully, does a pious action, for which he will be rewarded in the next life. His word is accepted without question when he states that he has returned the goods.

The books of *adab* are full of anecdotes concerning the unfaithful bailee. They abound also in stories of animals lost and found, the chief subject of tales told on the grazing grounds. The owner owes a reward and an indemnity to him who returns his strayed camel, whether or no he makes of the business a profession.

The Doctrine forbids lending to interest. The *riba'* (increase) was forbidden by the Qur'ān (2.276), as a reaction against the habits of usury prevalent among the Qurayshites, who were accustomed, in case of non-payment of a debt and the accrued interest, to grant the debtor a delay, but to exact twice the sum due. It is not known what circumstances caused Muḥammad, whom traditions present to us as a former merchant, to prohibit so completely all lending to interest, and to regulate so strictly the exchange of precious metals and articles of value; this prohibition has weighed, and still weighs, heavily on dealings between Muslims. With variations in detail, the Doctrine, keeping in line with the ḥadīths, permits only the exchange of two quantities of equal value of the things aimed at by the law, and the exchange must take place immediately, and not with effect at a future date. On the other hand, it is unlawful for a lender to make any profit out of his loan: it is an act of pious generosity which will have its reward in the next world.

It is also interesting to note that it was in that very society in which this code of rules was in force that there developed, in the 9th and 10th centuries, the banking institutions and commercial customs which were to become those of Europe, and which are quite inconsistent with the Qur'ānic law. This arose out of the fact that recourse was had, when necessary, to legal shifts, such as, for example, a double sale; the borrower sells a piece of cloth to the lender and receives the price in cash, but he had previously bought it from the lender for a higher price and on credit. This is the *mukhāṭara* contract which the European Middle Ages called *mohatra*, and which was allowed by Muslim Doctrine. In banking practice one just had to forget the Qur'ānic prohibitions, an omission which came easily to Jewish and Christian bankers, who centralised their business in Bagdad, and to the Christian merchants who controlled all foreign trade. The bill of exchange and the promissory note, both of which were condemned by the Doctrine, were in use from one end of the Muslim world to the other.

The exchange of precious metals gave rise to endless transactions. The coinage had, in the early days of Islam, been of gold in the West in the Byzantine provinces with the *dīnār* (*denarios*), and of silver in the East in the Persian provinces, with the *dirham* (*drachme*): in the 10th century the two coinages competed with each other in Bagdad. From this there resulted continual exchange transactions with the intervention of a coinage of base metals. When the caliphs had struck coins of various values, the market was flooded with coins of different origins and values, for which the money changers, acting under the supervision of the *muḥtasib*, had to find equivalent rates. On the other hand, Jewish and Christian bankers lent considerable sums to the State and to traders, and dealt in money; Greeks also engaged in the money business; it was only in the Turkish period that they were joined by Armenians.

SOURCES

Plessner: *Sûq*, E.I., 4.531;—Grohmann: *tirāz*, E.I. 4.825; Schacht: *riba*, E.I 3,1227; Juynboll: *Handbuch* (S.88).

CHAPTER THIRTEEN

INTELLECTUAL LIFE

Umayyad Poetry and Art—The 'Abbāsid 9th Century: Prose, Poetry, Art—The 10th Century: Artistic Prose, Learning, Art—Decadence—The Modern Renaissance—Iran and Turkey—Philosophy and Science.

THE second chapter of this book sought to give a general survey of the history of Muslim society, which was to be an introduction to the study of its institutions. In this chapter we begin once more the same journey through the centuries, in order that we may assign to literature and art their proper place in the history of the institutions.

It is the religious factor that determines the continuity of Muslim society, in which there is no separation of the temporal and the spiritual. Always and everywhere, we come back to the Qur'ān. Not only because literature and art repeat Qur'ānic verses, or are inspired by them, but also because it is the very form of the holy book, its language, its style, its rhythm, that have determined the way in which Muslim thought and feeling find expression. While poetry remained, as it were, pagan, and had great difficulty in finding a new framework and fresh sources of inspiration, prose took its form under the influence of the Qur'ānic harmony. It is the rhythm of the Qur'ān, carried into prose writings, that satisfies a natural taste of the Arab mind for balance and parallelism in ideas, for verbal abundance, for antithesis, ever ready to insinuate itself into paired passages of rhythmic prose, as if they were two poetic hemistichs. In Arab music it is rhythm that constantly dominates the arabesque of a melody that divides, and again combines, in symmetrical and complicated patterns. Similarly, monumental decoration is the prolific development of the rhythm of geometrical and floral ornamentation.

When describing the state of spiritual poverty in

which the energetic Europe of the 19th century found Muslim society, controversialists have maintained that the decline was due to the depressing influence of the Muslim religion.

A priori, to attribute the weaknesses of a social group to its institutions, and, in particular, to its religion, as if a religion were a force independent of the society itself, is to make things rather too simple. It is permissible to reason in this way only if we believe religion to be a revelation, like the Law that the Divine Being imposes on his people in exchange for his protection, and to which the people submit without question, and sometimes even without understanding. But if one looks upon religion as a social fact, simply occupying the first place among institutions of human origin, then one must believe that a people has the institutions it deserves; and this is so no matter whether they have framed their institutions by their own free will, or whether these have been received from another people, using either peaceful or warlike methods; for, in this last case, if the nation does not deserve to perish, the necessary reaction to the contingencies of history is in its own hands. If one denies the power for action of the personal and collective will, human life appears to be governed by an absolute determinism which makes every effort useless and ends in speedy annihilation.

We do not believe that the religion of Islam has been the cause of the weakening of Muslim society. For several centuries it did not in any way detract from the vitality of literature, science and art, a fact with which we shall deal very briefly.

The history of the intellectual and artistic life of Islam opens, like that of its institutions, with the period of the Umayyad caliphate, of which our knowledge is still insufficient, so rich is it in activities and tendencies. Poetry is purely Bedouin at that time, and resembles so closely that of pre-Islamic days that it has recently been possible to think that the two were contemporary. The religious influence was so weak that a few slight alterations would suffice to assimilate it completely to the *jāhilīya*. The life of the court merely accentuated the love theme. It is remarkable that this poetry, although contemporary with the conquests or immediately subsequent to them, is uninfluenced by them, and contains no trace of the epic form. The god who ordered the holy war having spurned the poets, the latter appear to have ignored his victories. Of Umayyad prose only indirect documents remain; they, for their part, belong to the religious milieu. It was the period in which the ḥadīth took final shape, that of a short narrative of which the quick and lively movement anticipates the anecdotal form of the later 'Abbāsid literary anthologies. The orations, often very secular in character, in which the chiefs, from the mosque pulpits on Fridays, address the faithful, the *khuṭba*, rise to eloquence through the use of that rhythmical prose whose value the Qur'ān has demonstrated once and for all. The language of the ḥadīth, and of the quite concrete khuṭba, is not yet suited to serve as the instrument of abstract and connected thought.

While the language, like principles and institutions, was struggling to break out of its chrysalis, it would seem that art found immediately a perfect form. We might be tempted to say that the needs of worship were more pressing than those of doctrine, and that Islam built mosques before acquiring a theology or a body of law: not an unusual event. Perhaps, too, the conquerors, great admirers of the Christian churches, wanted to show that they could equal the beauty of them. Moreover, it was not only mosques that the Umayyads built, but palaces as well, so that in them they might enjoy their marvellous good fortune. There arose, on the edge of the waste, noble dwellings, surrounded by farmlands, where the purest architectural proportions were adorned with a sumptuous ornamentation which was not by any means ignorant of the art of depicting the human form. In the large towns, Jerusalem, Damascus, Medina, at the Ka'ba in Mecca, the Umayyads, and especially al-Walīd (705-715), erected mosques of a very original Syro-Byzantine type, magnificently suited to that decoration with coloured marble and golden mosaic, which was so dear to the artists of Byzantium. It is in this that the enthusiasm of the conquerors would appear to have expressed itself; but it was given a visible form by the hands of native artists, who had adapted Byzantine traditions to their own genius.

The great century of Arab literature lies within the hundred years of the 'Abbāsid caliphate; the succeeding years developed what that period had created. Just as thought and art were born in the Umayyad period by the contact of the Arabs with Byzantine civilisation, so the mingling of peoples and cultures gave rise, in a few decades, under the influence of Iranism and Hellenism, to a magnificent surge of literary activity. The language disciplined itself and strove after the greater accuracy required for the expression of abstract thought; translations from Pehlevi (Ibn al-Muqaffa') and Syriac, received, these last, from the Greek, made necessary the effort required for the accomplishment of this transformation. Religious controversy sought expression in books, as well as by word of mouth, and searched the Qur'ān and the Tradition for its proofs; grammarians borrowed methods of reasoning, the art of dialectics, the *kalām*, from theologians and lawyers who, shortly before, had inherited them from the Greeks. Thus, as a kind of supplement to the Qur'ānic exegesis, grammar, at Baṣra and Kūfa, and then at Bagdad, became a science, the findings of which retain, even today, all their value. The language was thus made ready for a prose that could serve a variety of experiments in literature, short critical treatises, works of pseudo-scientific interest, of controversy, or anecdotal works intended solely for pleasure. Some of those essays have been collected into larger books, which can be enjoyed in spite of their incoherence. The charming animal book of al-Jāḥiz is, like his Bayān, a succession of essays, in which the taste of the Arabs for anecdote, vividly told and with a delicate point, is combined with a novel attempt to bring about the comprehension of thoughts subtle or profound, which gently insinuates a pinch of seriousness into minds that had so far been strangers to philosophic or moral reflection. Books such as the *'Uyūn al-akhbār* of Ibn Qutayba are more or less essays in character training. In the absence of oral teaching people began to take an interest in the instruction of the secretaries in the offices of the caliphate (*kuttāb*), for whom, until the 15th century, books were written summarising contemporary knowledge.

If foreign influences had contributed to the rapid development of this literature, the erudition that found, in the newborn prose, the instrument that was essential for its expression, grew out of the pure religion. Collections of ḥadīths, commentaries to the Qur'ān, treatises on canon law, controversial essays, all assumed a literary form which contributed to their diffusion among men who had always cared for beautiful language.

History appears, in great part, as a science auxiliary to the Qur'ānic commentaries and the ḥadīth, as well as to the lives of the Prophet, the tales of the conquests, and the biographies of the Companions; while taking on the amplitude of a world history after the Persian model, it yet serves the Tradition, and preserves the outward form of the ḥadīth. The need for defining the nature of taxation and for determining the routes to be followed by the postal messengers of the caliphate, brought into existence geographical descriptions which, during the succeeding period, were based on Ptolemaic data, with a padding made up of travellers' reports. In this period Arab philosophy was founded on the fringe of Islam.

During this so rich period of Arabic literature poetry had a curious fate. Living poetry discarded Bedouin and Umayyad traditions. In the refined, yet violent, society of the two great 'Abbāsid centuries, there prevailed a sensuous joy of living which is well expressed by Abū Nuwās and his imitators; violent and coarse satire continues to record the vicissitudes of social life. There we have something quite apart from religion. Loftier spirits, such as Abu l-'Atāhiya, make poetry speak words of grave import, which religious authorities described as zindīqism. At last a poetry of mysticism is born, expressing the divine love in the outward guise of earthly love, which it is somewhat disturbing to see practised by Abū Nuwās, a debauchee given to every vice. The old poetry is practically dead, but, being raised to classical status, is more and more admired. It profits by the battle that is joined between the exclusive partisans of Arabism and those who would place in the foremost ranks of the Muslim community the new converts, and especially the Iranians, the *shu'ūbīya*. On the other hand, this pagan poetry, damned by the Qur'ān and by Muḥammad for representing the human ideal of the *muruwwa* as opposed to the religious ideal of the *dīn*, became suddenly an auxiliary of the Qur'ānic exegesis. Certain expressions of the Qur'ān and the ḥadīth had to be explained to the 9th century faithful, but were hardly understood by the commentators who discussed them. In order to make clear the analogical relationship, the *qiyās*, one had only examples taken from the old poets to fall back on, with the result that their verses were introduced, in a fashion most strange, into the Qur'ānic commentaries.

Architecture developed Umayyad traditions in a Mesopotamian direction (Sāmarrā). Buildings erected in regions that had no stone, and where recourse was had to the fragile bricks of Assyro-Babylonian times, have not been preserved. No doubt, too, the palaces were either, like the Tāj of Bagdad, slender and flimsy buildings, or light pavilions placed here and there in gardens, whose sumptuous ornamentation constituted their chief beauty. Music and singing were a universal taste in spite of the Doctrine's condemnation; the lute, guitar, harp, zither, lyre, hautbois (*mizmār*), trumpet, drum and tambourine were all known. In the 10th century the Turkish amīrs had aubades (*nauba*) performed before their residences several times a day; the practice was passed on to the Mamlūks and the Ottomans and, by that route, doubtless reached Europe.

The period of the 'Abbāsid dynasty, which extends from the 10th to the 13th century, was still very rich in intellectual output; it was a time of grave disturbances, both religious and political, and the weakness of the caliphs of the time was extreme. But economic life was very active and town society, in which the merchants were most prominent, took an interest in the things of the mind. Literature, instead of keeping close to life, abandoned the vigorous prose of the writers of the preceding period, and became ornate and affected. Those earlier writers used rhythm only to give to the expression of their thoughts a harmony, an orderliness, which had heightened their value. The true rhymed and rhythmical prose (*saj'*) of the oldest sūras of the Qur'ān had been retained in the composition of the sermon, the solemn allocution, the *khuṭba*, and had overflowed into the correspondence of the chancellery of the caliphate. It became, in the 10th century, the habitual form of artistic prose, and gave to it a style whose constant charm lay in its showiness and addiction to antithesis. Except when it served to embody agreeable literary trifles, such as the Sessions (*maqāmāt*) of Hamadhānī (d. 1007) and Ḥarīrī (d. 1122), it produced a literature that was opulent in form but empty of thought. Thus the artistic summit was reached with a prose that was an end in itself, and that did not suffer from the embarrassment of expressing ideas.

Ordinary prose continued to be the medium of an abundant learned literature from which the ancient beauty of form is not always absent. Religious studies, very actively pursued in those centuries in which Shī'ism is dominant, are revived by Ghazālī (d. 1111), who was learned in all the knowledge of his time and was one of the best writers that Arab literature has known. He was the first to employ both Persian and Arabic, and to secure by this means the advance of Muslim thought in Iran. The adventurous lives of the merchants added to the wealth of information contained in the writings of those who described the country, and who were themselves travellers. "Human" geography, which has the air of being a modern invention, was practised by the Arabs, as it had been by the Greeks. Arab society felt a lively curiosity for exotic things and the marvels of distant lands. Historians occupied themselves, in addition to the subjects we have mentioned, with monographs on princes, tribes and cities, as well as with biographical collections (*ṭabaqāt*) of the works of poets, grammarians and jurists, according to a formula adopted by their learned predecessors.

Poetry retained its place of honour, for all the world continued to compose verse, but we should be able to discover nothing now, were it not that two real poets, Abū Firās and Mutanabbī, arose in the 10th century and in the curious environment of the Ḥamdānid emirs of Aleppo. For a moment, and in the extreme disorder into which the caliphate had fallen, circumstances led those Bedouin, barbarous and cunning adventurers though they were, to become the champions of Islam and Arabism against the Emperor of Constantinople. It was thus that, at the time when the power of the caliphate was at its weakest, a poet born at Kūfa came, after Bedouin adventures that earned him the name of Mutanabbī and by the irony of fate, to the court of Aleppo where he found his fortune. Gifted with an incomparable talent for verbal acrobatics, and a supreme master of rich and varied rhythm, he caught up, out of the storm of the Byzantine foray, a breath of epic. Employing the classic mould of Bedouin poetry, in which praise of the generous patron, however vile he may be, occupies the chief place, he sang of the proud honour of the Bedouin *muruwwa* in a brilliant flourish of words, rhythm and rhyme. To this double originality of matter and form Mutanabbī owes his enduring glory and his place as the poet of modern nationalism.

The incident of the Crusades is referred to only in the accounts of historians, of whom a few wrote in the fashionable style. While, in the mosques of the Orient, ornamentation is as super-abundant as it is in the rhythmic prose of literature, the Almoravids and Almohads in Morocco, recalling Islam to its early purity, restore to the art of the mosque a harmonious simplicity of line and decoration. This was the time, too, when Persian and Hindu-Muslim art, basing themselves on the ordinary pattern of the Muslim monument, produced works of complexity, and frequently of grandeur, which owed their beauty to local tradition and the native genius of the architects.

The rule forbidding the production of semblances of the forms of living creatures, proclaimed by the ḥadīth at the time of the Byzantine quarrel regarding images, has been constantly broken, save in the mosques. The Umayyad palaces had paintings and sculptures of human beings. In the 11th century the baths still had their statues and erotic paintings, of which some long survived. Carpets and hangings abounded in representations of animals, and the knick-knacks of domestic life, caskets, vases, trays and ewers, were covered with them, and with human figures as well. It is reported that the Umayyad Caliph of Spain caused the bust of his beloved Zahrā' to be carved on the door of his palace of Medīnat al-Zahrā'. It was the *fuqahā'* and the severely traditional spirit of the *madrasa*, certainly, that imposed a restriction which could well have been confined to religious buildings.

From the 13th to the 19th century Arab literature proper is one of pure imitation and quite uninteresting. Verses are still written; rhyme and rhythm are even employed in the composition of didactic works in praise of the Prophet, such as the *Burda* of Shaykh al-Būṣīrī, in the compilation of nautical instructions and grammatical treatises, for the statement of the rules of chess, etc. Erudition, too, produced a few works of use or merit: the Egypt of the Mamlūks has an important output of works of history, and the Prolegomena of Ibn Khaldūn are a work of exceptional value. In the field of religious controversy Ibn Taymīya is an original and influential figure.

This period of time, during which the originality of literature is so poor, left, on the other hand, buildings which testify, not only to the survival of the noblest traditions, but to the existence of new ideas in architecture. Ayyūbites, Mamlūks, Iranians, Saljūqs and Ottomans, Almoravids, Almohads, Merinids, and Naṣrids, have all left beautiful monuments, mosques, fortresses and palaces. The minor arts were applied to an infinite variety of objects which, because of the relative proximity in time, have been preserved.

The 19th century has seen a renaissance of Arab literature and the death of Muslim art. The new literature written in Arabic seeks to express the feelings and ideas that, for a century back, and especially during the last fifty years, have been seething in Muslim minds; its full development has been retarded by its very richness, as well as by the inadequacy of the means of expression. At the end of the 8th century the need had been felt for a prose suited to the expression of ideas that were very new to the conquering Arabs; neither poetry nor the Qur'ān, nor the language of solemn discourse, nor that of current conversation, provided the instrument that was felt to be needed. The efforts of translators produced a prose, abundant, elegant, and clear, which a few writers of talent perfected in use. In the 19th century what was required was not to create a prose, but to transform that in common use, to get rid of artistic prose, of all the rubbish that had encumbered the language since the 10th century, a style that could well be adopted by a humorist for the purposes of amusement, but which, applied to serious purposes, could not fail to be ridiculous. The problem was to return to the school of the simple and supple prose of the great writers of the 9th century, and, at the same time, with the object of translating and adapting European works, to rejuvenate the written tongue by bringing into it the living and ever-changing language of the street and the field. So far no great writer has appeared able to impress by his example, and to complete, in one stroke, the very heavy task that the Cairo Academy has undertaken. Besides, the Academy is, above all, and not without justification, concerned with the technical vocabulary because of the extreme confusion that prevails in scientific works.

Arabic script is inadequate. It is based, like other Semitic scripts, on the essential importance of the consonants, the vowels being, above all, derivative and inflectionary elements. Therefore, at first, Arabic script knew consonants only; then, at the end of the 7th century, at the same period as that in which Hebrew script was experiencing the Massoretic reform, Arabic script introduced, in the shape of little signs placed above or below the consonants, a very inadequate range of three short vowels, a, i, and u, to which were joined three corresponding long vowels, by the addition of *alif*, *yā'*, and *wāw*. Whether this notation has ever sufficed to render all the sounds of the language is very doubtful; today it is altogether inadequate. Moreover, seeing that a knowledge of this vowel system is deduced to a great extent from the rules of the language, educated people have thought it to be a sort of point of honour to neglect it in their handwriting, which is indeed formed with great material delicacy, above all in printed books. It is only with a view to fixing the unalterable text of the Qur'ān, to give exactitude to the meaning of a line or a passage that is hard to understand, or, finally, to indicate the exact pronunciation of a proper name, that people can consent to encumber their handwriting with those superposed signs.

The imperfections of this script form declare themselves more obviously at a time when education is spreading among Muslim peoples; the art of reading is about to cease being the privilege of a lettered class who acquired a kind of glory from their ability to decipher a writing full of mysteries. It would be necessary, first of all, to find a practical system of notation for the short vowels, a reform that would be easy if one limited oneself to the poor range of the classical Arabic a, i, u; but that would be to take no cognisance of living realities. The number of consonants might be reduced, but difficulties would be encountered when dealing with dialect pronunciations. Those who attempt to solve this very special problem come up against two tendencies which we have already mentioned: the one which retains the memory of the classical Muslim community under the domination of an Arab caliph, and would therefore like to keep the archaic orthography that enshrines it; and the other that has no fear of the diversity of national realities.

We can better understand the difficulties of a spelling reform that seems to affect the most sacred interests of Muslim tradition, when we remember that it required political revolutions and a rather hurried social revolution and a sudden transition from a "religious" to a secular organisation of society, before it was possible to touch the spelling of Turkish. The use of the Latin alphabet in writing Turkish was introduced in 1923 in Āzarbayjân, and has been compulsory in Turkey since 1st June, 1930. Religious influences, moreover, had inflicted on the Turkish language, together with the Arabic alphabet, a notation that was altogether inconsistent with its nature. Such a reform as this cannot fail to impress Arab public opinion. Secular nationalism has carried the day in Turkey against Arab Panislamism, and this attitude has been accentuated by the denial of the canonical value of the language of the Qur'ān: the solemn Friday homily, the *khuṭba*, as also the call to prayer, is nowadays delivered in Osmanli.

In the contemporary literary movement, poetry, in spite of a happy effort at rejuvenation, remains still in the Bedouin or 'Abbāsid tradition; it has, fortunately, ceased to imitate poets of later date than the 10th century, with the exception of Mutanabbī: in the past fifty years there have been several poets of talent. The novel and the short story, on the other hand, are entirely imitative of the European; we can find, for example, work in the manner of Maupassant or Tchekov; but a solicitude for personal observation and realism has produced works of real value. The theatre, foreign to old Muslim life, has been slow to appeal to the taste of modern society: it began with translations and adaptations of French or English plays; there has arisen in the past twenty-five years a theatre with moral and social tendencies, which has a certain originality. In scenic dialogue, still more than in the novel, the language of ordinary conversation and that of the streets introduce a pleasant element of reality and life. It is hard to understand why light and satirical vaudeville has not flourished in Arab society as soon as the latter began to take an interest in the theatre; the taste for verse has not declined; the sense of the ridiculous and the out and out grotesque is very well developed; from the 10th century on, the Near East has had a shadow theatre, the ancestor of the future Karagoez, and the public used to give a warm reception to men gifted with a great talent for imitation; the al-Fanā Square in Marrakesh was recently the theatre in which a very clever and audacious mime amused the strollers with its comic silhouettes of local people. In drawing, this same sense of comical exaggeration is everywhere evident. It looks as if such natural tendencies might develop into an art.

Classical Arab prose used to find scope in critical essays and polemics; the moderns, too, are past masters in that genre; the press offers them a wide field in which to exercise their talents.

Throughout the whole Muslim world a literary renaissance is accompanied by a pitiful stagnation in art. One might have expected, as in other countries and other times, a vulgar and complicated superabundance of decoration, but Turkish influence has coupled it with a sinister architecture, which seems to be copied from the French military style of construction in vogue since the days of Louis XIV. The result has been a crop of lamentable buildings and pitiful "restorations". The minor arts are crushed by the competition of the machine and modern economics: carpets, leather work, embroidery, porcelain, copper work, all are vanishing or adapting themselves to a duller European taste. A few years ago, Japanese imports into Syria killed the local industry that produced coffee cups. European protecting powers are seeking to restore life to the dying crafts by opening new markets to their products.

The development of Arab science and philosophy has been along lines diverging sufficiently from those followed by literature and art to have made it seem preferable to deal with it only at the end of this rapid review of the different stages of the intellectual life of the Muslim world. In the third chapter we enumerated the subjects of the controversies carried on by the theologian-philosophers, and which so felicitously gave breadth to the religious thought of Islam. It is on the fringe of Islam that we find the philosophers and men of science to whom we have still to assign a place in general history; they have exercised no influence on the institutions of Islam, but their works dominated the science of the Christian Middle Ages.

With them the union of science and philosophy is complete: those philosophers are, in theory, anatomists and physiologists, physicians and chemists, and, in practice, physicians, astrologers, alchemists, and constructors of hydraulic machines. Their learning is outside Islam. Like the theologians, they profit by the Greek heritage, but not by its teaching of the art of reasoning; they make use of the whole range of Greek learning, first through Syriac translations, and later, directly from the originals. The Monophysite medical centre at Gundēshāpūr was, from the 5th century, both a university and a school of medicine, to which the 'Abbāsid caliphs turned for their physicians, and which gradually migrated altogether to Bagdad. On the other hand, Arabs by birth appear rarely in the list of philosophers, where we find few other than Iranians or Syrians, Iraqians or Egyptians of Christian or Jewish origin; all the more reason to make special mention of al-Kindī, who is an Arab. We should therefore speak of philosophy in Arabic, rather than of Arab philosophy.

The Muslim East, between the 9th and 13th centuries, achieved considerable progress in mathematics (algebra is an Arabic word), in astronomy, anatomy, the art of healing, and chemistry. No doubt those scholars, too, often studied the books of their predecessors with an assiduity greater than that which they brought to bear on the observation of Nature, or else they evolved useless theories that further research disproved; but they also made exact experiments and knew how to record the results. Until the 15th century the scientists of the Christian West were never without the books of the Arab scholars and the works of Aristotle.

Aristotle was already the revered master of Arab philosophy before he became the sovereign guide of the schools of the West and a source of laughter to Molière's audiences. But it was chiefly through neo-platonism that the Arabs got to know him.

We find their doctrines to be based on Aristotle's four causes: the active cause (*fā'il*), matter (*hayūla*), form (*ṣūra*), and purpose (*ghāya*). These are joined to the idea of power (*quwwa*) and action (*fi'l*), and to that of emanation, to form the divine whole. The cause that acts and creates, which is related to the *logos* of the Stoics (*kalima*), works through a succession of intellects (*'uqūl*) which the Ikhwān al-Ṣafā' for example, call: the creator (*khāliq*), the active intellect (*al-'aql al-fa''āl*), the universal soul (*al-nafs al-kullī*), and the things that exist (*al maudjūdāt*). The philosophers used their scientific knowledge for the construction of world systems, doctrines of the soul, theories of evil, which separated them from Islam, but which were closely interrelated among themselves, being all more or less a syncretism of Greek ideas. It being impossible to give a clear account of them all, we have thought it best to summarise the teaching of one of the oldest of them, al-Rāzī, who died about 925, a physician and alchemist well known in the West by the name of Rhazes.

In Rāzī the man of science rises superior to the philosopher. He formulated with rare clarity a principle that seems a truism today, and which is essential to all scientific progress, namely, that one must take into consideration the opinions of one's predecessors, look on them as capable of revision, and strive constantly to go beyond their researches, in the hope that others will be able to perfect them later. The respect for the opinions of the ancients which caused the European 17th century to reject the theory of the circulation of the blood, prevailed in the intellectual life of Islam, and Rāzī's heresy was vigorously opposed. His metaphysic admits five eternal substances: the Creator, the Soul, Matter, Space and Time. The Soul, which is ignorant, and learns only by experience, has had the desire to unite with Matter; then the Creator, who is all knowledge, combined the atoms of matter according to the five elements, earth, water, fire and sphere, in a decreasing density, so as to form a large number of compounds. In them there remained of evil what it had not been possible to remove. Then the Creator gave to the Soul the spirit (*'aql*) and intelligence (*idrāk*), so that it might remember its former purity and aspire to separate itself from the world of Matter, the evil in which caused it to suffer. But each one of the individual souls that make up this Soul is incapable of freeing itself by a single effort. The human soul, following a conception derived indirectly from Aristotle, and which has persisted in the minds of all Arab philosophers, is made up of a soul of desire, inferior and vegetative (*nabātīya*), a soul of anger (*ghaḍabīya*) which is animal, and a "soul of reason" (*nāṭiqa*) which is divine. So that the soul shall purify itself, it is necessary that this last should direct the second, and permit the soul, after it has passed through other beings, to return to its first purity. To avoid evil, man must avoid extremes of feeling, and achieve that middle attitude of equilibrium which the Doctrine also recommends to the Muslim.

Man is therefore a part of a general system comprehending the universe. A doctrine common to Arab philosophers is that of the perfect concordance of the elements of the universe with those of human nature. This is a microcosm in the macrocosm and the concordance is extended to include the smallest details. The intellect of the world, a direct emanation of the Soul of the world, rules the world, in the same way as human intelligence governs a man's body.

Science and philosophy flourished at the same periods as religious speculation, literature and art. This great movement, external to Islam, lasted from the 8th to the 13th century, and we are indicating only a few outstanding figures if we mention Jābir b. Ḥayān (*d.* 803), al-Kindī (*d.* 873), al Farābī (*d.* 951), Ibn Sinā' (*d.* 1037), al-Bīrūnī (*d.* 1048), and Ibn Rushd (Averrois, *d.* 1198). After the 14th century we find not a single man of science of any worth. It must be acknowledged that, if the Muslim religion itself has not been the cause of this decadence, it is a consequence of the way in which the sects have dealt with their religion. The jurists (*fuqahā'*), the clerical party of the *madrasa*, has been hostile to all science that progressed, in astronomy, beyond the construction of astrolabes with which to fix the times of the Prayer, and in mathematics the calculation of the shares of an inheritance; all else was dangerous to the faith. It is not only in the lands of Islam that religion has incited parties to smother scientific research: but, as in this case there was no opposition to their tyranny, the scientific spirit itself, which was observed to be so firmly implanted in a physician of the 10th century, is now so weakened by long inertia that it can be revived only in an infinitely small number of Muslims.

SOURCES

Nicholson: *Literary History of the Arabs*, 2nd Edition; Gibb: *History of the Literature of the Arabs* (S. 101); Brockelmann: G. A. L. 3 vol. (S.62); Abd al Jalil: *Brève Histoire de la Litérature Arabe*, 1943; Kratchkowsky: E. I. Suppl. 26; Saussey: *Prosateurs Turcs*, 1935; *Bréhier*: *Philosophie du Moyen Age*; *Ibn Sina*, *Ibn Rushd*, *Rhazi* in E.I.; Wensinck: *Ghazali* (in French); G. Marçais: *L'Art de l'Islam*, 1946; *Manuel d'Art Musulman*, 2 vol.

CHAPTER FOURTEEN

MODERN ISLAM

WE do not propose to end this short work by anything so ambitious as an attempt to estimate exactly the present condition of Islam, and to forecast its future. At a time when the organisation of peace appears to be more difficult than was the conduct of war, we do not feel ourselves at all qualified to predict the destiny of the Muslim peoples. It is clear that there can no longer be any question of a Muslim community directed by a sovereign caliph, as at the time when it was a political and military power of the first order in the very small world of Europe and Western Asia. Scattered throughout regions which, except in India and the East Indies, have but meagre economic resources, the Muslim populations do not appear to be capable of forming a compact separate group of states. The religious unity which had brought about the institutional unity which is the subject of this little book has today lost its value: it is now only a façade, a slogan.

Religion has been the ruling force in the cultural development of all men who have adhered to Judaeism, Christianity and Islam. Yielding to the evolution of society, religion has, no doubt, loosened its hold; in spite of which fact it still retains considerable authority, the actual value of which it is supremely important to assess. The acceptance of a religious creed is based on a revelation which claims to have brought to men eternal truth and instruction in the law of Him who is omniscient; revelation has determined for all time knowledge of the world and the conception of what life is. Meanwhile, what revelation has given to men as incontestable truth is shown to be a confused mixture of error; and this happens again and again as the tenacious striving of the human mind carries men step by step up the ladder of knowledge. It is terrifying to watch how religion, shackled by revelation, makes no effort to join in this ascent. It seems, on the contrary, to insist on continuing to advise men to fix their thoughts on a lifeless mould, to refrain from all reflection and discussion, and to content themselves with religious observances which confine 20th century believers within the circle of magic rites that circumscribed the lives of their remotest ancestors. Religion is bound hand and foot by the bonds of its dogmas and rites, like a mummy in its wrappings. Words and gestures that may serve well as signals with which to rally a political party are worthless for the purpose of calling a soul to communion with the God of truth. Science is striving to break down the first of the obstacles that have hidden from the human mind the vastness of the infinite; religion must renounce the poverty of an anthropomorphism that makes man subject to the God made in his own image. When it resumes its forward march in search of the Spirit, religion will cease to encourage souls to seek refuge in a materialism which is also an attempt to find a faith. Islam, which is not ruled by a clergy that is in the grip of a routine of dogma and rite, might perhaps once more return to the free religious discussions which shed such a brilliant light on the pages of its history between the 8th and 12th centuries. But it is still dominated by the clerical spirit of the old class of *fuqahā'*, the jurist-theologians who have reduced its thought to the level of scholastic tittle-tattle. Even if Muslims of the 19th century did not return to the discussion of fundamental questions, they did at least give a completely new form to certain of their institutions. In that fact we may find a reason for hoping for the growth of a modernism that would more anxiously desire to find the Spirit. This spiritual blossoming would be possible only in a democratic society that was founded on a real union of free wills, ruled, as Montesquieu put it, by "virtue". Meanwhile, this "virtue" is extolled in eloquent discourses, but no social or political group is prepared to subdue the passions that inflame it, to modify what it holds to be to its advantage, or to change its own attitude to life.

Turkey has destroyed the conception of the Muslim community and of the caliph as a veritable Emperor-Pope occupying the place of the Prophet, the lieutenant of the ruler of the world. She has secularised herself. She has adopted the principle of the representation of the people, and has recast her whole administration. The West has been surprised by such a rapid and complete adaptation of the Turkish people to modern life: government, legal codes, education, economic activities; even fashion has accepted the suppression of the female veil and the change in dress. It was thought that, even if the middle classes were, through their contact with Europe, fairly well prepared for the acceptance of such sudden developments, the masses of the people would agree only very unwillingly, and that the moral unity of the nation would be a very fragile thing. The years that have passed have shown that the Turkish Republic has the ability to assert and maintain its position as an independent state (thirteen million inhabitants).

At the other end of the Muslim world, Wahhābism appears to have built, around the two holy cities, an unshakable fortress of the most ancient traditions of Islam. It holds to the most severely traditional orthodox rite, the Ḥanbalite, and to the teaching of the stoutest exponent of this rite, Ibn Taymīya (*d.* 1335), whose works have inspired the teaching of 'Abd al-Wahhāb (*d.* 1792). Wahhābism seeks to restore to Islam absolute respect for the Qur'ān and the Tradition, and condemns all innovations (*bida'*), such as, for example, the worship of the saints and the sacrilegious veneration of the places in which they lived, and the tombs in which they were buried. Amīr, later King, Ibn Sa'ūd has founded a kind of brotherhood of Wahhābite *Ikhwān* who provide him with a clan and military forces sufficient to safeguard his authority. The rigidity of those principles and the harshness with which they are applied would seem to condemn Wahhābism to remain aloof from the modern urge for material progress; but here again, it is the spirit of Ibn Taymīya that animates the leader and gives him his dominating concern for the public interest, the *maṣlaḥa*. The King of Arabia is trying to modernise the equipment of his little community of six million souls for the battles both of peace and war. He excludes from his programme of reforms only those innovations which appear to him to be a danger to the faith and to morality. We cannot believe that it will be in the region of the two holy cities, and on the inspiration of the cult of the House of Allāh and the tomb of the Prophet, that the religion of the Qur'ān will find a new spirituality. Meanwhile, the discovery of oil and metals has introduced into Arabia a new possibility of disintegration!

Half-way between the "free-thinking" Turks and the old Ḥanbalite Wahhābites, in the lands of the East, the *Salafīya* represent a middle opinion, capable of carrying with it the mass of believers and bringing about the evolution of Islam. They think that the Qur'ān remains the law of the 20th century, as it was that of the 7th, but that it should be interpreted anew, and that *idtihād* should be revived, that is, the right to express a new opinion on the subject of the application of Muslim law to present day conditions. Following the example of Aḥmad Riḍā and Shaykh 'Abdu, the Salafīya have so thoroughly refashioned the Qur'ānic Exegesis that certain of their adherents have, with a daring artlessness, found in the holy books microbes and aeroplanes. Others have occupied themselves more usefully with social problems, such as that of marriage and the organisation of family life. Like the Wahhābites, they are opposed to the magic rites of the cult of the saints, and to the practices of the brotherhoods and the Ṣūfī communities. Yet they do not appear to be sufficiently revolutionary to revive Islam by means of less anthropomorphist conceptions of the world and of God.

Thus the Near East is torn by the necessity of choosing between three points of view; and that of the Salafīya which might have brought about their reconciliation cannot, because of its very moderation, exercise the influence that the two extreme parties know how to use by their appeal to the passions. Moreover, neither appears to possess, whether in Egypt or 'Irāq or Syria, the good points of their brothers in Arabia and Turkey. The old believers continue to be immovably attached to the ancient formulae and to maintain undiminished their contempt of a satanic Europe; the "free-thinkers" do not possess the constructive impulse or the firmness of purpose of the modern Osmanlis. Behind the façade of a somewhat elementary encyclopaedism they display a dogmatic self-assurance which cannot claim to rest on any scientific foundation and which forbids that spiritual tolerance and understanding which are the essential condition of any general progress.

Within the circle of an apparent union of all Muslim and Christian elements the Arab League speaks with a loud voice: eloquent voices have ever been raised, in the tent of the Bedouin, in the audience chamber of the caliphs, and in the pulpit of the mosques. That of the Arab League is listened to the more eagerly because of its call to the spirit of destruction and hatred. It calls for the sabotage of reform in those Muslim countries which are still under European tutelage and seeks to spread disorder within their borders. It, too, has appealed to the arbitrament of the bomb and the grenade, as an instrument for the modification of the regrettable adventure of the new Jerusalem. But the League appears to understand that it is powerless to construct the framework of the United Nations of Islam, contenting itself with the proclamation of the good tidings, for such an undertaking would be a work of peace, whereas it itself is organised for war. Behind this mask of anger there is a smiling countenance ever ready to turn towards the rich foreigner who might be of service, and the mariners of Tyr have discovered all the secrets of the Ocean of Darkness. Yazīd and ʿAmr are ever ready for mutual combat, as they are in the examples given in Arab grammar, for the possession of a watering place in the desert, for an oil well, or for a deposit of thorium.

The Near East is far from being a geographic unity. Its situation, which makes it, as it were, the hinge on which hang three continents, and a meeting place of races and civilisations, gives it a permanent importance out of proportion to its economic value and the number of its inhabitants. It contains, however, two fertile regions, Egypt and Iraq. Egypt, the "gift of the Nile", is one of the noblest and most ancient figures of humanity; she nourishes twenty million Muslims. She has always been envied her possession of the narrow and fertile corridor of the river, and it has often changed masters. Guardian of the gates of the Mediterranean and of the Red Sea, the aerodrome of three continents, she is aware of the uncertainty of her political fate. Just as Stalin is the successor of Peter the Great and Catherine II, and the Turkish Republic takes the place of the Hittite kingdom of the 20th century before our era, so the King of Egypt wishes to believe himself the successor of the Pharaohs. Cairo is the Muslim city in which intellectual life is most intense, and where the greatest interest is shown in present day problems. Iraq (three millions) preserves the traditional fruitfulness of the "black earth" of her two rivers and has given proof of the more recent riches of her oil. But she no longer possesses, as she did in the 'Abbāsid times, the capital of the Muslim world that had its gates wide open to the Persian Gulf, India and China; her oil flows towards the Mediterranean, and the intellectual life of Bagdad is feeble indeed. Syria (two millions and a half) has preserved, down the long centuries of her history, the traditions of her spiritual life. Muslims and Christians are there in the foremost ranks of the literary contest; religious life retains its activity, and political controversy is the occupation of the hour. But the variety of race and religious belief is an obstacle to the idea of political unity which is more cherished in Damascus. The divergent efforts of the Syrian political parties are powerless to weaken foreign influences, that of Turkey and of Russia, that of England, always attentive to the problems of the East, that of the United States and its world-wide plans. France, which contributed usefully to the cultural progress of Syria, failed in its attempt at political organisation.

Iran is somewhat isolated because of Shī'ism, the originality of her people, her language and her thought, and because of her geographical situation which makes of her the battle arena of Russian and English ambitions.

The people of Egypt, with the collaboration of Europeans, and especially of the British and the French, have restored to their country an economic and cultural value which enable her to occupy an advanced place in the race for power.

The immense Indian nation, which seemed on the point of bringing into harmony, under the régime of the Pax Britannica, the teachings of Islam and one of the noblest systems of philosophical and religious thought that humanity has conceived, has removed its name from the map of the world. Hindustan and Pakistan are at each other's throats, and are preparing the way for a return to a general anarchy which will be but a caricature of the freedom which had appeared in such beauty in the dreams of Ghandi's noble spirit. Will Hindus and Muslims understand in time that their bloody quarrels can but prepare the way for the dictatorship of their powerful neighbour?

It had been thought possible that the East Indies would gain an ample autonomy under the reasonable and skilful guardianship of the Netherlands. There, too, however, the claim is for full freedom; it is to be hoped that it will be attained peacefully and without disorder.

It is not possible to ascertain the position of the Muslims of Central and Western Asia under the dictatorship of Moscow.

The Muslim West had, from the 8th century onwards, its own life, and has, in course of time, developed in its own way: in Spain under its Umayyad dynasty, then under the provincial princes in the Maghrib, in Sicily and in the Balearic Islands under their successive masters, Idrīsid, Aghlabite, Fāṭimid, Zirid, Almoravid, Alhomad, Hafṣid, Merinid, Sharīf, etc. The twelve million Western Muslims have their favourite rite, Mālikism, their institutions that are tinged with Berberism, their aptitudes for literature and art. For the past century North Africa has moved in the orbit of France; inhabitants of Spanish and Italian race add to the European element. Whatever its future fate may be, it will be a Western state.

Important black communities in Africa have been converted to Islam. They still take little part in the life of the world.

Everywhere the Muslim peoples manifest a desire to achieve the complete independence for which, for the most part, they seem very badly prepared. It is therefore to be feared that those aspirations may lead to anarchy, and that they may be an obstacle in the way of the organisation of universal peace and freedom. We should like to see the Muslim communities incorporated, with their religion and their customs, in a state belonging to one of the new combinations into which the nations of the world have grouped themselves. Those communities could play an economic and political part within the group, and, if they could achieve a development of their attitude towards religion, they might make a notable contribution to the spiritualisation of humanity.

We fear, and we must say it frankly, a moral impoverishment of Muslim society against which nothing would prevail. The belief is persistently held that the ethic of orthodox Islam is weak. But a body of tradition has, until now, preserved in the mass a certain moral standard the social value of which cannot be denied. The Muslim mind is doubtless unprepared for its replacement by abstract principles, devoid of all tangible sanction.

We think that the leaders of Muslim and European society might be able to agree on a few common principles, which could be a basis for a sound education of the moral personality of the young. What seems most to be feared for the rising generations is the prevailing intellectual and moral poverty, their low ideal standards. One fears intellectual shams and substitutes, that brilliance of encyclopaedic memory which creates an appearance of knowledge, and that abundant verbal facility which permits of brilliant talk on a subject of which the speaker is ignorant. Faced with the many-sidedness of knowledge and an abundance of contradictory doctrines, it is necessary that young men, without being over-eager to choose from among them, should be moved above all by the very grandeur of this variety and of this uncertainty, and that they should devote themselves tirelessly to the study of the problems of the world and of life. Whatever be the nature of his activity, the young man, formed in this school of sound reason, will find daily growing within him the methodical will to accept nothing that he does not understand, and which he cannot link up with some whole.

It is not to be desired, we repeat, that the young Muslim should give up sounding the unknown, nor that he should reject the solutions that the Muslim religion traditionally offers him. But, convinced of the power of reason and also of its limitations, he ought to allot, within his own mind, their due share to intelligence and feeling, to what he understands and to what he desires to believe. Thus, for the better progress of his personality, he would have separated within himself the spiritual from the temporal.

Finally, we would desire that the young Muslim should not succeed in Americanising himself too completely, and that he should not lose all the charming qualities of the ancients: a kind of smiling resignation which was not without greatness;

an attention to outward bearing that achieved dignity; a profound sense of the solidarity which brought forth goodness and the charity that conceals itself; the taste for the happy life, with a tender feeling for colour, nature, and the harmony of things.

THE END